CW00428939

Europe without

Europe without Priests?

Edited by Jan Kerkhofs

SCM PRESS LTD

Translated by John Bowden from the Dutch
Europa zonder Priesters?, published 1995
by Averbode/Gooi en Sticht, Averbode, Belgium.

© Averbode/Gooi en Sticht 1995

Translation © John Bowden 1995

All rights reserved. No part of this publication may be
reproduced, stored in a retrieval system, or transmitted, in
any form or by any means, electronic, mechanical,
photocopying, recording or otherwise, without the prior
permission of the publishers, SCM Press Ltd.

0 334 02612 1

First British edition published in 1995
by SCM Press Ltd, 9–17 St Albans Place, London N1

Typeset at The Spartan Press Ltd, Lymington, Hants
and printed in Great Britain by
Biddles Ltd, Guildford and King's Lynn

Contents

The Contributors

Robrecht Boudens OMI is emeritus professor of church history in the faculty of religion of the Catholic University of Louvain.

Jan Kerkhofs SJ is emeritus professor of pastoral theology in the faculty of religion of the Catholic University of Louvain; he is co-chairman of the European Values Study.

Peter Neuner is professor of dogmatics in the Catholic theological faculty of the University of Munich.

Peter Schmidt is professor of New Testament and president of the major seminary, Gent.

Paul-Michael Zulehner is professor of pastoral theology and kerygmatics at the University of Vienna.

Introduction
Europe without Priests

Jan Kerkhofs

It is well known that with few exceptions, the Catholic faith communities outside Europe and North America have long been confronted with a chronic shortage of priests. What is new is the fact that in the Western world, too, the average age of priests is rapidly increasing; that the number of candidates for the priesthood in dioceses and the religious orders is continuing to decline or is stagnant at a very low level; and that more and more parishes no longer have a priest who is resident locally. For the priests themselves, this development means increasing pressure of work. The bishops are being compelled constantly to adapt their 'staff management'. Laity to whom full-time or part-time pastoral tasks are entrusted are raising urgent questions about their theological status and the limits that they are coming up against in connection with liturgy and administering the sacraments. The faithful, above all younger people, are asking for renewing and dynamic leadership at the local church level.

Responsible solutions are being sought throughout Europe, both East and West. There are no answers which are really satisfactory in the long term. But awareness of the problem is growing: pastoral councils are making it clear that things cannot go on like this and that new perspectives must be opened up. There is also an increasing recognition that one of the main determining factors in the crisis over the priesthood is a cultural change, coupled with a crisis over the content of faith and the way in which the church is understood. It would therefore be naive to think that it will prove possible to break through the present impasse quickly with a few measures, however tentative. What is at stake is much more than just an *aggiornamento* of the ministry. The faith communities themselves, in their many forms, are being challenged to a creativity and a responsibility the significance of which even Vatican II cannot have foreseen.

Furthermore, it is becoming increasingly clear that every step that is taken on the way to tomorrow has ecumenical implications. Finally, all the churches are experiencing time-lags in which one group is still living in the past whereas another is already at home in the future. This phenomenon is leading to sometimes painful polarization among the faithful and church leaders, not least over the question of the ministry.

This book seeks to take stock of the complex questions connected with the ministry in Europe. First of all it describes the situation. This panorama remains incomplete and fragmentary; in a number of countries the necessary scientific studies on which to base conclusions just do not exist.

Secondly, the question of the renewal of ministry is investigated at a greater depth from a variety of perspectives: what do exegesis, history, theology and sociology teach us? The absence of adequate comparative sociological and psychological material prevented us from devoting a separate chapter to this. In a last chapter scenarios are offered for solutions, in which constant reference is made to the limitations inherent in any of these formulae. In fact there are no answers which are satisfactory in every respect. Every new way raises questions of its own, even if the authors believe that to maintain the *status quo* offers no prospects and leads to further discouragement. Of course this contribution to pastoral policy is unfinished. The situation is constantly changing, not least because of the increasingly rapid changes being undergone by every national culture in a Europe which is laboriously becoming one, and as a result of which the younger generations are raising new questions about their place in society and the church. However, throughout Europe the challenges run parallel. We shall thus need to reflect at a European level on the way that needs to be taken. This reflection cannot be postponed: in almost all areas, around the magical year 2000 the situation will have developed even further. In fact it is hard to expect *aggiornamento* and inculturation from a body of priests whose average age is approaching seventy. And what does that mean for 'the new evangelization', however one understands it?

All the authors of this book are aware that a firm approach to tackling these these problems throughout Europe is extremely urgent. But each is responsible only for his own contribution. Finally, it should be noted that we did not succeed in involving a woman author. We hope that later it will prove possible to remedy this deficiency.

I

The Shortage of Priests in Europe

Jan Kerkhofs

In many countries in Europe priests and religious are almost automatically coming to be classified as being in the third age. They have
disappeared almost completely from schools and hospitals. There are
very few parishes with more than one priest, and many thousands of
parishes have to do without a resident pastor. All this has happened in a
period without war or persecution, at least in Western Europe, while the
democratization of education is making higher studies possible for many
millions of young people. In a number of countries priests and religious
are still part of the ordinary street scene. The problem of an approaching
shortage of priests has not completely penetrated the collective
awareness of the church, and those who do notice it to any degree react
with the objection that there have been many waves in history in which
smaller and larger numbers of priests and religious have alternated.
Those who go on to compare Europe with the other continents come to
the conclusion that the shortage of priests is a relative matter.

  This first chapter seeks to offer a matter-of-fact account of current
trends. In it, Europe is put in the context of the wider world, and the
situation in most countries of Europe is described. Here we have to be
aware that statistics can both reveal and conceal. Important socio-
cultural differences, and marked historically-conditioned differences,
can often be hidden by the figures. Quantity can hide great variations in
quality. Insight into growth or decline calls for many refined analysis.
But figures have an importance for any policy. The Bible, too, indicates
the need to take account of numbers.

1. Europe compared with the wider world

The statistical survey which follows here needs careful interpretation,
although it does indicate ratios and trends. Almost all the figures have
been drawn from the only available source, the annual publications of

the *Annuarium Statisticum Ecclesiae*,[1] produced by the state secretariat of the Vatican. Of course these facts are based on information provided by the individual dioceses and religious institutions. These are not always accurate and sometimes differ from studies carried out locally. But they offer a fairly reliable survey.

Here two trends immediately become evident. First of all, Europe still has the largest number of priests, about 60% of the diocesan clergy of the whole world and 47% of religious priests. Secondly, it is evident that a large number of religious are working in parishes. Furthermore, many other studies indicate that many religious priests in Latin America and Africa come from Europe.

Table 1. Active Priests

	Diocesan		Religious	
	1986	1992	1986	1992
Europe	159,682	154,556	70,805	67,920
World total	253,710	259,866	149,176	144,770

Between 1986 and 1992 the world total of diocesan priests increased (in Africa, Latin America and above all Asia, while the number declined in North America, Europe and Oceania). The world total of religious priests declined (generally, apart from Asia and Central America).

However, large differences in the ratio of Catholics per priest underlie these figures. This ratio is clearly best in the three areas where the number of priests is declining relatively, namely in North America, Europe and Oceania, as Table 2 indicates. However, between 1986 and

Table 2. Proportion of Catholics to Priests (Diocesan and Religious)

	1986	1987	1988	1989	1990	1991	1992
Africa	4,086	4,150	4,249	4,318	4,358	4,434	4,395
N. America	956	970	991	1,007	1,023	1,033	1,052
S. America	6,956	7,013	7,014	7,074	7,276	7,360	7,360
Asia	2,504	2,531	2,546	2,588	2,541	2,553	2,583
Europe	1,210	1,221	1,231	1,248	1,270	1,282	1,295
Oceania	1,205	1,219	1,261	1,289	1,294	1,346	1,385
World	**2,145**	**2,182**	**2,217**	**2,258**	**2,308**	**2,338**	**2,368**

1992 the situation deteriorated everywhere, with the partial exception of Africa, above all as a result of the increase of the Catholic population, which is not matched by an increase in clergy.

However, the positive situation in Europe and North America is undermined by a negative balance between ordinations on one hand and the number of deaths and retirements on the other, as is shown by Table 3. This gives the ordinations, deaths and retirements per 100 serving diocesan priests (1991).

Table 3. Ordinations, Deaths, Resignations and Balance per 100 Diocesan Priests (1991)

	Ordinations	Deaths	Resignations	Balance
Africa	8.18	1.04	0.23	6.91
America (North)	1.43	1.97	0.36	−0.90
(South)	5.19	1.46	0.46	3.27
Asia	4.84	1.01	0.38	3.45
Europe	1.73	2.11	0.16	−0.54
Oceania	2.06	1.35	0.46	0.25
World	**2.52**	**1.87**	**0.24**	**0.41**

In Europe, the largest concentration of priests is to be found in Italy, France and Spain, followed by Poland and Germany. Relatively, i.e. considering the number of Catholics per priest, the differences are very great (1992). We find the following order: Malta (369), Ireland (703), Great Britain (747), Belgium (883), Switzerland (894), Italy (962), The Netherlands (1,134), Spain (1,243), Austria (1,280), Germany (1,306), Poland (1,510), Slovenia (1,515), France (1,542), Croatia (1,682), Yugoslavia (2,141), Hungary (2,176), Portugal (2,193), Czechoslovakia (2,861), Ukraine (3,621), Lithuania (4,032). Of course in the 'diaspora' of the North and in Orthodox countries one finds distinctive ratios: Iceland (197), Finland (249), Denmark (331), Greece (565), Norway (608), Sweden (1,217), White Russia (7,977). From this it is evident that outside Malta and Italy, numerically the best ratio is to be found in the more northern part of Europe. It will be seen later that here too, more differentiation produces a somewhat different picture.

Between 1976 and 1992 the absolute number of serving diocesan and religious priests declined in almost all countries except Poland.

Here it is striking that Europe cannot be divided into a southern

Europe which is richer in priests and a northern Europe which is poorer in priests. One cannot find any correlation, taking into account the ratio of priests to the number of Catholics. It is striking that with the relative exception of Poland, Central Europe is in a far less favourable position; this is to a larger degree a consequence of half a century of Nazi and Communist occupation. However, in terms of mission vocations Central Europe was already far behind Western Europe. Numerically speaking, Italy has by far the largest number of priests; but in the last century it had far more. The decline began in 1861: in 1956–57 there were only a third of the number of priests there had been then. Moreover one can find great regional differences within the same country: thus the north of Portugal, Spain and Italy traditionally had far more vocations than the south (depending on the diocese, sometimes in a proportion of 15:1). In 1950, F.Boulard found a striking regional difference: areas where there were more children produced far more vocations of priests and sisters, and often these coincided with mountain areas.

Table 4. Number of Active Diocesan and Religious Priests in Europe (Individual Countries and Total), 1976–1992

	1976	1987	1992
Belgium	13,432	11,065	9,778
Netherlands	5,083	5,779	4,878
Ireland	5,906	5,921	6,321
Great Britain	7,861	7,405	6,877
Germany (West)	22,576	21,609	21,774
(East)	1,525	1,363	
Switzerland	4,308	3,974	3,579
Austria	6,099	5,533	4,952
Czechoslovakia	4,054	3,386	3,790
Yugoslavia	4,097	4,245	249
Croatia			2,190
Slovenia			1,105
Poland	18,529	21,386	24,452
France	41,163	34,261	30,909
Portugal	5,035	4,596	4,500
Spain	33,369	31,124	29,851
Italy	61,784	60,196	57,659
Europe	**241,379**	**228,511**	**222,476**

It is against this general background that the phenomenon of parishes without resident priests is to be set. By no means all parishes in the various continents are served by a local pastor. Moreover the structure of parishes varies greatly. Thus many South American parishes quite often have ten thousand baptized Catholics, while in Africa and Asia the extended parishes include many mission posts served by catechists. Moreover Europe, above all in Italy, Spain and France, has many very small parishes, some of which only exist on paper or have only a handful of the faithful.

This needs to be taken into account in interpreting Table 5.

Table 5. Types of Parish and Quasi-parish According to the Way in which they are Served (1976–1992) and by Continent (1992)

	World total (1976–92)			Per continent (1992)				
Parishes served by	1976	1987	1992	Africa	America	Asia	Europe	Oceania
Diocesan priests	129,810	129,942	136,854	4,633	36,017	11,172	83,425	1,607
Religious priests	24,247	26,335	25,502	3,240	9,463	3,326	8,979	494
Non-resident pastors	44,157	53,108	53,554	926	5,045	2,323	45,089	171
Permanent deacons	84	230	351	40	140	19	133	19
Religious non-priests (male)	60	82	98	11	44	19	21	3
Women religious	332	883	1,091	72	760	46	198	15
Laity	342	950	1,483	194	273	68	853	95
Vacant	1,474	979	1,659	141	260	263	994	1
Total	200,506	212,409	219,231	9,257	52,002	17,236	139,692	2,405

As far as Europe is concerned, it is striking that of the parishes with a resident pastor, about 10% are served by priests in religious orders (in Africa 43%, in America 21%, in Asia 23% and in Oceania 24%). The number of parishes served by permanent deacons is lower in all continents than the number served by religious (men or – above all – women) who are not priests. However, in Europe it is less and less possible to call on religious, far less priests, since their number is constantly declining (Table 6) and most religious do not feel called to lead parishes, nor are they trained to do so.

In 1992 the largest concentrations of religious priests were to be found in Italy (19,733), Spain (9,838), France (6,894), Poland (5,448), Germany (5,195), Belgium (3,642), the Netherlands (2,937),Ireland (2,661), Austria (1,923), Switzerland (1,478) and Portugal (1,086).

**Table 6. Trend in the Number of Religious in Europe
(1980–1992)**

	1980	1987	1992
Religious priests	74,411	69,513	67,920
Male religious, not priests	35,445	30,450	26,949
Women religious	527,707	474,249	431,929

They declined everywhere by comparison with 1986 except in Poland
and Ireland, but the age pyramid in Ireland is characterized by a rapid
increase in the average age. We also need to note that in 1980
Belgium, with a third the number of inhabitants, still had more
religious priests than Poland (5,019 as compared with 4,358).

The distribution of male religious who are not priests and of women
religious follows that of the religious priests. Only in Poland have
women religious increased (from 24,973 in 1986 to 25,530 in 1992);
male religious who are not priests have declined (from 1,598 in 1986 to
1,424 in 1992). In Italy between 1986 and 1992 women religious
declined from 137,431 to 124, 721, in Spain from 76,875 to 70,608,
and in France from 72,702 to 61,503. With the exception of Poland,
everywhere one can note a rapid increase of average age in the age
pyramid.

The number of diocesan seminarians (being trained in philosophy
and theology) increased slightly between 1986 and 1992, from 19,851
to 20,731. This increase is predominantly to be attributed to the
Ukraine, Roumania, Czechoslovakia and Lithuania. In Poland the
number decreased. Relatively, the greatest numerical decline is to be
found in Ireland, Germany, Belgium and the Netherlands. In France a
massive decline had already begun earlier. Between 1986 and 1992
there was an increase in religious seminarians from 9,346 to 9,869.
Thus in 1992 they formed 32.6% of all seminarians. The increase
above all comes from Central Europe. The greatest declines were in
Germany, Great Britain and Ireland. In the Netherlands and France
the greatest decline had already taken place before 1986.

The *Annuarium Statisticum Ecclesiae* also provides information on
trends in the ordination of diocesan clergy. We can immediately see
that Europe still has by far the largest number of ordinations, that the
greatest numerical increases are in Africa and Asia, while North
America and Oceania are stagnating. As we already saw, the

ordinations are not keeping pace with the increase in the Catholic population.

Table 7. Ordinations of Priests (Diocesan Clergy) per Continent (1986–1992)

	1986	1988	1990	1992
Africa	545	663	716	823
North America	542	568	517	551
Central America				
(and West Indies)	341	380	426	455
South America	719	787	820	935
Asia	681	767	959	975
Europe	2,253	2,533	2,456	2,586
Oceania	55	52	44	58
World total	**5,136**	**5,750**	**5,938**	**6,401**
Percentage in Europe	**43.8**	**44**	**41.3**	**40.3**

On closer inspection, it is striking in the case of Europe that between 1986 and 1992 ordinations increased above all in Poland, the Ukraine, Italy and Spain. In Western Europe the numbers remained at a low level or decreased further. In the same period the world totals in the figures of retirements of diocesan priests fluctuate between a minimum of 562 in 1990 and a maximum of 633 in 1986. The problem is discussed in another context later in this book.

Against the background of all these figures we now return to the parishes in Europe to investigate the development of parishes which are not served by a resident pastor.

Table 8 reflects a clear development: a reduction in the number of parishes with a diocesan priest as pastor, an increase of the parishes served by a religious priest, and a marked increase in the parishes served by a pastor from elsewhere (despite the fact that above all in France and Italy a large number of small parishes were abolished). In 1992, around 33% of what had hitherto been regarded as parishes had no resident pastor. If we add to these the parishes entrusted to a deacon (133), a religious who was not a priest (2), to sisters (198), to lay people (853), or left completely vacant (994), the percentage increases to almost 34%. Above all in France, parishes have been entrusted to lay people (775) and sisters (123), and above all in Italy (57) and Switzerland (28) to

Table 8. Number of Parishes with a Resident Pastor (Diocesan or Religious) or Served by a Pastor from Another Parish, 1976–1992 (Europe and the Main Countries)

Countries	With diocesan pastor		With religious as pastor		Served by a pastor from another parish	
	1976	1992	1976	1992	1976	1992
Belgium	3,281	2,439	352	434	284	1,070
Netherlands	1,333	1,004	427	637	39	112
Ireland	1,257	1,295	27	59	–	–
Great Britain	2,797	2,754	343	347	8	69
Austria	2,053	1,856	592	647	394	584
Switzerland	1,338	994	149	224	191	420
Germany (West)	9,002	8,296	873	731	1,812	3,702
(East)	732	–	47	–	117	–
Poland	6,590	8,818	465	700	46	76
Czechoslovakia	2,642	2,012	224	292	1,259	2,088
Hungary	2,152	1,703	142	54	141	515
Yugoslavia	1,831	174	372	25	475	37
Croatia	–	1,022	–	182	–	276
Slovenia	–	636	–	70	–	87
France	15,597	12,184	832	807	20,851	20,385
Portugal	2,612	2,358	117	167	1,593	1,769
Spain	12,133	10,353	696	978	8,543	10,137
Italy	23,041	20,892	2,014	2,028	3,237	2,833
Europe	**88,840**	**83,425**	**7,682**	**8,979**	**39,242**	**45,089**

deacons. It is not surprising that Latin Europe above all has many parishes without a resident pastor; here there are many small hill villages, and a marked migration to the cities has taken place. The situation is more serious further north in Europe, where even parishes with a higher population are quickly losing resident pastors. In the meantime more and more parishes have been entrusted to religious; this reservoir is being exhausted.

Of course the sometimes very marked differences in the structure of the age pyramid are concealed in these sets of figures. The analysis by country will go into this. Before that, in this general statistical survey it seems important also to bring together some demographic and sociological facts. They should make it possible to achieve a more differentiated picture both of the 'potential vocations' and the 'pastoral burden'.

The number of young men and women in Europe is declining. To keep the population level demographers estimate that there is a need for 2.1 children per woman. In 1991, in the countries under consideration (Table 9) this was the case only in Ireland and Sweden. A comparison between 1965 and 1991 indicates a decline everywhere (except for Hungary, where, however, the replacement index of 2.1 has not been reached). This means that the average couple in Western and Central Europe does not have two children. We can understand that despite all the views about the practice of the faith, this phenomenon has a great influence on the 'potential for vocations'. Here we need to note that the lowest figures are in Italy, Spain and Germany.

Table 9. Average Number of Children per Woman (1965–1991)

	1965	1991
Belgium	2.60	1.57
Netherlands	3.04	1.61
Ireland	4.03	2.18
United Kingdom	2.83	1.82
Austria	2.70	1.50
Switzerland	2.61	1.61
Germany		1.33
East	2.48	0.98
West	2.51	1.42
Poland	2.52	2.06
Czechoslovakia	2.37	1.92
Hungary	1.82	1.87
France	2.84	1.77
Portugal	3.07	1.50
Spain	2.97	1.28
Italy	2.55	1.27
Sweden	2.42	2.12

(Source: *Population* [INED, Paris] 48, 1993, 1060).

Traditionally, vocations are to be found above all in families of practising Catholics. According to the European Values Study (1990),[2]

weekly practice declined everywhere between the 1981 survey and that
of 1990. Furthermore, the figures given here are optimistic estimates;
the real figures are 5% or more lower. Those relating to the age-group
18–24 are even lower; in this age-group many virtually never go to
church, and the number of those who say that they do not belong to any
church is increasing. The figures from Table 10 relate to all Christian
churches.

**Table 10. Sunday Practice in Western Europe, Age-group
18–24 (1990), and Those who Say that They do not Belong to
a Church**

	Churchgoing at least once a month %	Less than once a year, in practice never %	Do not belong to a church %
Belgium	20	57	45
Netherlands	17	50	61
Ireland	81	6	7
Northern Ireland	58	28	14
Great Britain	14	67	59
West Germany	18	53	10
France	7	72	60
Portugal	37	48	42
Spain	21	54	20
Italy	36	20	15

(Source EVS, 1990)

For the ten countries mentioned, in the 18–24 year-old age group only
11% say that they have great confidence in the church (in the 65-plus
age group the number is 49%), 26 believe in the resurrection and 34%
in a personal God. Of Catholics (of all ages), 33% say that they find
'religious belief' important in upbringing at home (compared with
'toleration', 72%); according to a survey by the Eurobarometer
(European Commission, Brussels 1992) in which more items were
covered than in the European Values Study and in which former East
Germany and Greece were included, 'religious belief' reached only
10% (the highest percentage was Greece with 22%, the lowest East
Germany with 3%).

From this limited number of facts we may conclude that as far as young Europeans are concerned, in Europe we may speak of a minority church (only in Poland do we find a majority of the total population who find 'religious belief' important in upbringing at home).

2. North-West Europe

(a) The Netherlands

Thanks to the Catholic Social Church Institute (KASKI), for years the Netherlands has had excellent church statistics. Along with many other studies they show that in religious terms no country in Western Europe has changed so rapidly since the Second World War as the Netherlands. Some tables illustrate the development. We might note in passing that the Netherlands (1990) has 15 million inhabitants, of whom 37% are Catholics (with a Sunday practice of 14% as compared with 64.4% in 1965, 31.1% in 1975 and 17.5% in 1985).

Table 1. Number of Priests Actively in the Service of the Dutch Dioceses (b.p = active in the Base Pastorate, viz. in Parishes and Quasi-parishes)

	Secular				Regular			
	Total	Retired	Active	b.p	Active	b.p	Total b.p
1960	–	–	–	2,987	–	708	3,695
1965	4,174	–	–	2,902	–	955	3,857
1970	3,729	–	–	2,280	–	1,153	3,433
1974/5	3,263	727	2,536	2,027	1,472	1,146	3,173
1980	2,746	855	1,891	1,340	1,483	948	2,288
1985	2,377	875	1,502	1,091	1,159	713	1,814
1990	2,075	882	1,193	880	945	597	1,477

In the period between 1965 and 1980 religious began to serve parishes to an increasing degree. First of all, in the 1960s more religious became available for other activities as a result of the abolition of their own minor and major seminaries. Secondly, in the 1970s numerous religious returned to the Netherlands as a result of the political situation or because churches in Third World countries gained their independence. Many of them began to work in grass-roots pastoral care.

However, the reservoir of religious priests rapidly became exhausted. Moreover, the other religious who were directly or indirectly involved in pastoral work declined rapidly (Table 2).

Table 2. Number of Religious in the Netherlands

	Sisters	Brothers	Priests
1974	23,334	3,306	4,042
1980	20,147	3,159	3,699
1985	17,774	2,652	3,458
1990	15,197	2,156	3,047

In 1969, 9,302 Dutch religious were active outside the Netherlands; in 1990 the number was only 1,964.

In 1991 the Netherlands had 2,130 active priests in the service of Dutch dioceses, of which 942 (44.2%) were religious. Of the total number of secular priests, 885 (42.7) were retired. Of the total number of religious priests, 3,047, this figure was 1,116. Of the 14,304 sisters who belonged to a so-called active order or congregation, 11,313 (79.1%) were retired or otherwise inactive. Of the 841 brothers of active orders and congregations, 476 (56.6%) were still functioning.

Of the 1,754 'pastoral units' (parishes, quasi-parishes and so on), in 1991, 63.3% were served by secular priests and 38.7% by religious priests. Depending on the definition of 'pastoral units', in the Netherlands there are between 175 and 350 'parishes without resident priests'. A rapid increase is forecast. The number of ordinations to the

Table 3. Ordinations to the Priesthood and Resignations (1960–1990)

	Ordinations to the priesthood		Resignations	
	secular	religious	secular	religious
1961–65	411	981	29	79
1966–70	213	507	306	612
1971–74/75	49	120	227	542
1976–80	41	120	72	111
1981–85	68	37	23	56
1986–90	96	34	17	17

priesthood remains low, despite a recent increase in the number of secular priests.

Here it should not be forgotten that according to the European Values Study, 61% of those between 18 and 24 said that they did not belong to any church (51% of the whole population) and that the crisis among the Catholics and the Reformed is greater than it is among the Reformed.

An attempt has been made to find a provisional solution by fusing small parishes and parishes with a low level of practising Catholics. However, here there is opposition from the faithful: they see the parish as a support for basic community relationships. This implies a constant slimming down of the tasks of the priest, for example by the collective baptism of children, by abolishing celebrations of the eucharist at weddings and funerals, by concentrating youth services in one city church, and so on. In the meantime increasing recourse has been had to pastoral workers and – to a lesser degree – to permanent deacons. As in other countries it has been noted that too few people with theological training are available to be pastors in base communities. Moreover at the time of the special Synod of Dutch Bishops in Rome (1980), it was emphasized that as few of the traditional tasks of the priesthood were to be given to the laity in order not to damage the preservation of priestly identity. One really bright spot needs to be mentioned: the faithful are quite clearly involving themselves in parochial activities as volunteers to a greater extent than in neighbouring countries.

(b) Belgium

The federal structure of Belgium is also reflected in the church. So here Flanders, Wallonia and the urban province of Brussels will be considered separately.[3]

In 1991 the three Walloon dioceses and the vicariate of Walloon Brabant had 2,010 parishes, 984 of which were without a resident priest. The number of these has been steadily increasing: in the diocese of Liège (from 123 in 1981 to 214 in 1991), in the diocese of Doornik (from 170 in 1981 to 272 in 1991). In 1991 the extended diocese of Namur–Luxembourg had 454 parishes out of 740 – some of these with very few inhabitants – without resident priests.

Of course the age pyramid there has changed: below 30, 24 priests; 30–39, 157; 40–49, 290; 50–59, 494; 60–69, 660; 70–79, 293; above

80, 43. The average age is around 61 (1991). Between 1984–85 and 1988–89, on average only 15 diocesan priests were ordained annually in Wallonia.

Various strategies have been used to cope with this development: more use of lay people (through pastoral teams and parochial councils); the restructuring of 'pastoral units' (by reassessing collaboration at deanery and district level); teams of priests, together responsible for a number of parishes; the French model of Sunday celebrations of the eucharist without a priest (ADAP, see below, 23f.) in parishes led by lay people. Lay people are trained for pastoral work by various systems, but as yet there is no common approach. The conviction is certainly growing that some full-time lay people could provide an answer, both for the parishes and for the pastoral staff in hospitals. Priests and laity want more theological reflection on the function of laity and priests and on new forms of ministry for men and women, not to mention married men and women.

In the four Flemish dioceses and in the vicariate of Flemish Brabant, in 1990, out of a total of 1,830 parishes, 142 (7.7%) were without a resident priest. We need to take into account that most of the Flemish parishes have many more inhabitants than the Walloon parishes and are also more urbanized. The situation is changing rapidly. For example, in 1986 the diocese of Antwerp had 4 parishes (out of 313) without resident priests; in 1992 the number was 60 and at the beginning of 1994 already 106. In 1986 the diocese of Hasselt had 360 priests, active in 320 parishes; in 1991 it had 300; the estimate for 2010 is around 100. Since 1980 the number of pastoral workers trained or in training has increased to around 1,800.

The number of diocesan seminarians has constantly declined (678 in 1963, 518 in 1969, 186 in 1979, 150 in 1989, 118 in 1993). Compared with 106 ordinations to the priesthood in 1963, in 1969 there were 65 and for the period 1978–88 there was an average of 20 a year. Compared with 1966 the number of inductions and ordinations dropped by 70%. This has resulted both in a steady decline in the absolute number of priests (e.g. in Antwerp from 1,325 diocesan priests in 1963 to 781 in 1988, a quarter of them retired) and in a marked increase in average age.

Not only are the same solutions sought as in Wallonia, but there are also other responses here; in particular the use of well-trained 'pastoral workers'. Great efforts have also been made to set up pastoral teams as well as parochial councils (of 1,403 parishes surveyed in 1989, 390 had pastoral teams). The number of full-time paid laity is gradually rising (in hospitals, as in other places). Financial restrictions prevent the appointment of more full-time lay workers. Since 1971 the Inter-diocesan Pastoral Council, the only one of its kind, has constantly pleaded for the ordination of married *viri probati* and for the admission of women to the diaconate and possibly to the priesthood. Here it is supported by the powerful Catholic women's organizations.

The situation in the capital, Brussels,[4] is complex, not least because of the multilingual situation. It is becoming dramatic, as the following age pyramid indicates.

Age group	Flemish-speaking parochial clergy	French-speaking parochial clergy
71+	6	11
61–70	19	53
51–60	21	51
41–50	13	23
31–40	7	15
–31	1	1
	68	154

In the period between 1970 and 1980 numerous religious priests (including returned missionaries) were appointed to parishes in Belgium. In 1978, about 33% of the clergy in the archdiocese of Malines–Brussels consisted of religious (515). But the number of male religious is also decreasing rapidly: for Belgium from 6,172 in 1990 to 5,637 in 1993, and religious priests from 4,554 in 1987 to 3,722 in 1993. Of male religious, 68,6% are over 60 (1993). The average annual number of ordinations to the priesthood between 1988 and 1992 was 21.

(c) The Grand Duchy of Luxembourg

The development in Luxembourg follows the general tendency.

Year	Active priests	Retired	Total in service
1960	392	83	475
1970	360	82	442
1980	237	107	344
1990	177	92	269
1994	160	88	248

In 1994, there were 160 active priests for 266 parishes. Between 1987 and 1993, on average 10.4 priests died and 2.4 were ordained annually. The progressive ageing is evident from the following graph.

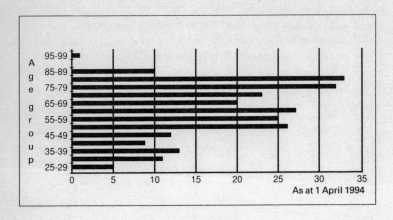

Active Priests by Age-group

According to the *Annuarium Statisticum Ecclesiae,* in 1976, of 274 parishes in the Grand Duchy, 69 were without a resident priest. In 1992 the number had risen to 126. Of the remaining 148 parishes, 36 were served by a religious priest.

(d) West and East Germany

Of the 22 dioceses of West Germany, in 1991 two had less than 11% of parishes without a resident priest: Berlin (7.3%) and Fulda (10.7%). Two dioceses had no resident priest in more than 40% of parishes: Trier (48.2%) and Augsburg (41.4%). Seven dioceses had between 30% and 40% of parishes without resident priests, e.g. Rottenburg –Stuttgart (35.5%), Limburg (32.2%), Passau (35.6%) and Freiburg (32.6%). On average 29% of German parishes have no resident priest.[5]

It should not be forgotten that three dioceses have more than 3,000 Catholics per parish priest and that there are only two with fewer than 2,000 Catholics per priest. Depending on the diocese, between 5% and 20% of priests are appointed to non-parochial work. The great ageing of the clergy means that many are in retirement: in two dioceses (Berlin

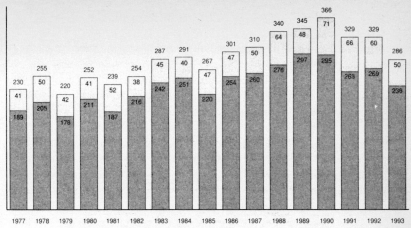

Graph 1. Newly ordained priests, 1977–1993
(In both graphs, the lower part of the column represents
diocesan priests; the upper part priests in religious orders)

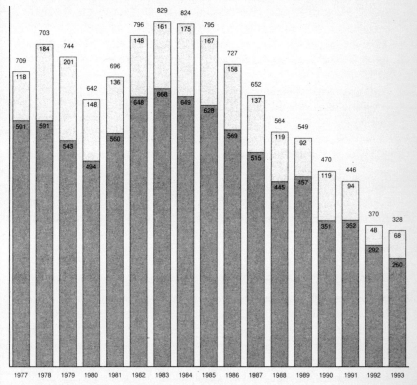

Graph 2. New candidates for the priesthood, 1977–1993

and Fulda) two out of three; only in two dioceses is the proportion one out of five.

In the period up to the year 2000, around 4,000 of the 11,000 active priests will be retired (in 1991 there were 19,707 priests in the service of the German dioceses, including retired secular and religious priests).

According to a survey, in 1989–90 97% of all Sunday services were still celebrations of the eucharist, 2% were liturgies of the word and 1% communions. Of priests, 47% had three eucharistic celebrations per weekend, 14% four and 5% five. In the diocese of Trier, with many small parishes, 35% of the clergy serves 1 parish, 39% 2, 18% 3 and 3% between 4 and 6, whereas 5% of the parishes have no celebrations. Around the year 2000 only every other parish will have a resident priest.

In former East Germany the situation is very different. According to a recent survey only 4% of the population is Catholic. There the church is completely a diaspora church. In the diocese of Dresden – Meissen, 17 of the 147 parishes have no resident priest (and 15 of the 23 quasi-parishes); 15% of the clergy are retired. In Görlitz, the smallest diocese, 12 of the 56 parishes have no resident priest; it is expected that around the year 2000 the present number of 77 active priests will have declined to 45.

Thanks to good organization and the church tax, in many places it has been possible to involve deacons and lay theologians in pastoral care (see below).

In 1991, unified Germany had 13,334 parishes and quasi-parishes. Of these, 8,313 had a resident priest (of the quasi parishes, 661 had one and 1,027 did not). Of the 11,327 priests working in pastoral care, 9,985 are secular and 1,342 religious.

The recent pattern of ordinations and entry into major seminaries, priestly training by dioceses and religious orders is evident from the graphs on p. 17.[6]

(e) Austria

According to information from Canisiuswerk, Vienna, in 1994 Austria had 730 parishes without a resident priest (176 in the archdiocese of Vienna, 129 in Gurk–Klagenfurt, 105 in St Pölten, 103 in Graz–Seckau, etc.). In 1970–71, there were 773 enrolments of Austrian students in the theological faculties in Austria reading theology as their main subject (706 men, 65 women); in 1980–81 there were 1,252 (985 men, 408 women); in 1990–91 1,508 (1,086 men, 422 women): in

1993–4 1,359 (951 men, 408 women). In addition, in independent courses of religious education in 1980–81 there were 231 enrolments of Austrian students (129 men, 102 women), and in 1993–94 832 (529 men, 303 women). Enrolments do not coincide with persons (one person can enrol several times, depending on the course of his or her education). The increasing number of women is striking.

(f) Switzerland

There had already been parishes without priests for a long time –before the rapid decline in the number of priests. As a result of the constant migration of the population from the mountain villages in the diocese of Lugano and Chur, in 1970, 34% and 20% respectively of the still extant canonical parishes had no resident priest. Gradually the number of parishes without a resident priest also increased elsewhere, to the point that in 1990 one out of four parishes in Switzerland had no resident priest. The following table[7] gives a general survey of the situation.

Table. Leadership of Parishes and Quasi-parishes

	Parishes with resident pastor						Parishes without resident pastor						Total parishes
Diocese	Diocesan priests		Religious priests		Total		(a)	(b)	(c)	(d)	Total		Total
Diocese	N	%	N	%	N	%	N	N	N	N	N	%	N
Basel	357	67.4	59	11.1	416	78.5	72	17	25	0	114	21.5	530
St Gallen	105	73.4	13	9.1	118	82.5	25	0	0	0	25	17.5	143
Chur	225	66.0	49	14.4	274	80.4	63	3	1	0	67	19.7	341
Lugano	105	41.5	19	7.5	124	49.0	129	0	0	0	129	51.0	253
LGF(e)	187	64.5	3	10.7	218	75.2	70	0	0	2	72	24.8	290
Sion	94	61.0	29	18.8	123	79.9	31	0	0	0	31	20.1	154
St-Maurice (f)	0	0.0	5	83.3	5	83.3	1	0	0	0	1	16.7	6
Total	**1073**	**62.5**	**205**	**11.9**	**1278**	**74.4**	**391**	**20**	**26**	**2**	**439**	**25.6**	**1717**

NB: (a) = looked after by a non-resident priest; (b) entrusted to deacons; (c) entrusted to laity; (d) totally vacant; (e) Lausanne–Geneva–Fribourg; (f) under the jurisdiction of the Abbey of St-Maurice.

During the period between 1980 and 1990, the number of active priests in the service of the dioceses steadily declined (from 1,842 in 1985 to

1,700 in 1990). These priests have almost all been replaced by lay persons. In this decade the relationship between priests and laity has fundamentally changed: in 1980 only one full-time pastoral worker in six was a lay person; by 1990 this had already become one in three. Between 1960 and 1990 the total number of diocesan priests declined from 3,139 to 2,217 and that of religious clergy from 1,945 to 1,253, with the result that the number of Catholics per diocesan priest steadily increased from 602 in 1940 to 1,367 in 1990. In the meantime, however, almost half of these (47%) have reached legal retirement age (sixty-five). 96 priests were ordained in the period between 1980 and 1990, as compared with 275 deaths and 19 resignations. We may project a further reduction and ageing for the near future. The number of religious priests, which increased up until 1956, declined more rapidly than that of diocesan priests from 1970 (33% as compared to 25%) and their age-pyramid is even less favourable.

Only recently have complete statistics become available for women religious: between 1985 and 1990 there has been a decline of 11.8% (more among the active apostolic institutions than among the contemplative orders). Their age pyramid is even less favourable than that of the religious priests.

The effect of this whole development on some dioceses can be illustrated quite precisely by the previous figures. In the largest diocese (Basel) in 1993 there were 290 parish priests and 53 assistant priests in 454 parishes (in 1960 there were still 800 priests). A decline to 205 and 43 is projected for 1998. There are not enough full-time theologically trained deacons and laity to fill the empty places: around 1998 it is expected that 40 parishes will be without a community leader, priest or lay.[8] In the diocese of Chur the development is parallel: in 1978 the deanery of Chur had 25 parish priests, and in 1988 still about 15; in 1987 Zurich had 113 and still around 77 in 1994. In the diocese of Lausanne–Geneva–Fribourg there were 519 priests in 1974; in 1994 377.[9] If the present situation continues, in 2015 there will be only 50 diocesan priests for 600,000 Catholics.

(g) Ireland

In 1989, Bishop Konstant of Leeds published a pastoral letter in which he referred to the number of priests in his diocese. He mentioned not only the ageing of clergy but also the diminishing number of priests who traditionally came from Ireland.

Statistics show that Ireland in fact still has no parishes without priests. However, the number of ordinations to the priesthood is constantly declining.

We have general information about diocesan clergy only up to 1989. The episcopate decided that the Council for Research and Development in Maynooth should publish statistics only every five years. Between 1970 and 1981 the number of active diocesan priests declined by 6.5% (in this period the population increased by 15%). In the period mentioned, on average 72 diocesan priests were ordained annually, while on average 76.5 died and 12.4 resigned. The number of candidates for the priesthood remained stable. Meanwhile the ageing has increased: in 1970, 51.8% were below fifty (in 1981 47.9%) and 26.7 above sixty (in 1981 32.3%). In 1970 3,080 priests were serving in 1,195 parishes; in 1981 2,869 priests in 1,311 parishes. According to the Council for Research and Development's report *Vocations in Ireland 1989*, since 1981 the number of vocations has been declining uninterruptedly for all groups (diocesan seminarians, religious student priests, sisters and brothers) from a total of 750 in 1970 to 322 in 1989. The decline has been most marked among religious. Between 1983 and 1989 the overall total of priests and religious declined from 26,490 to 24,546.

It is also less and less possible to appeal to religious. In 1989/90 the Association of Superiors carried out a thorough enquiry into personnel.[10] The age pyramid given below speaks for itself.

Ireland: Age Pyramid of Religious (1989–1990)

Age group	Sisters %	Brothers %	Clergy%
–29	2	5.2	8.8
30–39	4.8	7.6	8
40–49	16	19	14.5
50–59	20.2	21.3	28.1
60–69	23.2	20.8	19.6
70–79	22.2	19.9	16.8
80+	11.6	6.2	4.2
Total 15,634	**11,415**	**1,178**	**3,041**

(h) Great Britain

In 1976, Great Britain including Scotland had 8 parishes without priests; in 1991 there were 53 such parishes.

It emerges from the report made by Mgr P. Hypher of Peterborough on behalf of Cardinal Basil Hume for this study that he received 100% answers from 22 dioceses. As elsewhere in Europe, Sunday practice among Catholics is steadily declining (by about 10% since 1980). This development is coupled with a decline in available priests, an increase in the age pyramid and a number of other factors. It is estimated that in the coming decade 1,350 will be lost through death, while no more than 400 newly ordained priests will replace them. Roughly speaking, this means a reduction in the priesthood of about a third, whereas in the next ten years about a thousand parishes without priests are expected. 60.2% of parish priests are older than fifty (37.3% older than sixty). In 1991 England and Wales had 3,616 diocesan priests in active service, including a number who had already retired. The 2,703 parishes have on average 1.34 priests per parish; the archdiocese of Liverpool estimates that 2.3 priests per parish are needed if account is also taken of specialized forms of apostolate.

The main way in which the problem has been dealt with hitherto is by a progressive reduction in the number of assistant priests. During the last five years this has taken place in more than 210 parishes (more in urban areas than in the country). Of the 53 parishes mentioned, 27 have been taken over by a neighbouring parish, 10 have been entrusted to religious, 3 to a religious community (but without priests) and two to a deacon.

Some dioceses began by reducing the number of celebrations of the eucharist. Three or four attempts have been made to link parishes and to entrust them to a team of priests. Some want to have more parishes led by deacons. A number of communities of sisters have given up their work in schools and hospitals to devote themselves to pastoral care in parishes. However, the lack of vocations is a threat to their existence. The process that has been intensified for about ten years and in which parishes are entrusted to religious priests has increased (this is now true of 11.6% of parishes: already 25% in Menevia, 27% in East Anglia and 29% in Cardiff). In the years to come, however, parishes will be handed back to the dioceses because of the ageing in religious orders.

The faithful have not been sufficiently prepared for this state of affairs, although developments are under way, stimulated above all by the diocesan pastoral councils (though these exist in only 50% of dioceses). The use of part-time or voluntary lay help is being steadily organized. Full-time work is far more exceptional. Priests themselves are disturbed by the increasing role of the laity, above all because of a lack in their training. For a number there is an explicit or latent crisis of identity resulting in frustration among the laity and despair among the clergy.[11]

Finally, there is no coherent form of study aimed at coping with the situation and giving objective information to the diocesan authorities. In the immediate future a further decline of more than 10% in the number of priests is expected (from 3,616 to 3,239 between 1991 and 1996).[12] After that the decline will accelerate. In 1991 there were 56 theology students in the first year, 73 in the second and 84 in the third. In this period the great diocese of Westminster did not have a single candidate.

3. Southern Europe

(a) France

Like other southern European countries, France has numerous very small parishes, even a large number of parishes which still exist canonically but in which no one lives any longer, although many of these have been abolished over the last decades. Alongside this there are the urban parishes with many thousands of baptized Catholics. In many rural areas one priest is responsible for 1, 5, 12 to 27 'parishes', though here the practice is often very low. The number of priests has been declining steadily from as long ago as 1938 – with a small interruption in 1951 – from 40,981 diocesan priests in 1965 to 28,629 in 1985 and about 19,700 in 1995, according to a maximal estimate. In 1965 40% were under 44; in 1989 5% were under 40 and 60% over sixty. In 1989 the average age was 66. Ordinations of priests declined from 1,355 in 1938 to 1,028 in 1951 and 370 in 1969. During the last twenty years the annual number of ordinations has fluctuated between 100 and 150, whereas 600 are needed annually to keep things stable. Of course this situation weighs heavily on the physical and spiritual health of the clergy. Thus in *La vie diocésaine de Rennes* (15 March 1993), Mgr Jacques Jullien, Archbishop of Rennes, commented: 'Fatigue, heart problems, sudden deaths and all kinds of health problems of which priests are victims are so many warnings.' Priests are more concerned over the future of their communities than over their own future (although many are living in a wretched state).

Since 1976, Monique Brulin has been studying the situation of parishes without priests on behalf of the Centre National de Pastorale Liturgique.[13] The ADAP system (Assemblées Dominicales en l'Absence de Prêtre = Sunday celebrations in the absence of a priest) has been introduced in more and more parishes to cope with the shortage of priests. In 1977, there were 1,136 such parishes; by 1987 their number had grown to at least 2,754. About 50% of these ADAPs involve communities with less than 500 inhabitants; 21% take place in communities of more than 1,000. In 70% of parishes women play a leading role. In an increasing number of dioceses – often as a result of diocesan synods – pastoral teams have been set up both for the ADAPs and for regional pastoral care. Priests support and co-ordinate these teams. This practice is leading to reflection on the role of the laity, the identity of the priest and the search for new forms of ministry.[14]

Despite the marked development of the ADAPs, their actual influence should not be exaggerated: the attendance at celebrations varies between 10 and 500 and more than half have a congregation of less than 50. Women make up two-thirds of those present. In the meantime awareness has steadily grown among believers. They are becoming aware of their responsibility; knowledge of the Bible is improving through the preparation of celebrations by the team; the faithful have also taken more responsibility for other tasks. In a number of places better attendance at celebrations can be noted. However, many problems remain: the ageing of the country population; a number of teams have experienced meagre and inadequate renewal; not all animators enjoy the trust of the faithful and a number are not suited for teaching. All observers emphasize the great need for continued training.

During the last decade synods have been held in many French dioceses. These have markedly contributed to the sharing of responsibility by the faithful. At the same time, in many places a wish has been expressed that ministries should be opened to married men and to women.

(b) Spain

According to the most recent information provided by the Oficina de Estadistica de la Iglesia en España,[15] in 1990 the church there comprised 22,305 parishes (as compared with 22,488 in 1986). The following table gives a picture of parishes with and without resident priests.

In interpreting this table it is necessary to note that Spain has many very small parishes: in 1984 there were 4,946 with less than 100 inhabitants, 6,619 with between 101 and 500 inhabitants, and also 1,490 with between 500 and 1,000 inhabitants. 1,058 had more than 10,000 inhabitants (above all in the agglomerations of Madrid and Barcelona).

Table. Parishes with and without Resident Priests (1986–1990)

Parishes	1986	1987	1988	1989	1990
With resident diocesan priest	11,178	10,990	10,941	10,826	10,797
With resident religious priest	920	955	973	985	1,003
Without resident priest	10,390	10,598	10,623	10,502	10,505

The age pyramid of all priests born in the Spanish dioceses shows a picture of ageing (1988): 11.3% under 40; 19.1% between 40 and 49; 31.7% between 50 and 59; 21.1% between 60 and 69; 10.1 between 70 and 79; 6.5 over 80. 30.4% of the clergy are below 50 and 37.8 above 60. In 1988 the average age of diocesan clergy was 56.8, and of religious clergy 53.6. In Spain in 1990 19,966 diocesan priests and 9,020 religious priests were involved in pastoral care.

After a marked decline in those at major seminaries for diocesan clergy (only 1,505 in 1979–80), the figure stabilized at around 2,000 between 1987 and 1992.

Between 1950 and 1975 large parts of Spain changed in a striking way: the rural population emigrated to the cities. In 1950, 38% of the population lived in urban areas, whereas in 1975 this was 71%. Thus many dioceses were forced to make a basic reorganization of pastoral work: parishes became small groupings, all the elements in which were entrusted to one priest. In the meantime more communities of sisters devoted themselves to pastoral work in the impoverished rural areas. The increasing shortage of priests led more and more bishops to introduce the French model of ADAPs. They set up courses to train the laity. This was particularly the case in the rural areas of Catalonia, where many parishes without a resident priest had to establish the system (1989): 1,539 priests were available for 2,237 parishes, and 1,174 parishes had no resident priests (with the result that many priests were burdened with two parishes, 106 with three, 38 with four, 19 with five and 47 with more than five).

At the same time the Spanish clergy were challenged by: 1. millions of foreign tourists who stayed for a long time, often also in the winter months; 2. excessive loads for an older clergy in the large cities; 3. the need for trained priests for a rapidly secularized milieu with better trained laity. It is still not sufficiently recognized that Spain is increasingly becoming a diaspora. Many observers hope for more initiatives to train lay people and demolish the sometimes deep-rooted clericalism.[16]

(c) Italy

Thanks to the collaboration of A.Filippi[17] it has been possible to make a first, still incomplete, survey of the Italian dioceses. Answers were received from 126 of the 224 dioceses (with 16,294 parishes); 98 (with 9,340 parishes) did not respond. Of the parishes which did respond, 2,255 had no resident pastor. Of these, 2,161 number less than 1,000 inhabitants,[18] 86 between 1,000 and 5,000 inhabitants, and 1 more than 5,000 inhabitants. Not long after the new 1984 concordat, on 30 July 1986 the Italian conference of bishops decided to abolish a number of very small parishes, mostly in the mountain villages, and to entrust them to pastors from neighbouring villages. These totalled 884. It is very seldom that one pastor has responsibility for three or more parishes. The situation differs markedly from diocese to diocese. It is above all parishes from the mountainous areas which have no resident priest, e.g. in the dioceses of Piacenza (129 parishes out of 428), Teramo-Atri (68 out of 187), Novara (66 out of 346) and Trent (82 out of 456). From the comments which one regularly hears, in the next decade the number of parishes without a resident priest will increase rapidly, not least because of the ageing of the clergy. According to the *Annuario Pontificio*, between 1968 and 1990 the number of diocesan priests declined by 15.75% (from 42,786 to 36, 058); in the meantime the population of Italy increased by around 4 million, which means that relatively the number of diocesan priests declined by 21%.

To judge by these responses it seems that people have hardly begun to reflect on the consequences of this development. Priests are increasingly concentrating on the celebration of the sacraments, which leaves less time for a thorough and direct evangelization and the guidance of a growth towards new ministries by trained lay people. However, in some dioceses efforts have been made to train the laity, both men and women, in taking up pastoral tasks in teams. The possibility of good training for a better future is certainly there: without doubt Italy, with Ireland and Malta, is sociologically the most Catholic country in Europe.[19]

4. Central and Eastern Europe

(a) Poland

This most Catholic country in Central and Eastern Europe has had an evolution which is markedly different from that in Western Europe. Before the Second World War and for quite a long period afterwards, the proportion of priests to Catholic population was far less favourable than for example that in Italy, Belgium of the Netherlands. Over recent decades, however, the number of ordinations has steadily increased to a peak in 1991.[20] The largest number of seminarians was reached in 1987–90. It is evident from the graph that the vocations increased most markedly between 1985 and 1987: compared to 1974 the increase of first-year religious seminarians was 119% (1985), of novice brothers 264% (1985), of novice sisters 103% and of first-year diocesan seminarians 62% (1987). Comparing these peak years with 1993 we see a decrease of 66.1 in the first-year religious seminarians, of 44.8% in novice brothers, of 41.2% in novice sisters and of 37.4% in first-year diocesan seminarians. Although there has not been a return to the level of 1974, the decline is striking.[21] Two possible explanations given are that the rapid increase was a consequence of the choice of a Polish pope, and only now is there a return to the 'normal' level, although Poland too has a crisis for roughly the same reasons as Western Europe has one. Future development will be able to give an answer here. Poland has hardly any parishes without a resident pastor, nor does it have a permanent diaconate.

Comparisons with the pre-war period are made difficult by the fact that Poland has had important changes in its frontiers. But it seems that for a long time Poland had relatively far fewer priests than many Western European countries.[22] Thus – of the Latin rite – there were 7,977 diocesan priests in 1925, 10,154 in 1939 and 12,713 in 1958.

Table. Development in the Number of Seminarians and Newly Ordained Priests

Year	Seminarians			Newly ordained			Total priests		
	Diocesan	Religious	Total	Diocesan	Religious	Total	Diocesan	Religious	Total
1982	5,018	2,207	7,225	571	204	775	15,942	5,117	21,059
1987	5,859	3,179	9,038	711	298	1,009	17,726	5,706	23,432
1993	4,679	2,720	7,399	760	372	1,132	20,555	6,504	27,059

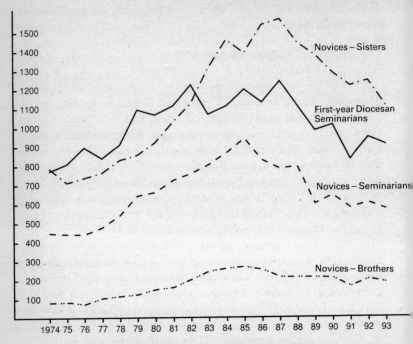

Graph. Development of Novice Religious and First-Year
Diocesan Seminarians, 1974–1993

The number of sisters has been far more stable: between 1974 and 1993 the total number remained approximately the same, with a slight decline in those who belonged to an active apostolic order (from 25, 902 to 24,551) and a slight increase in those belonging to a contemplative order (from 1,270 to 1,362). However, the number of novices has taken quite a different course (see graph above).

(b) Czechia and Slovakia

The decrease in the number of priests (as a result of persecution and the small number of candidates who were admitted to the seminaries)[23] is evident from the following table. The result of this has been that in 1990 about half the parishes had no resident priest. The period between 1990 and 1993 is too short to allow any prognoses of the future. A monograph by Dr Z.Bohac provides information about the recent situation in

Bohemia. During the last century the alienation of the church, above all in the cities, constantly increased. At the beginning of this century most intellectuals and workers no longer had any real links with the church. The vocations came almost exclusively from the villages. Between 1919 and 1921 a large number of the clergy and faithful went over to the newly established church of the Hussites. In the country, pastoral care remained largely limited to the administration of the sacraments. The apostolate among the young was virtually non-existent. At the end of the 1940s, the more active parishes (the German ones) were split off from the rest, and in 1948 many seminaries were closed and the religious orders banned. A limited number of priests and laity went underground. All this of course caused an increase in the number of parishes without a priest. Thus the diocese of Hradec Kralóvé (Königgrätz) had a resident priest in only 186 of its 477 parishes, and in the diocese of Ceské Budejovice (Budweis), 305 of the 430 parishes had no resident priest.[24]

Moreover, the age pyramid has been turned upside down, as we can see from the number of ordinations in the diocese of the church province of Bohemia (figures before 1989 and relating to the priests still alive):

Present State of the Clergy in Bohemia by Years of Ordination

Diocese	1940–49	1950–59	1960–69	1970–79	1980–89	Number of parishes
Prague	104	48	32	58	34	623
Ceské Budejovice	65	29	26	35	15	433
Hradec Kràlové	135	25	23	43	20	77
Litomerice	77	10	20	21	14	445
Bohemia	**381**	**113**	**101**	**157**	**83**	**1,978**

How the situation deteriorated this century is evident from the table of ordinations in the diocese of Ceské Budejovice:

Situation in 1949		Situation in 1989	
1900–09	72	1940–49	77
1910–19	93	1950–59	10
1920–29	20	1960–69	20
1930–39	98	1970–79	21
1940–49	115	1980–89	14
Total	**398**	**Total**	**142**

We note that around 1940, of the 1,978 parishes of the church province of Bohemia, 788 were predominantly German-speaking and 1,190 predominantly Czech-speaking.

Since 1990 the number of seminarians (studying theology) in Prague has again risen, but is far from enough to meet the needs of the four dioceses mentioned (figures for 1990/91):

	Diocesan seminarians	Religious seminarians*
First year	26	10
Second year	21	5
Third year	18	6
Fourth year	14	8
Fifth year	14	6

*This figure does not include religious who are trained in their own houses.

The situation in Moravia is clearly better. Perhaps an exchange of priests with Bohemia is possible, but there are a great many psychological problems. The author thinks more in terms of deacons, theologically trained laity, better co-ordination between urban and country areas.

Of course in Czechoslovakia the question is being raised of the place of married men ordained priests during the Communist persecution. The complexity of the situation cannot be summed up here. A number of priests were incorporated into the Greek Catholic Slovakian diocese of Presov. At the beginning of 1994 a Greek Catholic vicariate was established in Prague for the scattered Greek Catholics of Czechia. It is not impossible that some married priests have also been accepted here. Of course the whole adaptation of a Latin clergy to the style of Greek Catholics remains. In the meantime the situation remains very problematical for the Latin majority church, above all in Czechia. In 1994 the average age of the diocesan clergy was 65. There are 1,529 priests for 3,104 parishes (of which only 1,960 are served by priests), and this number includes all those who are retired and also the religious who live in parishes at the request of the bishops. Between 1991 and the end of 1993 there was a marked increase in the number of seminarians. This improvement now seems to be at an end. Entry into religious institutions is following the same curve. Given the very clerical and hierarchical past of the Czech church, it will be a long time yet before a sufficient sense of shared responsibility grows among priests and laity for more lay people to direct pastoral work and be integrated into it.[25]

In passing, it should be noted that according to the European Values Study (1990), in Czechia 31% claim to believe in God and 15% in the resurrection (Slovakia 64% and 39%); 72% have little confidence in the church (Slovakia 50%).

(c) Hungary

According to a study by E.Andraš,[26] the number of priests declined by at least 60 in the period between 1969 and 1980. The total number declined from 3,720 in 1960 to around 1,700 in 1990. The number of seminarians declined from 525 in 1954 to 130 in 1983.

Pastoral work is further handicapped by the abolition of the religious orders in 1950, which then numbered 2,582 priests and 8,956 sisters.

Between 1984 and 1994 the total number of priests declined from 3,117 to 2,005. For the year 2000 the number is estimated at 1,850, and for 2005 at 1,400.

A 1991 case study made by A.Maté-Tóth[27] of the diocese of Zeged–Csanad shows that between 1980 and 1990 the number of active priests declined from 147 (2,478 Catholics per priest) to 100 (3,643 Catholics per priest). In 1950 the diocese still numbered 247 priests (230 active in pastoral work). It is conjectured that there will be only 67 priests in 2004 (58 of them active). The number of ordinations declined from 11 (1980–82) to 9 (1983–85) and 3 (1986–90). The faithful are not aware of the seriousness of the situation, have no insight into the possibility of pastoral teams, and are not up with the renewed theological study of the relationship between priests and faithful. At the moment 27 out of the 113 parishes have no resident priest. In coming years a slight increase is expected in the number of seminarians, though the low birthrate continues to limit growth.

According to Dr M.Tomka, in Hungary the reality of the parishes without resident priests is disguised by the official statistics. For more than twenty years now, parishes which have no local priest have been incorporated as branches of one regional parish. Pastors are then responsible for five, six and even twelve branches. To ensure that the eucharist can still be attended in the country, relatively more pastors are appointed there than in the cities. The result is that there are country parishes with one priest for 800 faithful and urban parishes with one priest for 40,000 faithful. Masses are celebrated, but there is still little real pastoral care. As most priests are overburdened, they have no time to devote themselves adequately to the training of laity and making

Europe without Priests?

renewal possible in collaboration with them. Furthermore the old clerical mentality which has traditionally marked the church life of Hungary has a stubborn existence, so that priests and laity tend to get involved in suspicious confrontation.

Finally, E.Andraš and other observers note that the Greek Catholics, who have their own diocese in Hungary, have no shortage of priests and seminarians. Whereas only an eighth of the Latin clergy is under forty, this proportion among Greek Catholics is one third.

(d) Other Central and Eastern European countries

There are no detailed studies, nor is there reliable information about trends. According to the *Annuarium Statisticum Ecclesiae* the situation looks like this.

Table. Parishes With and Without a Resident Pastor (–1992)

	Parishes with resident		Parishes without
	secular pastor	religious pastor	resident pastor
Lithuania (1987)	459	7	165
(1992)	414	28	225
Latvia (1976)	107	11	60
(1987)	79	4	96
(1992)	69	10	120
Estonia (1992)	1	1	?
Roumania (1992)	967	36	807
Bulgaria (1992)	26	19	7

5. Summary facts about other Christian churches

Both the new ecumenical context and the request which is often heard for information about the other Christian churches justify this very brief survey.

(a) Roumania

According to the 1991 census, 87% of the population (around 22 million) is Roumanian Orthodox. A 1994 statistic from the patriarchate indicates that there are 8,400 parishes in the 21 dioceses of the Orthodox Church, served by 8,000 priests. There are 4,397 students (seminarians and other church workers) in the more than 20 seminaries. In the 367 religious houses there are 5,200 monks and sisters.[28]

(b) Hungary

After the Catholic Church (with about 7 million members out of a total population of 10 million), the Reformed Church is the most important (around 2 million). The four study houses for the training of ministers are full. There is still no shortage of pastors (around 1,500 for the 1,200 communities). The church is financed by its own system of church tax.[29] But the Greek Catholic Church has more candidates for the priesthood than the Reformed Church.

(c) Greece

The Greek Orthodox Church has around 9,000 parishes for a population of 10.5 million, serviced by 6,500 married priests and 1,000 unmarried priests or monks. There is no resident priest in 1,500 parishes. The priests are paid by the state (there is no division between church and state – priests are state officials). The priests are divided into categories from A to E depending on the level of their training (those who belong to category E may not even have completed school courses and are mostly retired). Parishes without priests are to be found above all in the villages in the north and east. Younger men who study theology opt to become teachers of religion in secondary education (religion is a compulsory subject in all schools); they do not want to become priests of a hierarchy which they regard as conservative. This also explains why few sons of priests want to become priests. Since normally they only celebrate the liturgy on Sunday, many village priests work on the land during the week. The Greek clergy feel very isolated. The hierarchy tries to protect them against secularization and thus furthers a degree of fundamentalism, but above all fear of other Christians of Western Europe (both Catholics and Protestants). Coupled with this is a markedly nationalistic spirit ('only Greek Orthodox are authentic Greeks'). Although the official statistics say that 98% of Greeks (according to their identity cards) are Greek Orthodox, only between 3% and 4% go to church on Sunday. The hierarchy points to the 'decline' of the church in the West (the question of the ordination of women among Protestants, the loss of priests among Catholics, the primacy and the infallibility of the Pope, the secular power of the Vatican and so on) in order to emphasize the worth of the Greek Orthodox Church and its loyalty to the tradition of the church fathers. To meet the needs of parishes without priests, the metropolitans entrust three or four village parishes to one priest (which given the long duration of the ceremonies is not regarded as normal). Because of their weak theological training, priests of categories D and E may not preach or hear confessions. Preachers and confessors from elsewhere are sent to help here. Reformed laity may also preach. From what has been said above, the absence of any ecumenical spirit, above all in the hierarchy, the priests and the monks, is evident; this contrasts with the ordinary faithful and those who are better educated; they are far more open.[30]

(d) Scandinavia

Although there are regional exceptions, in Sweden the Lutheran state church is struggling with a shortage of vocations to the priesthood. As in Denmark, the shortage would be even greater were there no women priests. According to A.Bäckström[31] 21% of the Swedish clergy are women. At the end of the 1970s there was a marked increase in the ordinations of priests, as a result of which the average age is now relatively young. In the 1980s the number declined again. In the diocese of Strängnäs, for example, one can see a very normal age curve (13% under 35, 43% 36–45, 27% 46–55, 17% over 56). Fewer children of priests than before become priests themselves: one in four of parents of the clergy had close links with the church, but most clergy were members of church youth movements. Among the new candidates, 50% are women (according to some observers a sign that the priestly vocation has become less valued in society). There is a clear ecumenical tendency among the clergy: 61% want to work with the Roman Catholic Church. About 65% of the male priests say that they accept the ordination of women, which is noticeably more than 10 years ago; above all the younger ones are more open. It needs to be noted that according to the European Values Study, 83% of Swedes say that they belong to a church, but only 4% go to worship regularly; 40% believe in God, 21% in the resurrection.

The Finnish Evangelical Lutheran Church, which is also a state church, has a numerous church personnel (18,813 at the end of 1991, with a decline after 1992 because of the economic recession).[32] The great majority have no theological training. In 1991 the clergy numbered 3,432 (608 on a pension), of whom 1,658 were active in the 600 parishes of the country (the size of which varies between 58,195 and 127, with an average of 12,584 in the urban and 4,460 in the rural parishes). In Finland 87% of the population belongs to the Lutheran church (90% were baptized into this church). In the period between 1988 and 1991, 207 men and 508 women were ordained (in 1988 the ministry was opened to women). For a long time the number of priests has remained very stable, but a decline in the number of theology students is expected: the economic crisis is reducing the income form church tax.

Although around 90% of Danes belong to the Lutheran state church, active Christianity there is very weak (around 3% practise regularly). In 1989 there were 2,073 parishes and as many ministers, 409 of them women (the proportion of women in the total is constantly increasing). We note that there are 28,000 Catholics above the age of sixteen (out of 5.2 million inhabitants), and their number has been stagnating for years (as in Finland and Norway, in contrast to Sweden). Of the roughly 100 priests, two-thirds are foreigners.[33]

6. New forms of pastoral ministry

Although in church law these new forms, deacons apart, are classified under the broad heading of pastoral workers, numerous men and women who come under them carry out an actual function of leadership, usually because there is no resident priest or because of the limitations which their age brings. This is the case not only for a number of deacons but also for those who belong to the broad range of pastoral assistants, 'workers', local moderators, at celebrations without priests, in hospital chaplaincies, in schools and movements. Many of them have in fact taken on the traditional leadership tasks of the priesthood, apart from the sacramental ministry strictly reserved to the ordained priesthood, including the celebration of the eucharist, confession and the anointing of the sick.

(a) The diaconate

Since Vatican II restored the permanent diaconate, the number of men ordained to it has gradually increased in the various continents, as is evident from Table 1. It is striking that the increase is greatest in those continents (Europe, and above all North America) where the relationship between priests and Catholics is still relatively most favourable. In most other continents catechists have already long taken over the tasks of deacons, locally often with broader competences than those of a deacon. Moreover the actual tasks of deacons have been carried out in a great variety of ways.

Table 1. Permanent Diaconate. Distribution by Continents (1972–1992)

	1972	1980	1985	1992
Africa	18	91	235	297
North America	283	3,257	7,522	11,040
Latin America	55	550	1,122	2,530
Asia	2	49	64	92
Europe	228	1,202	2,335	5,329
Oceania	2	52	55	107
Total	**588**	**6,456**	**11,333**	**19,939**

(Source:*Annuarium Statisticum Ecclesiae*)

In Europe the deacons are concentrated in particular countries. In 1992 these were Germany (1,618), Italy (1,270), France (830), Belgium (450), Austria (293), Great Britain (287), The Netherlands (178), Spain 167. None of the other countries has as many as 100.

In 1992, 133 parishes without a resident priest were entrusted to a permanent deacon. The greatest concentration is to be found in Italy (57), Switzerland (28) and Germany (21). Markedly more parishes have been entrusted to lay people (853) and to sisters (198).

(b) Laity involved in pastoral work

This section will simply offer a more statistical and in many respects incomplete survey, to be supplemented by the last chapter. For many countries there are no preliminary studies of this other very important area.

Above all from around 1970, more and more pastoral tasks have been entrusted to the laity. The way in which these unordained men and women are used, trained and appointed differs from country to country and often from diocese to diocese. A good deal depends on the finance available. In countries where there is a church tax, like Germany, or where there is a tradition of generous support from the faithful in the parishes, as in the Netherlands, lay volunteers have far more opportunities than elsewhere. Everywhere one finds a difference between laity trained for pastoral work who may well have had an academic training and others with only minimal training. The following survey does not aim at completeness. Only a few models and tendencies are described.

(i) Germany

A distinction is made between academically trained 'pastoral assistants' on the one hand and non-academically trained 'community assistants' on the other.[34] In order to achieve some stability and harmony at an inter-diocesan level, in 1977–79 the conference of bishops published important statutory texts: *Zur Ordnung der Pastoralen Dienste, Rahmenstatut für Pastoralreferenten(-innen), Rahmenstatut für die Ausbildung.* The difference between the ordained priesthood and non-ordained ministries is emphasized. Initially, above all supra-parochial tasks were entrusted to the 'pastoral assistants' to avoid confusion with parish priests. Since then the statutes have been regularly adapted and there is a very great difference between the various dioceses. In the meantime questions have increased about the theological position of these lay theologians, about their spirituality and their relationship to the church. There is noticeable vocational uncertainty. Whereas the number of lay theologians has steadily increased, the bishops have limited the number of places available for pastoral work (already in 1983 there were only 3,000 places for 13,000 lay theologians). In the meantime, in more and more parishes lay theologians are becoming 'reference persons', though the real responsibility lies with a pastor from elsewhere. The bishops want to avoid the distinctive profile of the lay theologian (or deacon) being blurred by the acceptance of priestly tasks. It is also clear from a number of studies that in general lay theologians are more progressive and critical of the church than the average priest.[35] Their quantitative presence differs greatly from diocese to diocese; for example in 1990 in Regensburg there were 11.5 full-time pastoral lay workers to every 100 priests in Regensburg, as compared with 55.8 in Mainz. In 1990 there were 5,163 full-time lay workers in pastoral work, of which 1,551 were 'pastoral assistants' and 3,612 'community assistants' (male and female), i.e. 8 and 18 per 100 priests respectively. Thus there are approximately ten times more

full-time lay workers than deacons (552 out of 1,469). Pastoral
assistants comprise 1,059 men as compared with 492 women, but
community assistants comprise 672 men and 2, 940 women.

(ii) The Netherlands

As in Germany, so in the Netherlands the gradual preparation and
employment of academically trained laity in pastoral work began around
1970. They were given a church mandate with a salary laid down by legal
statutes. These laity are called 'pastoral workers'. Their number is
constantly increasing. They work at the level of the diocese, the
diaconate, the parish and in hospitals. Table 1 indicates how many of
them are employed in pastoral care at the base, in other words have a
relationship to a parish.[36] For every 100 priests who are working for the
dioceses, in 1985 there were 19 pastoral workers and in 1990 33 (22 of
them in pastoral care at the base level). There are great differences
among the dioceses: in 1990 Groningen, Utrecht and Breda had more
than 40 pastoral workers for every 100 priests working in the diocese. In
addition, in the Netherlands a large number of voluntary workers work
in church ministries.[37]

Table 2. Pastoral Workers (Men and Women) in the Netherlands (1975–1990)

	Absolute figures				percentage in base pastoral care			
	1975	1980	1985	1990	1975	1980	1985	1990
total number of	154	302	392	543				
women	13	45	81	166	55	63	53	47

Since the pastoral workers have been assigned more and more
leadership tasks in the church and some bishops have also been asked to
ordain married men among them as priests, a discussion has arisen in
both the Netherlands and in Rome over the identity of priests. The
Special Synod of the Dutch Bishops in Rome therefore led to a number
of decisions which in fact amounted to a reassertion both of the celibacy
of priests and of the essential difference between priests and laity.[38]
There have also gradually been interventions in the bishops' policy of
nomination, as a result of which the homogeneity of the conference of

bishops has been demolished. However, the small number of ordinations during the last decade is keeping the position of pastoral workers alive.[39]

(iii) Belgium

In contrast to Germany and the Netherlands, it is impossible to provide a clear survey for Belgium. Not only are there great differences between Flanders and Wallonia, but even within Flanders the dioceses have their own formulae for the employment of laity. The dioceses of Antwerp and Gent and the Flemish-speaking part of the archdiocese of Malines–Brussels have a system of 'pastoral workers' who have been specially trained. However, in contrast to the Netherlands, most have no academic training. In addition there are many forms of training by catechists, 'pastoral helpers', 'pastoral animators', parish assistants, and many thousands of volunteers. For the whole area of the Flemish church in 1989–90 twenty-five times as many laity as paid workers were active in parishes or deaneries. The two obstacles which markedly prevent further development are an inadequate theological training and above all the very limited financial means (although 'Catholic' Flanders is one of the richest regions of Europe). Hospital chaplains however, are paid by the institutions which recruit them: here moreover one finds a number of academically trained laity.[40]

Over the last thirty-five years the theological faculty of the Catholic University of Louvain has trained around 1,100 theologically educated laity, i.e. for the last fifteen years around three times more than the diocesan student priests who completed their theological studies. Half of these lay people who have completed their studies are women. By far the majority of academically trained laity become teachers of religion, among other reasons because that is the only place where they can be trained.

In French-speaking Belgium there are no 'pastoral workers'. Each diocese has its own system of recruiting and training lay volunteers.[41] However, there are fewer academically trained lay theologian there than in Flanders.

(iv) Austria

Lay theologians are working in church ministry in all nine dioceses of Austria.

	In parishes			In a pastoral category		At diocesan level		Total
	Male	Female	Total	Male	Female	Total	Male	Female	Total
1980			33		37		47			117
1983			71							
1990	106	48	154	62	19	81	79	19	98	333

In addition to these academically trained lay people there are numerous others with less training in pastoral theology by comparison with the German 'community workers'. The payment of these lay people differs, depending on the level (parochial and diocesan), and is helped by the form of church tax which exists in Austria.

(v) Switzerland

In 1970 in the six Swiss dioceses there were still no lay people in pastoral ministry. In the meantime their number has constantly increased, from 220 in 1975 and 500 in 1980 to around 1000. It was evident from a careful investigation in 1985 that at the time 795 lay people (376 women and 419 men) worked professionally in the service of the dioceses. This comprises 21% of the total (10% women and 11% men, 48% active diocesan priests, 16% religious priests, 14% retired priests, 1% deacons). Of the 795 laity, at the time 27% were active in parishes as pastoral assistants, 49% in parochial catechesis, 18% in specialized tasks, 12% in movements, 7% as directors of schools, 12% in the diocesan administration or in training. In addition to that a very high number of lay volunteers are active in the parishes.

The pastoral planning committee of the Swiss conference of bishops envisages that the number of laity employed will constantly increase. The strong financial structure, including forms of church tax, has made the development of the employment of laity by the church possible, more in German- than in French-speaking Switzerland.

It is already clear from this summary survey that in German-speaking Europe the organized application of the employment of lay people has led to striking results in a relatively short time. Although in Latin Europe many thousands of pastoral laity are involved, given the very great difference and the lack of comparable statistics, it is as yet impossible to give any survey.[42]

II

Ministries in the New Testament and the Early Church

Peter Schmidt

1. To begin with, an old story

When Samuel became old, he made his sons judges over Israel. The name of his first-born son was Joel, and the name of his second, Abijah; they were judges in Beersheba. Yet his sons did not walk in his ways, but turned aside after gain; they took bribes and perverted justice. Then all the elders of Israel gathered together and came to Samuel at Ramah, and said to him, 'Behold, you are old and your sons do not walk in your ways; now appoint for us a king to govern us like all the nations.' But the thing displeased Samuel; when they said, 'Give us a king to govern us.' And Samuel prayed to YHWH. And YHWH said to Samuel, 'Hearken to the voice of the people in all that they say to you; for they have not rejected you, but they have rejected me from being king over them. According to all the deeds which they have done to me, from the day I brought them up out of Egypt even to this day, forsaking me and serving other gods, so they are also doing to you. Now then, hearken to their voice . . .' (I Sam.8.1–9).

An attractive story from the Old Testament, that nowadays is better denoted by the acronym Tenach.[1] The Tenach came into the world very slowly. Its formation took many centuries. The thousand-year history of its growth has made the book an extremely complex construction, but the complexity of a long and slow growth also has unmistakable advantages. The book of the first covenant illustrates more clearly than the New Testament the degree to which what we call 'Word of God' and 'revelation' is characterized by the good and ill, the to-ings and fro-ings, of centuries of contingent history and evolution.

I chose the Samuel text as an introduction to this chapter because it has some interesting motifs which are well worth considering. For a long time the kingship was the highest and most holy office in Israel. As the anointed pastor and leader of the people (*meshi'ach*, Messiah), as the supreme sacrificer, as the mediator between YHWH and Israel, indeed as 'son of God', the king was a model of the relationship between God and his people. Since the kingship ideology of David and Solomon, the kingship had become the dominant expression of God's pastoral care of his chosen people. The king was as it were the sacrament of God's concern for his people. The Bible has abundant texts which confirm this view of the kingship. Among the many I need mention only the prophecy of Nathan in II Sam.7.4–17 and the messianic Psalms 2 and 110. The kingship was so much seen as the expression of God's will for Israel that after the exile the kingship ideology became a real theology, 'messianic theology', to which the people's dreams of salvation were attached. In ancient Israel a long search was needed to find a pastoral office which was more 'by divine right' than kingship. The Christian confession of Jesus as 'Messiah', 'Son of God' and 'Son of David' could be understood precisely on the basis of the Davidic model of the Old Testament kingship theology. The Christian belief is that God's will has found its eschatological fulfilment in Jesus. This is what we confess, and therefore we call Jesus the Christ, i.e. the anointed one, after the model of the king of Israel, the pastoral office *par excellence* by the will of God.

The high sacrality of kingship and the view that it was 'by the will of God' lasted for centuries and centuries. In antiquity Christians saw the Christianized Roman emperors in the same light, as the pastors of the people appointed by God. The Byzantine emperors revered this same theology up to the fall of Constantinople. When the mediaeval rulers, emperors and kings of the West had themselves anointed, this was with a clear pointer towards the sacral, even sacramental, dimension of their kingship, with just as clear a reference to the Davidic model.[2] Thus many people interpreted the beheading of Charles I or England or the guillotining of Louis XVI of France as a blasphemous act, and contemporary church reactions also took this line. The kingship of the Christian rulers derived from a sacred tradition which was almost thirty centuries old.

Still, kingship in Israel certainly did not begin with the general acceptance that it was the expression of the will of God. First and foremost there is the bare historical fact that there was a period of a couple of centuries when there were no kings. The confederation of twelve tribes was a much more 'democratic' reality, with quite autocephalous tribes, whose 'princes' (*nasim*) were the authorities and elders (*zeqenim*) the representatives. The office of 'judges' *(shopetim)* was regarded as a co-ordinating institution; according to biblical tradition Samuel's sons were the last two judges. Centuries-old anti-royalist traces have survived in the Old Testament from the old tribal theology of the people of God in which God was the only true king (and thus there was no human king).[3] In this earlier phase of Israel's history the term 'theocracy' means that God himself, and not a man, was king over Israel. This is not the place to go into the literary strata of the book of Samuel,[4] or to reconstruct the precise origin of the monarchy in Israel. But it is important to see how the biblical notion which connects the pastoral office of the king to the idea of God's eternal will is not eternal, but developed in history.

In the story about Samuel which I quoted, neither Samuel nor YHWH himself are favourable to Israel's proposal to anoint a king. For YHWH, this is yet one more sign of the disloyalty of the people. But he seems ready to allow them to do what they want, and so he advises Samuel to yield. The story offers one of the many illustrations in the Bible in which God as it were 'adapts' himself to the historical situation and makes the best of it. The biblical God – above all in the pre-prophetic view – is not a God who himself plans and marks out history at every point; he is a God who so to speak sees how human beings make their history, and shows enough inventiveness to allow his covenant with humankind to grow in history. YHWH constantly creates a new future. This idea of God already begins with Adam and Eve in paradise, and with the story of the flood and the tower of Babel: human beings go against God's will, and God can even repent of his own decisions and actions, but he continues his adventure with humankind along new ways. That is also the case with the birth of the kingship. Once the Israelites have their king, God will attach his covenant to this office as his sacrament, and the pastoral office of the king will become a privileged expression of God's will. The view of history which underlies such a notion is attractive and liberating; history is not determined *a priori* by God, but God adapts his will flexibly to the changing context of historical circumstances.

The Tenach knows many such examples, and Judaism to the present day confirms the historical view which underlies this. Kingship disappeared with the exile and became an eschatological ideal, a kind of utopia. But specific offices for leading the people of God continued to be necessary, even if the king was sadly no more. Therefore in the Persian period the function of high priest developed into that of religious leader of the people. And when the prophetic office – for that, too, had been in existence – disappeared, counsellors are still to be found in what was later to become the Sanhedrin, and the rabbinic scholars took over the role of the expounders of God's will. After the exile, when in accordance with the precepts of Deuteronomy there was only a single temple for the whole of Judaism, and synagogue communities developed everywhere, there, too, offices developed which had not existed under the monarchy. The individual synagogue communities were led by a 'ruler of the synagogue'. After the destruction of Jerusalem in 70 CE, the office of priest in the temple finally disappeared. Judaism lived on with other types of leadership, necessitated by circumstances. These other forms have developed and matured down to the present day. A community always needs an order. In biblical terms, the ordering of the faith community is a work of God's spirit.

The Samuel story teaches an important lesson: the paradigms in which God's guidance of his people takes full form have changed in the course of time, although God's will remains the same. Throughout history God's will for a covenant with his people follows as it were the vicissitudes of historical events. Here the Bible offers a consistent picture of human freedom to decide and act. And to return to the kingship: who would now dare to argue that kingship formally derives from the explicitly revealed will of God and must therefore remain unchanged? The harsh fact of the guillotine put an end to this theology. But on the other hand, what believers would claim that other political offices like presidency and parliament are not in the end called 'to fulfil God's will'? The only question is what God's will really means in the social system, and how people are called to do it in changing times. The will of God remains the same in a democracy as in a monarchy. It is not focussed on political forms, but on the challenge to build a just society as a sphere for the covenant between God and humankind.

We could sum up this brief survey as follows: offices and functions change, but God's covenantal will remains. Furthermore, if this fundamental covenantal will is to remain, offices must show sufficient historical flexibility to adapt. A reference to the Old Testament in its long, thousand-year-old history calls for a fundamental reflection on the relationship between history as it evolves in practice and what we call the will of God.

The Old Testament provided the model for the historical views of the first Christians. Of course the New Testament makes a new contribution, which could be summed up as the eschatological fulfilment of God's saving will in Christ. But the view of the New Testament writers about the relationship between revelation (of God's will) and history – in other words, their view of the covenant – is almost literally the same as that of the Tenach. For the first Christians, too, what we want to call God's word or God's will does not present itself as a pre-existing structure the forms of which are fixed once and for all, which remain external to the conditioning of a culture by time and space, and which can be impressed on history from outside. On the contrary, they allowed themselves to be led by historical circumstances ('the signs of the time') in the quest for order and leadership in their communities.

It could not be otherwise. One cannot force living history into given structures. Those who have attempted to do so have always both caused a good deal of torment and experienced great disillusionment. This is what fundamentalist reflections and totalitarian patterns of thought are still trying to bring about in our time: for them, history has to adapt itself to principles. When this does not prove possible, it is thought that it is not the principles which are wrong, but the whole of history. When those who cherish such ideas are fanatics, they do not hesitate to exclude people whom they hold responsible for a course of history which does not accord with their absolute principles. So they often use only the argument of power, seize power, or, if they possess it, sacralize it and hold on to it tenaciously. History is full of examples, in the political systems and the religions of many cultures.

Now such a mentality, of which perhaps fear of chaos is the deepest foundation, is contested by the story from Samuel. It has been the cause of many wars and much unjust violence, of the blind use of force, of hatred, condemnations, exclusions and countless mutual hostilities. To put it in Platonic terms, this form of thinking seems to me to be a kind of rigid application of the theory of ideas to historical reality. The concern is to derive concrete history from ideal patterns of perfection with which they must accord. Or, facts don't count against arguments. This is essentially a deductive and essentialist way of thinking. The concern is to derive the actual course of history from prior principles, which are thought of as already existing – divine? – essences.

It is above all totalitarian ideologies or systems which want to force history into a mould. Religions, too, are open to this temptation, perhaps most of all those religions which came into being in the biblical and

Mediterranean cultures. Past history teaches that they must always be on their guard against totalitarian mechanisms. Philip II and the rearguard action of the nineteenth-century church against modern freedoms provides a painful illustration here. Today we can also see from certain fundamentalist tendencies within Islam to what consequences this can lead.

In fact this mechanism is not at all what it imagines itself to be, namely an attempt to make history correspond with the will of God. It is more a matter of identifying a particular system with God and therefore absolutizing and sacralizing it, and wanting to make or keep history in conformity with that. In reality, however, history is not being conformed with God's will but with a self-made image of God. That is why such mechanisms are so close to the 'will to power'. But they are pursuing illusions. The concrete fulfilment of God's will is *never given in advance*; it is not an already formed mould into which reality can be poured. We cannot take seriously enough the basic intuition of biblical faith that God reveals himself in and through history. There is no revelation of the will of God outside history which one can take down the centuries like a suitcase always containing the same immutable content. Some of the signs of the time can teach where the will of God must be sought. Or, to put it another way, it is not the past from which we come that is the ultimate norm, though it is very true that we cannot understand our own situation without the past, and that there is much to be learned from the past. Rather, the norm must be sought in the way in which the present has to be experienced so that it becomes the future.

It is clear that the experience of history among people today, including Christians, largely escapes existing church structures. That does not mean that there should be no structures. Quite the contrary. Even Paul, the advocate of freedom, endorses them. Without structures any community goes to rack and ruin and succumbs to the right of the strongest, to a fundamental lack of freedom. The 'will of God' cannot be realized in a community without structures. This will is fundamental and always directed towards building up a human community in justice and love. In my view, this alone should be sufficient foundation for the ministry as sacrament. But another insight seems to me to be extremely important: no single concrete structural form is God, nor is any tradition, however venerable; nor are these absolute. Now, as then, structures must constantly seek new paradigms for realizing God's covenant will sacramentally, so that these can be signs of the will of God in this world. This is what the Old Testament constantly did – as it were without standing still.

Jesus himself was also a new paradigm of God's sacramental presence in the world. In fact, according to the Christian confession of faith Jesus is the definitive paradigm. But that does not mean that this paradigm is formally fixed. What is definitive is the direction he indicated for doing God's will: opting uncompromisingly for human well-being. *Gloria Dei vivens homo* – the glory of God is the living human being. However, this is a trend, a movement, and therefore is possible only with changing models. Jesus' own attitude was a new paradigm. His attitude towards publicans and sinners, the prostitute, the leper, the Samaritan, was a living image of this. In the name of the new paradigm Jesus healed the women who was bent over (Luke 13.10–27) and the man with the withered hand, on the sabbath, against the letter of the sabbath law. From the standpoint of a religious structure which has been absolutized, in so doing he was going too far, and 'the Pharisees and the Herodians made plans to do away with him' (Mark 3.1–6). It would be a misconception to think that a phrase like 'new wine in new skins' applied only to the short period of his historical appearance, and that one could then freeze this moment as an unchangeable model to be applied to the further course of history; in other words, that one could formally fix the further course of history in the forms in which Jesus' own history and that of his disciples ran their course. Neither the Old nor the New Testaments are recipe books from which we can prepare the forms of our experience of history. 'New wine in new skins' is a phrase which serves as a model, not only for the New Testament period, but also for the church of today and all days.

2. From an old story to a long story

In a fundamental reflection on the relationship between God's will and concrete history I now want to open another register which in my view is far too neglected in thought about forms of the church and ministries. At first this register may sound strange and unusual, but I am convinced that it urgently needs to be incorporated into the theological organ, not only in connection with forms and structures, but also in connection with dogmatic and ethical questions.

We must reflect on what concept of time underlies the attitude of those who think that church structures can be kept unchanged in conformity with a predetermined model all down the ages. There is something strange about the idea that traditions can go through the whole of history unchanged and that this immutability is an adequate expression of God's will. This notion can only arise when time is short enough. In fact one gets the strong impression that church arguments are still presented within a temporal framework which is not fundamentally different from that of the Bible. What I mean is that the Bible thinks of the course of history taking place within a very short temporal perspective, a few thousand years, a time-span which one can survey as a whole. Of course the Bible presents itself as a book which offers a survey of history as a whole, from creation to the end. Here we must not forget that the appearance of Jesus and the first disciples, and of course almost the whole of the New Testament, lie in a period when people could think that the end was near. There is no doubt that for example both the Qumran people and the early disciples of Jesus – and in all probability Jesus himself – lived in the expectation of the possibility that history had come to an end. And that creates a really remarkable horizon of thought: those who were familiar with the biblical history could have the illusion that they were surveying the whole of history, from alpha to omega.

For someone like Paul the time had 'become short' (I Cor.7). He thought that he himself would still be alive at the return of Jesus, when the curtain would fall on history (I Thess.4.17). It is true that the expectation of an imminent parousia is already fading in the New Testament (Luke, II Peter). Nevertheless, the biblical picture of time (and that of all Westerners down the birth of modern astronomy and palaeontology) is very short. The history of the world and of human beings still lies within the human perspective and can be surveyed.

In such a view of time and space one can indeed think that there are things which will go on 'for ever', in other words as long as history lasts. More precisely, in religious communities it can then be imagined that certain structural forms can survive fundamentally unchanged throughout world history. In these matters thought is not in terms of a cosmic or biological time-scale. Those who argue in this way give the impression that Paul's view of the age of the world is still to be taken literally. For him and the Christians of Thessalonica or Corinth in one way or another the end of the 'age' was drawing near. But whether we like it or not, we can no longer talk of history generally, or human history, in terms of this model of time. None of us still really thinks that time has become short. Who really stands every week in the eucharist, in the literal sense, 'watching hopefully for the coming of Jesus, Messiah, your Son'? This has become a timeless expression.

In fact human beings are no longer quite sure where they stand on the ladder of history. We come from a history of many hundreds of millions of years, and however young human beings themselves are, Adam lived not just five thousand years ago but ... sixty thousand? one hundred thousand? More? At any rate his ancestors did. The age-old pyramids are brand-new, and after some thousands of years they will have been eroded, long after all our ancient cathedrals have ceased to stand. For many many thousands of years before Copernicus and Galileo, people – with the exception of Aristarchos of Samos – thought that the sun revolved round the earth and that the earth was motionless. And this conviction was deeply rooted in the most venerable religious traditions. People were very emotionally attached to it. But that has changed, just as even all the eternal immovable mountains and oceans have moved and changed in the course of time.

Of course I am aware that not a single society or church can begin to plan its concrete historical projects or organization in such long periods. Of course for each one of us life now is the eschatological kairos, at the time when we experience it; now is decisive for *our* covenant with God. But to realize this is something different from reflecting on absoluteness and relativity with reference to the further history of God's church in the world. It may perhaps sound somewhat Darwinian, but would it not show greater wisdom if we began to think of our time-scales differently, above all when we want to talk about the relationship between God's will and our history? We now know incontrovertibly that the world must be thought of in incomparably different time-scales from those in the Bible and church history. A minimal attachment to the frame of reference of scientific discoveries about world history may perhaps not be completely useless here. From a biological perspective *homo sapiens* is still young, and Christians too belong to the species *homo sapiens*.

It is not at all a crazy or a theologically unworthy thought to suppose that humankind could continue to exist for a number of thousand years yet. If an incoming asteroid or human folly do not put an end to our existence, this calculation may even be on the low side. Is it then nonsensical to think that God's people still has many centuries in front of it? Perhaps hundreds? At any rate we cannot think of the history of church forms with a mentality of 'we'll keep them immobile as long as possible and then ... après nous le déluge'. But if we begin to take a longer-term perspective, things begin to seem fundamentally different.

Theoretically the immutability of traditions and structures can be maintained as long as people think that 'the time has become short'. And situations can be kept immobile for a number of years, generations or indeed centuries by laws, prohibitions, and possibly the exercise of force. But even the divine right of kings, a tradition which lasted almost three thousand years, could not stop the French Revolution, the republics and democracy. We now know better than people did then that kingship is simply one possible, relative way – in certain circumstances perhaps the best way – of leading and uniting a nation. History has taught us this.

Furthermore, while one can immobilize forms of ministry for a while or put them on a ventilator if they cause problems because of the tension between them and the conditions of the time, even the smallest child knows that such a condition cannot last for another thousand, three thousand, ten thousand years. That is no naive remark. I am very well aware that it would be a delusion to look at the needs of the church from a perspective of three thousand years on. But precisely for that reason it is good to think in terms of the forms that can best serve the community now, today. The mere possibility – and perhaps actuality – of a very long span of time (which means nothing cosmologically) now shows that forms and traditions, however venerable, are by definition relative and subject to evolution, because they are temporal. They *cannot* be absolute, and the immutability of God's will cannot depend on the immutability of their historical form. To appeal here to the inspiration of the Holy Spirit or to divine law must inevitably end up in abuse. Moreover, as far as 'divine law' is concerned, there have always, everywhere, been people who have defined what in the church is divine law and what is not. The real question which needs to be put to ministries and orders is not whether or not they are immutably willed by God, but under what form they best realize God's will with the human community. For the ministry as such is not part of the formal purpose of the Good News. Ministry is not an end, but a means. The purpose of church ministry can ultimately only be to help to build up the community of Christ. A church therefore cannot deny time nor begin to stand above it; it cannot put itself outside the temporal evolution in which it is itself involved. Anyone who wants to persist in this attitude is finally to be described by a saying which has alternatively been attributed to Talleyrand, Fouché or Boulay de la Meurthe: 'C'est plus qu'une crime, c'est une faute.'[5] We do well to realize that ministries, however sacred, are human realities, and that human affairs are necessarily conditioned by history. Moreover, as long as the end of time has not dawned, the age-old wise principle of Heraclitus applies: *panta rei*, everything is in flux.

I am not concerned to make a cheap effort to bring Bible and science into line. The level of truth that the Bible intends lies elsewhere than that of cosmology and biology. As I have sketched out above, the Bible in fact regards time as being very short and the cosmos as being very small. Nevertheless, it remains true that the biblical history of revelation in particular opens the door to another view of the relationship between God's will and time than one in fixed terms. God's revealed will is not a solid mould. Revelation as a whole is neither a history nor a mould. The biblical interpretation of history takes another course: after the event, chance historical events and developments are interpreted as 'God's will' because within the limited horizon of their time, among chance historical circumstances and needs, they are experienced as the best way of giving form to God's saving will, which itself remains the same. God's saving will is that in all circumstances men and women should experience their humanity – in justice and love – in such a way that the building up of their community can become the historical realization of God's love as its ultimate ground and meaning. God's will, which is always true to itself, is as flexible as history.

One of the clearest examples of this theological intuition is provided by the Mosaic Torah itself. If we compare legal texts from Exodus with texts from Deuteronomy or Leviticus, there too we can see the evolutionary stream of centuries of history. The laws and customs are adapted to changing circumstances of time: regulations from an agrarian culture before the kings were changed and replaced by others when an urbanized society during the monarchy needed different regulations. These laws still stand side by side in the Torah, as an expression of God's one unchangeable covenant will.

3. Ministries in the New Testament: God's covenant in Jesus becomes concrete in human society

(a) Introduction: what does the terminology tell us?

Philological approaches to historical or theological questions are risky. The mammoth undertaking of Kittel and Friedrich is an illustration of this. Their *Theological Dictionary of the New Testament* contains the results of a gigantic exploration of the semantic linguistic horizon of the

New Testament vocabulary. One cannot do without this tool if one wants to penetrate the thought-world of the New Testament. But the giant work also reveals the limitations of the historical method used. The exegesis of a text has not been settled by a lexicographical investigation of the whole historical field of a word or expression and a mapping of this field. The precise nuances of meaning which, for example, a poet gives to a particular term in the context and structure of a poem can escape the existing lexicographical horizon or transcend it by creating a new meaning. This is the distinctive feature of a living language, and that fact is of great importance if one reflects on the relationship between scripture and tradition.

Here is an example which is interesting for the New Testament ministries. The terms *presbyteros* (elder, presbyter) and *episkopos* (overseer, leader) never come within the lexicographical field *hiereus/sacerdos* at the moment when they make an appearance in the New Testament. But that does not mean that it was wrong to make the later connection with '*sacerdos/hiereus*'. Here the term *sacerdos* is given a new content, which came about precisely because of the experience of the first Christian centuries. The experience of the Christian ministries itself began to function as a new element in the hermeneutic of the old term 'priest'.

Despite its limitations, a philological approach to a theological question is important, for a variety of reasons. We always learn how people think from their language. The words which they use to describe things and situations show how they think about them. For instance, is it not remarkable that in discussing ministry the famous *Dictionnaire de Théologie Catholique* has no article on 'ministère' but only one on 'ordre'? This says something about the thought-world of the people who compiled this encyclopedia.

Another argument which is important for our discussion is a historical one. A lexicographic picture is very useful for showing the historical situation of a term. An approach like that of Kittel may not be able to establish the hermeneutics, but it can investigate the relationship between the later content of a term (perhaps today) and the meaning given to it in an earlier historical period. To be specific, an examination of the horizon of meaning of terms for ministry in the time of Jesus and the early church do not allow this meaning to be laid down for ever, so that it could be stated, for example, that later developments are illegitimate. This investigation shows very well how the people of the New Testament themselves filled the term with content, and consequently what must be attributed to the contribution of evolution and to historically free decisions.

In the survey of the early history of ministry which follows, we shall therefor first allow ourselves to be guided by terminology. Many interesting facts come to life as a result.

(b) Church office

The term 'office' when applied to the early Christian church communities already poses difficulties for the New Testament. With Jürgen Roloff we can begin from present-day terminology: 'The term "office" is focussed on a function of leadership which is clearly laid down by law and socially recognized, which exercises authority in the name of a particular institution and has the power to implement decisions.'[6] We also find the Greek terms used for this notion of office (*arche, telos, time, leitourgia*) in the New Testament. However, there they are used for the exercising of office by Jewish priests or Gentile civic officials, for the angels (good and bad) and finally for Jesus himself. The terms for priestly office (*hierateia*, Latin *sacerdotium*) or the exercise of priestly office (*hierateuein*) are also reserved for Jewish priests. The term *(arc)hiereus*/Latin *sacerdos* is reserved for the Jewish or pagan priests or for Jesus himself. The book of Revelation applies the term *hiereus* three times to the followers of Jesus (1.6; 5.10; 20.6). As is well known, the word *hierateuma*/Latin *sacerdotium*, 'priestly body', is applied only to the baptized, to the church as a whole, in I Peter 2.5,9.[7]

This brief summary of terms and concepts is simply meant to show that the obvious terms for denoting an office are nowhere used in the New Testament of those whom we now call ministers, any more than words which denote priesthood or the priestly task (for the latter see below). Such an absence of terminology is not the whole story, but it inevitably raises the question: how did the early Christians then regard themselves, their communities, and their responsibilities? This state of affairs in all probability still shows traces of the original situation of Christianity. Initially Christians formed a socially insignificant group, membership of which in religious terms at first still came under Jewish officials and in civic terms for a long time still was under the Roman imperial authorities. The Christians initially also formed a group which regarded itself primarily as charismatic; it did not think in terms of structured office, nor was it regarded in this light by others. So the existing terms for office were not used in the New Testament communities. Thirdly, this was a group which initially had a marked eschatological expectation and therefore did not begin with long-term perspectives on organization. Its charismatic and eschatological character also meant that in the light of Christ the early church did not regard itself directly as an institution, all the more so since Jesus' own attitude to the religious (and political?) establishment was, to put it mildly, very problematical.

The fact is that in the present state of the investigation we must be on our guard against over-hasty systematization. Granted, the gathering of all the writings into a canon makes them contemporaneous in a theological sense and equally normative for the church, although they come from different times. Nevertheless, if for example we want to argue from the historical Jesus and disciples about offices, we must also take account of the historical evolution which can be noted within the relatively short period of time covered by the New Testament. The safest and most correct standpoint here is to take due note of the plurality of manifestations.

(c) Apostle, the Twelve

The term *apostolos* occurs 80 times in the New Testament.[8] The Pauline literature uses it 34 times (Paul 27, Ephesians 1, Colossians 1, Pastoral Epistles 5); Luke also uses it 34 times (Gospel 6, Acts 28). Thus Paul and Luke clearly have the lion's share of occurrences. The other passages are spread over the rest of the New Testament.[9]

The sparse usage in Matthew, Mark and John is striking. Matthew and Mark use the term in the appointment of the Twelve (Matt.10.2; Mark 3.14), and in addition Mark uses it once in 6.30, to say that the apostles returrned to Jesus. John uses the word once, when he makes Jesus say that the one who is sent is not more than the one who sends him.

This Johannine passage shows us the original semantic field of *apostolos*.[10] Both the noun and the verb (*apostellein*) denote sending and being sent. The apostle must first and foremost be regarded as one who is 'sent' (*missus*) and therefore is working on behalf of a higher authority who has sent him. In this sense Epaphroditus is said by Paul to be an 'apostle' of the community of Philippi (Phil.2.25): he is acting on their behalf, but there is always the connotation of an authority which derives from the sending. Thus Jesus himself is once called 'apostle' (Heb.3.1), but in the Gospel of John the verb *apostellein*/send is always used to indicate that Jesus has been sent by the Father, and consequently has God's authority as revealer.[11] This theme of having authority is an important feature of ministry in the New Testament.

The term *apostolos* has been connected with the Hebrew root for send (*sh-l-ch*), from which the noun *shali'ach* ('one who is sent') is derived. This is the meaning that we find in John 13.16. In Judaism there was the institution of the *shali'ach*, a plenipotentiary who could perform specific tasks for which he was sent in the name of a person or group (e.g. the Sanhedrin). In this sense rabbis regulated the calendar in the Diaspora or the high priest appeared for the people. Paul's authority in Acts 9.1ff. must also be understood in this light. The *shali'ach* also acted in secular affairs, for example in betrothals, divorces or selling goods. It is quite possible that the notion of the authority which the Christian apostles receive on the basis of their being sent must be connected with this. At any rate, what is an office in the New Testament has grown out of the term 'sending' for which the sending of Christ himself was a model. The apostolicity of the church, rightly emphasized down the centuries, finds its roots and its *raison d'être* here. Authority in the church also comes from mission, the 'apostolate'. Paul is a privileged witness to this. In his letters he often speaks of his authority as an apostle. For him the word almost exclusively means being sent by the Lord. So true is this that in Galatians Paul does his best to explain to the Christians of Galatia that his authority is based on the fact that he was sent, not by the authorities in Jerusalem, but by God himself, at the moment when Jesus Christ was revealed to him. For that see his autobiographical account in Gal.1.11–2.10.

The word *apostolos* in the New Testament is far from being applied only to the Twelve. The Pauline use of the term already indicates this. Paul applies it to others than the Twelve. First of all he calls himself an apostle, and he is fond of using the title as an authoritative introduction in the prescripts of his letters. Called by the Lord, he has also been sent by him. 'Am I not an apostle? Have I not seen Jesus our Lord?' he exclaims in I Cor.9.1. 'With this term he describes his task of preaching the gospel: as a messenger and representative of the crucified and risen Lord he is authorized to bring the gospel to Gentile Christians.'[12] Paul so incarnates the very type of the apostle of Christ that in early Christian terminology the term 'the apostle' always referred to him.

However, Paul also uses the word for other people who are engaged in preaching. In I Cor.9.5 he speaks of his right to take a woman with him on his journeys 'like the other apostles and the brothers of the Lord and Cephas'. Whereas 'other' in the expression 'other apostles' connects them with himself, and he mentions Peter (Cephas) separately, it is probable that by the apostles he also means others than the Twelve. In I Cor.15.5,7, where he is speaking about the appearances of the risen Lord, he draws a clear distinction between 'the Twelve' and the 'apostles'. In I Cor.12 he speaks of tasks and gifts in the church community. He goes on to say: 'And God has appointed in the church first apostles, second prophets, third teachers' (v.28). It is clear that here by apostles he understands others than the Twelve. In Gal.1.19 he includes James the brother of the Lord among the apostles, though he was not a member of the Twelve. The well-known list of greetings at the end of Romans concludes with the names of Andronicus and Junia, fellow-workers of Paul, whom he terms apostles (Rom.16.7).[13]

It is not always easy to make out precisely what function Paul's 'apostles' perform, but the authoritative preaching of the Good News is never out of Paul's mind, and this is even more the case in the Deutero-Pauline letters, i.e. the letters not written by Paul himself which nevertheless inherit his thoughts. We may be sure that all his letters (with the possible exception of Philemon, though that is by no means certain) have an official character. However, paradoxically enough he regards his ministry, although recognized by the 'Jerusalem pillars' (Gal.1), essentially as a charismatic one, which has not been bestowed on him by predecessors but by Christ himself. He interprets his office of apostle as empowerment by the risen Christ himself, and this is one of the reasons why Paul forms such an important part of the dossier on the resurrection and appearance traditions. He associates the authority of his mission with the risen Lord, without ever having known the earthly Jesus.

Only later is the term 'apostle' identified with the Twelve, and this is predominantly the result of a deliberate action on the part of Luke. In the Acts of the Apostles Luke never gives Paul the title apostle – though he is still his great hero. He clearly reserves the term for the Twelve, whom he sees as the nucleus of the disciples of Jesus, who were with him in his lifetime 'from the beginning, the baptism of John, until the day when he was taken up into heaven' (Acts 1.22). Above all in the account of the early Jerusalem church which occupies the first chapters of the book, this terminology seems abundantly clear.[14] The later custom of reserving the word 'apostle' in the church almost exclusively for the 'twelve apostles' must be derived from Luke's restrictive use. However, this does not mean that Luke himself invented the application of the title 'apostle' to the Twelve. On the contrary, it seems very likely that they were already called apostles at an early stage – though not exclusively.

There is also every reason to think that the historical Jesus himself stands at the origin of a special group of twelve disciples, who later formed a kind of college in the early church. I want to mention this fact here, because it is not immediately evident. Since Jesus without doubt had more disciples than the Twelve – the Gospels provide unambiguous evidence of this – and since the lists with the names of the Twelve in the Gospels do not precisely correspond, a number of writers have expressed the view that the institution of the Twelve really came into being in the early church and that the Gospels have projected it back on to Jesus' own time. Mention could be made here of W.Schmithals, G.Klein and P.Vielhauer as exegetes who hold this view. Strictly speaking such a process is quite possible, since other features of the early church are projected back on Jesus' time, like the idea of the expulsion of Christians from the synagogues or the mission in Samaria. But it is very probable that we should prefer the view that the origin of the Twelve is to be attributed to a deliberate choice on the part of Jesus himself. The fact that the traditional lists of apostles do not correspond precisely points more in the direction of an independent testimony to authenticity. An artificial construction would not run the risk of inconsistencies. Moreover – above all? – the fact that in the earliest traditions of the passion Judas is called 'one of the Twelve' points strongly in this direction. Would the person who betrayed Jesus have been reckoned one of the Twelve if this college had only come into being in the post-Easter church?

Another question is how far Jesus saw this Twelve as an office, and whether here he was thinking of a distant future. The first and historical significance of the Twelve can be derived with reasonable certainty from some texts in the Gospels. In Matt.19.27, Peter asks Jesus, 'Lo, we have left everything and followed you. What then shall we have?' Jesus replies: 'Truly I say to you, in the new world, when the Son of man shall sit on his glorious throne, you who have followed me will also sit on twelve thrones, judging the twelve tribes of Israel.' The parallel text in Luke, set at the time of the Last Supper, says: 'As my father appointed a kingdom for me, so do I appoint for you that you may eat and drink at my table in my kingdom, and sit on thrones judging the twelve tribes of Israel' (22.29f.).[15] The primary significance of the choice of a group of twelve persons must be sought in the symbolism of the new assembled people of Israel. The twelve apostles were symbolically the patriarchs (and also the rulers and judges) of the twelve tribes of Israel. Their role was associated with the last judgment, and this indicates the eschatological character of the symbolism. Jesus' mission is to gather the eschatological people of Israel round him for his Father, and the apostles are the 'fathers' of these new twelve tribes. They are a symbol of the whole people. In other words, Jesus' choice must be put in the category of prophetic symbolic actions, which are very well known from the Old Testament.

Two comments should be made here. First, it is evident from Jesus' words about the significance of the Twelve quoted above that 'mission' was not the exclusive and perhaps not even the primary purpose of their choice. What judgment is made here will depend on our picture of the immediacy of the eschatological expectation among them and with Jesus himself. However, this is not clear. Did Jesus himself expect that the breakthrough of the kingdom of God was imminent? There is much to point in this direction, but it is a tricky point for exegesis. In any case, the number twelve cannot immediately be connected with the notion of sending which is contained in the term 'apostle'. Any other number would be appropriate for sending as apostles. In both the Gospel of Luke and Acts, where sending to preach the word is mentioned, more people than just the Twelve are involved. Luke 24.33 mentions 'the eleven and those with them'. These are the ones who have been sent by Jesus to bear witness to the world. In the account of Pentecost in Acts 2.1ff. it is said that 'all' were present. 'All' refers to the group in Acts 1.13–14, or rather to the group in 1.15; at all events more than the Twelve. All those present are strengthened in the Spirit and sent by the Spirit. The term *apostellein*/send is also used in the Gospel of Luke for the messengers and the seventy(-two) disciples whom Jesus sends out to preach the kingdom of God (cf. Luke 9.52; 10.1). This does not mean that Luke does not bring the Twelve to the fore as the authoritative original witnesses and reserve the title for them. But precisely this is a later combination of 'apostle' with 'the Twelve'. That there were twelve beyond question has to do with the eschatological symbolism of the tribes of Israel. In the vision of the new Jerusalem in the Apocalypse we read: 'And the wall of the city had twelve foundations, and on them the twelve names of the twelve apostles of the Lamb' (21.14). It could hardly be clearer than that. But this means that the college of Twelve have a characteristic that was meant for them alone and cannot be passed on to successors. The element 'Twelve' as judges over Israel is something that cannot be passed on to the later bishops and therefore stands alongside the apostolic succession. The office of bishop cannot be derived directly from the function of the Twelve in this sense. We cannot even know whether Jesus himself ever thought in terms of a succession to the Twelve. Of course it is impossible still to make out in what sense the Twelve functioned as a college or institution in the early church. In Acts they were initially the leaders of the Jerusalem community. That may well have been the case, since they were the original witnesses to Jesus.

It is possible that the Twelve came up to Jerusalem from Galilee as a leading group (somewhat contrary to Luke's view), because it seems highly likely that the tradition of the appearances to the Twelve must be set in Galilee. However, it is unclear how this group functioned and for how long. The majority of them must have gone on missionary journeys at a very early stage, and we lose track of them in history. When Paul arrived in Jerusalem some years after his conversion, of the Twelve only Peter and John still seem to have remained there. And perhaps at that time James the brother of the Lord was already the leader of the Jerusalem community. Together they are called the 'three pillars' of the church, and perhaps they formed its leading body. Even this was not to last long, since John and Peter departed, in the directions of Ephesus and Rome respectively. Moreover the authority of the Twelve in the first church will have rested primarily on their personal status as the closest disciples of Jesus who had known him intimately and had had the experience of Easter. This, too, could not be handed down as an office. Today's bishops may see themselves as successors of the apostles in the sense of having inherited their authoritative mission, but they cannot be regarded formally as successors of the Twelve *qua* twelve, i.e. as patriarchs of the eschatological Israel and the original witnesses to the Lord. There are links of a different kind between the Twelve and the bishops.

Secondly, it is strange that in discussions within the church the symbolic function of the Twelve as patriarchs is so often passed over when it is stressed that they were males. Claims that in his choice of the Twelve Jesus was not in any way bound by the sociological or cultural limitations or ideas of his time manifestly overlook this primary fact. It is generally known that there were women among Jesus' followers (see e.g. Matt.27.55ff.; Mark 15.40f.; Luke 8.1–3). But the symbolism of the core group of Twelve points too emphatically to Genesis and the twelve patriarchs of Israel for it to have been possible to include women in it at that time. Can we see Wagner, in his express reference to well-known and heavily loaded symbolism, including any female knights of the Grail in Parsifal? The symbolism of twelve patriarchs is sufficient explanation why no women could figure in this group; the intended symbolism would not have allowed anything of the kind in the contemporary context. It would have become impossible to interpret or would have been broken. Thus Jesus was quite limited in his choice of twelve males by a cultural and time-conditioned context, namely the explicit reference to the symbolism of scripture itself, which was so firmly fixed.[16]

Here the historical Jesus had thought even less of a *sacerdotium* in appointing the Twelve. The automatic association of the apostolate of the Twelve with the notion of the priesthood is inadmissible at the level of the New Testament. One of the most striking features of the New Testament is that the terms available to denote the priestly function or dignity are not used for any ministry. As I have already pointed out (53 above), the priestly terminology was reserved for Jewish or pagan priests, and within the Christian context for Christ himself and believers (men and women). Neither the apostles nor the Twelve were ever presented as '*hiereis* – priests'. This is inexplicable if Jesus had spoken in one way or another about the priestly function. It may be true that the New Testament did not call its ministers priests because this was unthinkable within the sociological context of the Judaism of the time, but the total absence of this terminology indicates that the New Testament never regards ministers as priests either. One can find traces of this well into Christian literature. The 'sacedotalizing' of the ministry emerges relatively late there. Edward Schillebeeckx is correct in writing: 'It emerges above all from the pre-Nicene literature that the ancient church had difficulties with calling the church leaders "priestly". According to the New Testament, Christ and the Christian community alone were priestly; the leaders were at the service of Christ and the priestly people of God, but are themselves never said to be priestly.'[17] Nor do we do not find any indication in Clement of Rome or even Ignatius of Antioch that *episkopoi*, presbyters and deacons should be regarded as priestly.

However, the mention of *episkopoi*, presbyters and deacons is anticipating our further analysis of ministries. It is sufficient for the moment to see that the notion of 'priesthood' or 'high priesthood' would later be associated with the apostles and the Twelve at a secondary stage. This association has to do with the growth of the idea of the *representatio*

Christi by the ministers, and the absorption of the whole of the Old Testament, including the laws on priests and sacrifices, as a prefiguration of Christ. In fact the Christian notion of priesthood took on a new content as a result.

The identification of the Twelve with apostles and the succession to them in the later *episkopoi* clearly does not go back to the explicit will of the historical or risen Lord. There is no indication whatsoever that Jesus himself ever thought in terms of *episkopoi*, presbyters or deacons. As far as the authoritative sending of disciples is concerned, we must be very careful to make a distinction between the words of the historical Jesus and the commissions which according to the Gospels and Acts he may have given after his resurrection. I am thinking especially of the conclusion to the Gospel of Matthew, 'Go and teach all nations . . .', the conclusion of the Gospel of Luke and the beginning of Acts, 'Bear witnesses to all these things beginning from Jerusalem . . .', and the words of the risen Christ in John, 'As the Father has sent me, so I send you . . .' (John 20.21). The following comments need urgently to be made on such texts. The current view of Jesus' mission charges after the resurrection is still far too much one which sees the appearance stories as being of the same order of reality as those about the historical appearance of Jesus before his death. In fact the appearance stories are understood as though Jesus gave his disciples a number of precise orders which were perceptible acoustically. With the best will in the world, this view of things can no longer be regarded as correct. Here we have a different language-game. The post-Easter mission charges which Jesus gives in Matthew, Luke and John should in reality be attributed to the resurrection hermeneutic of the early church, if not for the most part to the theological redaction of the evangelists.

The literary genre of the resurrection stories is now too well known for it to be claimed that A could not have been said after B. These stories are not live reports, but are regarded so to speak as word-of-God stories, which are presented in an apocalyptic garb and use a mythological language. It can be said beyond any doubt that these stories express the truth of Christ's resurrection, and that the charge to engage in an authoritative mission which the disciples read from the resurrection corresponds to God's will. We express the belief that what they write about the risen Lord is 'true' in intent by saying that the stories are inspired by the Holy Spirit. But it is impossible to use these stories as if they contained audible *ipsissima verba* of Jesus and to incorporate them into a historical argument as is so often done. In such a view, the period of the Easter appearances is imagined as a kind of extension of the way in which the earthly Jesus was present to his disciples. Here the communication which he had with them is thought to have been just the same as before, with the only difference that he now communicated from beyond death. This is typical mythological thought. The insights of literary criticism have consequences for the mission charges of Jesus which have not yet been sufficiently taken into account in arguments about the ministry. It is high time that this was done.

The line which leads back from the bishops through the episkopoi to the Twelve as the only legitimate apostles can therefore be defended with good reason as a legitimate development in the church – and as such as a development 'in the spirit' which links them with the apostles – but it is impossible to see this as the expression of an explicit will of the historical Jesus or the risen Christ. As is generally known, at the earliest this view dates from the period of the Pastoral Epistles, the letters of Clement and Ignatius of Antioch. Of course, at the end of the first century it still stood alongside other views of ministry, especially those current in the Johannine and Matthaean church(es).[18] The present-day line of the development of the ministry proves precisely what I emphasized in connection with the story from Samuel: that the 'will of God' does not impose any pre-existing and already fixed structural mould on history. Rather, a particular development was accepted as the best translation of the gospel in certain circumstances in the church, and it was therefore read as the historical expression of God's will (as tradition). An eternal immutability of structural forms is not part of this attitude of trust in the original inspiration – preparing a covenant people for God.

The prime link between the church and the historical Jesus runs through the prophetic mission of the apostles. Of course Jesus' own activity must not primarily be seen as the exercise of an office; it was charismatic. Jesus is first and foremost a prophet, and the first 'messengers of the gospel' saw their task of preaching as an extension of his prophetic mission. The theology of the so-called 'Sayings Source' (Q) which expresses an early Christian prophetic view still shows this in texts like Luke 6.22f.; 10.2–16; 11.49–51. Paul himself was really to be a representative of this view. His call in Gal.1.15f. is expressed in terms which are also characteristic of the accounts of the calls of Jeremiah and Deutero-Isaiah (Jer.1; Isa.49.1). In Rom.10.15 Paul calls those who bring the gospel God's eschatological messengers of joy, alluding to Isa.52.7 and Nahum 1.15. The first proclamation of Jesus and the formation of the church are so to speak integrally made by itinerant Christian prophets: 'apostles, prophets, evangelists, teachers'. Paul is clearly the figure-head and the greatest example of this, but we also see people like Barnabas, John, Mark, Apollos, Peter, Philip and many others in this role.

(d) A charismatic beginning

All this has brought us to an important point: the charismatic beginning of the church as the 'Jesus movement'. Luke attests the almost immediate formation of a community in Jerusalem and Judaea. We have very little information about the situation elsewhere. A Jesus movement must also have come into being in Galilee, perhaps at the same time as in Jerusalem (or even before?). It is thought that the traditions of appearances in Galilee are a clear indication of this. Jesus' conversation with the Samaritan woman and its sequel in John 4 suggests that preaching of the gospel must also have taken place in Samaria at an early stage, with the formation of a community. Samaritans who became Christians must have been members of the later Johannine community, a development which perhaps was not congenial to some people. Exegetes are more or less agreed that John 4.34–42 must be seen as a text which projects the mission of the first Christians in Samaria on to Jesus. The conviction that Samaritans were also called to accept the gospel was by no means obvious, and it is therefore quite possible that a projection of this back on to Jesus' own activity was a welcome support for the community.[19]

We also hear of the formation of communities in other places, though briefly and in passing. Was Damascus an outpost of Galilean communities, and was Ananias a kind of episkopos there? The story of Paul near Damascus, both in Acts and in Gal.1, presupposes that there was a structured community in the place. Further north in Syria, at an early stage Antioch was to develop into an important community with a variety of responsibilities. It was to be the 'headquarters' for Barnabas and Paul. The church of Antioch was doubtless a mixed group made up of Gentiles and Jews. We have no explicit information about areas like Rome and Egypt in the earliest texts. However, without doubt communities must have developed there at a very early stage. When Paul writes his letter to the Romans, the community is evidently no longer brand-new, but has developed to some degree and enjoys a certain prestige in the outside world. The gospel must also have spread rapidly in Egypt. However, unfortunately we hear nothing from the New Testament about the specific forms in these Christian groups.

In the early communities of which we do get a glimpse, we must start from an institutional form in which there are no offices. Paul really sees the whole Christian community as charismatic, a community of brothers and sisters, and his picture of the community is also an expression of this. In saying this I am not excluding the possibility that Paul had a deliberate plan in engaging in his missionary journeys, and that he wanted to found steadfast Christian communities in select centres. Only the mission among the Galatians seems to have been a chance encounter. Paul himself writes that sickness – and thus a hindrance to his plan of a journey further afield – was the cause of his having preached the gospel in this area of central Asia Minor. However, for all the planning, the fundamentally charismatic image of a church community as brothers and sisters in the Spirit of Christ is an integral part of his thought. He sees all tasks, responsibilities and functions as the gift of the Spirit, and I Cor.12–14 gives us the most attractive picture of his ecclesiology. One of his greatest achievements was to have democratized in the 'Spirit'. Far from being convinced that the Spirit is the privilege of some elite special people, he sees everything that builds up the community to be the body of Christ as the gift of the Spirit. To put it simply, what is good for the community and what nurtures faith in Christ the Lord is the work of the Holy Spirit. Only there are no notions of an institution in any of this. Paul would have been shocked by the thought that some of the leaders of a community possessed the Spirit or could speak from the Spirit. Here we should not forget that Paul himself never completely got away from an imminent expectation of the parousia, although this is not a notion which dominates his specific advice and actions very strongly. His own authority is of the order of what Max Weber calls 'charismatic rule'.[20]

In all this it should never be forgotten that the first Christian communities were house churches, with a house liturgy. This small scale alone cannot be reconciled with a strictly hierarchical concept of office.

Only at a later stage, after the end of the first century, were structures of office gradually to be built up. On this development, Paul Hoffmann comments: 'Here social and historical factors played a major role. Now the urban communities came to control developments. The role of itinerant charismatics became less important. This is the situation of the second and third generations who lived in a transitional situation as a result of the failure of the parousia to materialize and the increasing chronological distance from the founders. On the one hand attempts were made to secure the future with the idea of tradition, and on the other hand there was a challenge to consolidate as a group in society and history. Max Weber says that in sociological terms such situations always lead to charisma becoming more trivial and losing importance. Despite the distance from society of which, according to the texts, the Christian communities seem to have been sharply aware, there was some adaptation to their surroundings in terms of internal order. The formation of stabilizing structures was encouraged both by outside pressure on the Christian minorities (social pressure and persecution) and by crises within the church.'[21] The Catholic Epistles and the letter to the Hebrews are clear evidence of this situation. The growth of the communities was also to lead to a distinction between a leading elite and a larger 'mass' of ordinary Christians. Granted, the Pauline requirement of mutual submission and love of neighbour still shaped the general awareness of the communities. But in fact, again under social pressures, religious stratification and inequality were to grow. The office of leader was to attract to itself functions relevant for the community, above all those of teaching and presiding at the eucharist. The other church charisms were gradually to lose importance, or were made subordinate to the office of leader, whereas in Paul a real juxtaposition of charisms is still more prevalent.

(e) The ministries which will shape the future

(i) Deacons[22]

As is well known, the Greek word *diakonos* (Latin *minister*) denotes someone who performs a service. The basic meaning is that of waiting at table. This service is called *diakonia* (*ministerium*) and waiting at table *diakonein* (*ministrare*). This meaning occurs, for example, in Mark 1.13 and Matt.4.11, where the angels come to 'serve' Jesus. Martha waits at table in Luke 10.40 and in John 12.2. At the wedding at Cana Mary speaks to the 'deacons', i.e. to the waiters. The word is also used for Peter's mother-in-law, who serves Jesus and his disciples (Mark 1.31; cf. also Luke 12.37; 17.8; 22.27). In Acts 6.2., seven men are appointed to serve tables, which in this situation perhaps also means 'supervise'. In the tradition they have become the first 'deacons'. But in the same context the service of waiting on tables (*diakonein trapezais*) is set over against the *diakonia tou logou*, i.e. the ministry of the Word. So the meaning of *diakonia* was a broad one.

A more general meaning of service also already occurred outside the New Testament. For Flavius Josephus, the term *diakonein* can even mean 'obey' and 'perform a priestly service'. In Matt.25.42–44 the term is used as a summary for feeding the hungry, giving drink to the thirsty, clothing the naked and visiting the sick and those in prison.

It is important to mention that for classical Greek culture the term is not an honourable one, far less so for Hellenistic and Roman culture. *Diakonein* is work for servants and slaves. Adult men should not strive to serve but to rule. So the fact that among Christians an office or dignity is called by the term *diakonos* indicates a change of values. This changed mentality can already be perceived discreetly in Acts 6.2. The fact that the same term is used for waiting at tables and for the lofty task of preaching the word already indicates that for Christians, 'serving' is an honour. There are already indications in Old Testament and Jewish thought that service is a work which is honourable in God's eyes, but here the first church was inspired by Jesus himself. Jesus' lowly social situation, his refusal to seize and use power, and moreover his humbling self-surrender in suffering and death became for Christians the basis of serving others after his example, as the highest expression of love which is not self-seeking. There are plenty of clear texts: the foot-washing in John 13 as an example for the disciples and the text of Mark 10.42–45 in which, prompted by a discussion among his disciples of the question who among them is the greatest, Jesus contrasts the will to rule with the will to serve, following his example: 'for the Son of man has not come to be served but to serve (*diakonein*)'. Luke sets the parallel text at the Last Supper: 'The kings of the Gentiles exercise lordship over them; and those in authority over them are called benefactors. But not so among you; rather, let the greatest among you become as the youngest, and the leader as one who serves. For which is the greater, one who sits at table, or one who serves? But I am among you as one who serves' (Luke 22.25–27). Throughout this context words derived from the verb *diakonein* are used for 'servant' and 'serve'.

From this it seems clear that in the Christian communities life could be seen as a life in *diakonia*. The *diakonia* of Stephanas in I Cor.16.15 is an attractive example of this. In I Cor.12.28 *diakonia* is put between prophecy and teaching as one of the gifts of the Spirit in the church. In I Cor.12.4–6, gifts (*charismata*), service (*diakonia*) and work (*energeia*) are used so to speak as synonyms to express all the different things that

Christians can do as one service to the one God. In Rev.2.19 *diakonia* is associated with love, faithfulness and steadfastness. On the basis of I Peter 4.10, H.W.Beyer rightly comments that all charisms or gifts of grace are given in the church to serve one another: 'Serve (*diakonein*) one another, as good stewards of God's varied grace with the gifts which each has received.' Moreover Acts and the Pauline literature understand the whole work of mission as *diakonia*: Timothy, Erastus, Onesimus and Onesiphorus are 'deacons', i.e. helpers in Paul's missionary task (see Acts 19.22; Philemon 13; II Tim.1.18). The connotation of concrete material service is still markedly present in Paul's texts about his great collection for the poor of the church of Jerusalem. He calls this campaign for support quite specifically a *diakonia* (see e.g. II Cor.8.19; Rom.15.25).

Paul himself clearly sees his apostolate as a *diakonia*. He often calls himself a *doulos*, i.e. 'slave', of Christ. But he sometimes uses the term *diakonos* as a synonym: 'deacon' of the gospel, servant of God and Christ (II Cor.6.3ff.; 11.23); servant of the church through his divine mission (Col.1.25). He calls himself and Apollos 'deacons' of God and the church in I Cor.3.5.

None of this as yet sounds very much like an office. Only in a few passages in the New Testament must the term *diakonos* be understood as an expression of specific service in an office. Where that happens the Vulgate does not translate the term as *minister* but as *diaconus*. More specifically this is the case in Phil.1.1: 'Paul and Timothy, servants of Jesus Christ, to all the saints in Christ Jesus who are at Philippi, with their leaders *(episkopoi)* and deacons.' There is also the well-known text in the Pastoral Epistles, I Tim.3.8–13, which clearly refers to a church order. The deacons are mentioned after the episkopoi, and they have to have roughly the same qualities to be worthy of their ministry. Verse 11 mentions 'the women'. Strictly speaking, it is not evident here whether these are the wives of deacons, or deaconesses. The latter is far more probable.[23] We know one female deacon by name: Phoebe, from the community of Kenchreai near Corinth, to whom Paul perhaps entrusted his letter to the Romans. Strictly speaking, here too we cannot say with certainty whether the term *diakonos* is meant to denote an office or is more general. Were the latter the case, Paul would mean that Phoebe, like many other fellow-workers, had done great service to the gospel. But here too it is more probable that Paul in fact had in view the office of a woman deacon. So the office could have existed in Kenchreai as it did in Philippi. In later Eastern Christian literature (and from the fifth century also in the West) there is even mention of deaconesses, who among other things teach and baptize women. As we know, the role of women deacons did not last in the Catholic church.

We do not know what the precise task was of the deacons in Philippi or in the Pastoral Epistles. From the mention of them next to the episkopoi it seems that a distinction was made between the two offices, and on the basis of the title we should suppose that their task did not so much consist in real leadership within the community as in service and material administration. It is improbable that the office of deacon developed from the 'Seven' of Acts 6.2. Perhaps we have a more or less parallel but independent development. The term *diakonos* was so widespread in the secular Gentile world of the time that we need not assume dependence on the Jerusalem Seven to explain the ministry. Any service which involved material help or administration could be called *diakonia*.

(ii) Presbyters[24]

The words 'priest, prêtre, prete' are derived from the word presbyter (Greek *presbyteros*). However, if we look in a lexicon we see that the word for priest in Greek is *hiereus*, in Latin *sacerdos* (cf. 53 above). Since our word priest now has the meaning of *hiereus/sacerdos*, this of course means that the Christian tradition has transferred the function of the *sacerdotium* to the presbyters (and of course to the episkopoi). But the shift in terms equally points to the fact that the first churches did not see their presbyters as priests. In fact the word *presbyteros* is a comparative of *presbys*, which means 'old'. Thus it means someone who is older, an 'elder'. In general the term has connotations of venerability. We find it as a (secular) function in many cultures where the leadership of a community or organization is in the hands of elders. That is of course why in certain Reformation churches the term 'elder' has been reintroduced to denote leaders of the community. Because in many cultures the term was already focussed on a leadership function, it has often been detached from the literal meaning of great age, and simply denotes a dignity in the group. We find the same phenomenon in words like 'senate' and 'senator', which also come from a root that means 'old' but has lost its connotation of age.

What is important for the New Testament is the fact that the 'elders' are represented in various ways in the Old Testament and Judaism. We need not go into this at length, but in all strata of the Old Testament we find 'elders' as leaders: as heads of great families or clans in the early Israel of the tribal alliance; as a group which Moses gathers to support him in his work (e.g. Num.11.16f., 24f., which are perhaps anachronistic; the later rabbis traced their own 'elders' back through tradition to the time of Moses); in the time of the judges as authorities and delegates (see I Sam.4.3; 8.4; II Sam.5.3; 17.4). We also meet them during the monarchy, though with less influence. In Deuteronomy they are mentioned as having legal competence; they also play a role during the exile as leaders of a community which no longer has a king.

Most passages in the Gospels refer to a group of 'elders' in the Sanhedrin, who are mentioned alongside the 'high priests' and the 'scribes' (see e.g. Matt.16.21; 26.3; 27.41; Mark 8.31; 14.43, 53, etc.) This is in all probability an influential group of aristocrats, originally lay people, who formed a group in the supreme council before the scribes had access to it. After 70, however, the council in Jamnia was to consist only of scribes. Elders no longer had a seat.

In the debate in Mark 7.1ff., Jesus contrasts God's commandment with the traditions of the *'presbyteroi'*. In this context, however, the reference is not to the elders of the Sanhedrin but to the 'forefathers', for whose tradition according to Gal.1.14 Paul also fought. As in his rebukes in Matt.23, Jesus puts the will of God above the traditions of the elders.

As for the office of presbyters in the New Testament churches, it is clear that various communities took over the 'institution' of elders to hold responsibility. We must not forget here that at the time of Jesus and the apostles, as from antiquity, towns and villages in Palestine were governed by a small group of elders, one or more of whom could exercise the function of magistrate. To some degree giving responsibility to elders is the most natural thing in the world: their experience and dignity makes them as it were spontaneous authorities in all cultures. Therefore it seems very natural that the first communities, which still had a very domestic character, should have resorted to this form. Acts makes it abundantly clear that the institution must have existed in Jerusalem quite close to the apostles. The presbyters of Jerusalem are mentioned in Acts 11.30; 15.2ff.; 21.18. In 11.30 and 21.18 they clearly seem to be representatives of the community, something which can be compared with the Jewish synagogue councils. In 15.2ff., the text which describes the apostolic council in Jerusalem, they are mentioned alongside the apostles. The 'council' was held as a meeting of apostles and elders (15.6). It strongly reflects the composition of the Sanhedrin.

But whether all communities had this structure at a very early stage is an open question. Remarkably, the term does not occur in Paul, although in Acts presbyters are mentioned in the communities of Ephesus which Paul founded (Acts 20.17).

It is well known that for Paul the functional aspect played a greater role than formal office in his church communities.[25] The order of a community has to be able to develop like a body in which each member has its place and function, and therefore leadership is also one of the charismata given by God's Spirit. In I Cor.12.28–30, Paul seems to divide gifts and tasks more or less into categories. First he mentions those who do the work of spreading and teaching the gospel. These are the apostles, prophets and teachers.[26] Then he mentions those who serve the Christian community with their specific gifts and build it up as the body of Christ: those who have the gifts of miracle-working, healing, governing, speaking in tongues. Romans 12.6–8 takes the same line. The leadership of the community is mentioned alongside and among the gifts of service, instruction, encouragement, sharing possessions, mercy. When Paul asks his Christians to show respect and recognition of those who 'lead and instruct' them (I Thess.5.12ff.), this is primarily the work that the leaders do, not on the basis of a view which distinguishes them ontologically from other Christians who, just as the leaders are guided by the Spirit, possess other gifts or perform other tasks. In Paul himself there is no mention of sacralizing of the office of leader on the basis of an equality with Christ with an ontological foundation. As we know, in Philippi these authorities were episkopoi and deacons; in Ephesus they were possibly presbyters. We have no clear specification of their task. However, *a priori* and by comparison with elsewhere, we can guess what must have been necessary for the leadership of a community.

In the New Testament period after Paul, the function of presbyter has already undergone a development. Acts 14.23 has Paul and Barnabas appointing presbyters in Gentile churches. This function has a permanent authority. Of course it is important that in Acts 20.28 the presbyters of Ephesus are also called episkopoi. Here presbyter and episkopos are evidently synonymous. The function is not differentiated.

In I Peter the factor of age still plays a part in the mention of the elders, since in 5.1,5 the author compares the elders with the young men. But the context suggests that these elders have a pastoral task: the care of the flock which has been entrusted to them. The anonymous author of the letter calls himself a 'fellow-presbyter' of the elders. The letter is pseudonymously attributed to Peter and therefore is not authentic, but the fact that the author presents it as though it were written by Peter himself at least indicates that it was thinkable and acceptable to call the apostle Peter a presbyter. The advice given in I Peter 5.2ff. is strongly reminiscent of that in the Pastoral Epistles. Note that in this letter only Christ is called 'episkopos'.

As for deacons and episkopoi, the clearest New Testament reference to an evolution of the presbyterate as an office is to be found in the Pastoral Epistles, and more specifically in I Timothy.[27] The letter speaks of a 'presbyterium' as a college: 'the assembled elders'. The custom of the laying on of hands by the assembled company at the ordination of a priest, which still exists, comes from this text. The qualities that elders need are further discussed in I Tim.5.17ff., along the same lines as the comments in the letter on deacons and episkopoi in ch.3. Remarkably, only in connection with the elders does the author remark that they must be paid if they do good work, and also that they must be protected against frivolous accusations. According to the text they have a special responsibility for preaching and teaching. From the author's treatment one would be inclined to infer that the presbyters are regarded as the most special people in the community. Therefore it is difficult to discern whether the role of the presbyter and that of the episkopos (overseer) were already differentiated. However, it should be noted that the letter speaks of the episkopos in the singular, but of the deacons and presbyters in the plural. This could already point in the direction of the episkopos as a one-man function and the two other offices as being a collegial function.

It is also interesting that the author of II and III John calls himself as 'the elder'. However, whether this refers to an office is open to question. The author opposes a certain Diotrephes, 'who is fond of taking first place in the community' – an episkopos? – and who does not recognize the author's authority. Here we could equally well think that the title 'elder' does not refer to a specific office that the author holds in the community but, as Bornkamm writes, to the fact that he is the bearer of special authority as a witness to the apostolic tradition.

The mention of the *presbyteroi* in Revelation is less important for our purpose. They are the real elders, who offer praise to God as a kind of heavenly council (clothed in white and crowned).

(iii) Episkopoi[28]

In classical Greek the word *episkopos* denotes someone who oversees tasks, an overseer, a supervisor and thus also a guardian, a patron. The religious use of the term is reserved to the gods who oversee and protect the course of events in the world. Otherwise it denotes profane functions. For example the city of Athens had 'episkopoi', i.e. officials sent as supervisors (controllers) to the other cities of the Attic alliance. Comparable functions are also known elsewhere.

The word is applied to God once in the Old Testament (LXX), in Job 20.29, but with a clear reference to his power as judge. The LXX also uses the term to denote supervisors of all kinds (cf. Judg.9.28; Isa.60.17 – a text which was to be used by Clement of Rome as a foundation for the office of bishops and deacons; II Kings 11.18; II Chron.34.12,17 Neh.11.9).

Of the five occurrences of the word in the New Testament, one refers to Christ himself. In I Peter 2.25, Christ is called the 'shepherd and episkopos' of our souls. We may confidently translate it 'guardian', and then we see how much the term episkopos is bound up with the role of pastor.

The other four occurrences relate to an office within the church community. As I have already pointed out, in Acts 20.28 the presbyters of Ephesus are called episkopoi. Thus the words denote the same task: guiding the flock as pastors. So in the church of Ephesus various episkopoi are at work side by side and with one another. This indicates that in the New Testament the task of episkopos may not directly be identified with that of the later bishop. Interim stages would be necessary, caused by historical developments. That the text of Acts, although written by Luke, can describe the situation of a Pauline community is confirmed by the greeting in Phil.1.1 in which Paul greets the community of Philippi 'with its episkopoi (plural) and deacons'.

In the Pastoral Epistles (I Tim.3.1f.; Titus 1.5ff.) we seem to have reached a further stage. The task of episkopos already has to be described as a firm and stable function. It is said to be something that can be striven for, and for which qualifications are necessary. These qualifications have to do above all with fitness at a general human level. Nothing is really specified technically, so that the precise task of the episkopos is not clear to us. Leadership and instruction will certainly have been part of it. But as I have remarked, the difference from the text about the presbyters is not so clear. The episkopos is mentioned in the singular, and if this is not a type but in fact a number, we could already have an indication of a development which was later to become clear: the episkopos as sole leader of the community.

It is difficult to find a formal parallel with the function of the Christian episkopos in the functions which are denoted in the Greek world by this term. The comparison with the Jewish leader of the synagogue (*archisynagogos*, cf. Luke 13.14) is more promising; this official led worship, supervised external order and was supported by 'elders'.[29] However it is difficult to claim that Christians derive the function of an episkopos directly from the leader of a synagogue. Here, too, we may suppose that a quite natural development led to the forms of community. Jesus entrusted the apostolic mission to the Twelve and others, primarily as prophets and teachers. They read this mission charge at least from the appearances to them. Where communities were founded, people with a special charisma had to be found for pastoral leadership in the community, to guarantee teaching and preaching, and also to have responsibility for community life. Just as Judaism provided the term for the 'presbyters', so in the Greek world the terms *episkopos* and *diakonos* were found, which could serve well to describe the specific functions in the community. As communities grew and became more stable, there was less need for travelling preachers, and these functions became a kind of permanent structure. Initially the titles emerge from the function, and relate to 'lower' functions. Of course the designation of Christ himself as episkopos (cf. I Peter 2.25) gave the office an extra theological dimension.

Only with thought like that of Clement, who in a more 'haggadic'[30] interpretation of scripture draws a direct hierarchical line from God through Christ and the apostles to the bishops, can the view of the apostolic succession which still prevails in the Catholic Church be explained (I Clement 42–44, see below).

We may ask to what degree the apostolate as an office goes back to the explicit will of Jesus. We may also ask to what degree Jesus thought in terms of a future church, the basic structure of which he wanted to provide. Without doubt he began a movement of disciples, but the very anti-structural life-style of his disciples (radical following, leaving everything behind, to join an itinerant group of men and women as described in Luke 8.1–3) points in the direction of a marked eschatological mentality. It is virtually certain that Jesus himself did not limit the 'apostolate' as a mission to the Twelve. It is a fact that the Twelve also recognized others as apostles of the risen Christ. James and

Paul are the best-known examples of this. But there are still honest questions and doubts on all these points.

What we certainly cannot doubt is that not a single one of the community offices mentioned, episkopos, presbyter and deacon, goes back to an explicit will or institution on the part of Jesus. If we study the New Testament systematically, the first thing we note about the structures present in it is negative: the community offices as such, in their concrete form, cannot be connected with Jesus. If we want to attach to Jesus with historical arguments the forms of ministry which in fact developed, we end up in quicksand. Historical arguments based on Jesus are extremely suspicious on this question. In reality they have no force. Therefore a distinction must be made between the legitimacy of a development and its immutability. That a development is legitimate means that it embodies the best way of being faithful to the gospel of Jesus for the situation of its time and place. In this sense any legitimate development can be called the 'work of the Holy Spirit' and the 'will of God'. If a church form really serves to build up the community of Christ, it is based on the gospel. But to be 'based on the gospel' means something different from being 'formally willed by the historical Jesus'. So there need be no doubt of the legitimacy and the evangelical foundation of a church development towards the threefold ministry that we have known for centuries. But this legitimacy need in no way of itself mean immutability. The argument that one cannot change a form of ministry because in so doing one is going against the explicit will of the historical Jesus is historically groundless. The actual forms of ministry grew out of the concrete need to structure, order, lead and instruct a community. The titles were taken from parallels in the Greek world and Judaism. Such offices were not regarded as sacerdotal in the New Testament period, nor did they have a sacral character. The social and cultural environment played a great role. Why then is there a need to look for arguments for immobility? The ontological way of thinking about the ministry also comes from a later period than the New Testament itself, above all the notion that attaches the priestly *representatio Christi* to the male gender. In the New Testament on some occasions it is said that the baptized are priests (I Peter 2.5,9; Rev.1.6; 5.10; 20.6). This means all the baptized, men and women. Paul expresses his idea of *representatio Christi* with the image of the church as the body of Christ . The community represents as it were the presence of Christ on earth. It realizes itself. But again the apostle is thinking of all members of the body, men and women. The specific sacerdotal view of ministry is post-New Testament. It is possible that we have to say that the evolution towards a more ontological pattern of thought was legitimate, like the sacerdotalizing of the ministry. But these thought-patterns cannot be attributed to an explicitly expressed will of Jesus, and even less so the consequences which are derived from them.

4. The post-apostolic period: the ministry develops towards *ordo* and consecration

Already in Ephesians (towards the end of the first century?) we see a change taking place from the primitive Pauline view and practice in the direction of a community structure built on 'evangelists, pastors and teachers' and based on the foundation of 'holy apostles and prophets' (Eph.2.20; 3.5; 4.11). In this Deutero-Pauline document from the last two decades of the first century we can see that a chronological gap separating the churches from the original apostles has already developed. The Christians are aware of this and the church is being 'built up'. But there is still a juxtaposition of ministries: apostles, prophets, evangelists, pastors and teachers are mentioned side by side and are distinguished from one another. The task of apostle, pastor and teacher is not yet fused in the one function of the bishop. So here we can see that a distinction must still be made from the later period.

The Didache or 'Teaching of the Twelve Apostles', a didactic work about church order from the beginning of the second century, is ambiguous about functions. On the one hand it still speaks of itinerant apostles and prophets of the kind found in Palestine and Syria: 'Let every apostle who comes to you be received as the Lord, but let him not stay more than one day, or if need be a second as well; but if he stays three days, he is a false prophet' (11).[31] The apostles have their authority as 'representatives of the Lord', the prophets on the basis of their charismatic words: 'Do not test or examine any prophet who is speaking in a spirit . . .' (11). It seems that these people have no fixed abode, and have renounced possessions and perhaps also marriage. Many specialists think that the texts about these apostles and prophets bear witness to an older tradition (11.4–12). At any rate they provide attractive extra-biblical evidence of the first life-style of the itinerant preachers. On the other hand the work also attests the existence of an institutionally accepted group of 'episkopoi and deacons' in the community (15.1ff.). Here episkopos is clearly not a synonym for apostle. Episkopoi have a function alongside prophets and teachers. They must be 'worthy of the

Lord, meek men, and not lovers of money, and truthful and approved', characteristics which recall the Pastoral Epistles. But the 'ministry' is closely bound up with the community. The episkopoi and deacons are democratically chosen by the Christians: 'Appoint for yourselves bishops', we read in 15.1.

Around 120 Bishop Polycarp of Smyrna wrote a letter to the Christians of Philippi. In this letter he mentions only presbyters and deacons (5.2f.; 6.1f.; 11.1). This is an interesting fact, because more than sixty years earlier Paul himself had spoken of episkopoi and deacons in this community. Have Paul's episkopoi become Polycarp's deacons? Or has a single episcopate developed in the meantime which Polycarp does not mention? At all events, here again is a sign of the possibility of change in the development of ministry and the terminology used to describe it in the early Christian period. The tasks of the presbyters include financial administration, discipline, pastoral care and preaching.

It is significant for subsequent history to note how the idea of a mono-episcopal structure became established. The Letter of Clement and above all the letters of Ignatius of Antioch are of great importance here.

Between 90 and 100, perhaps around the time of the death of Emperor Domitian in 96, Clement of Rome wrote a long letter in the name of his church to the community in Corinth in reaction to turbulent events which had taken place there. Some younger men there – evidently with the support of the majority of the community – had deposed some presbyters/episkopoi. In the eyes of the Roman community this would not do; it was a godless revolt leading to schism in the community. From this whole reaction it is abundantly clear that the episkopoi/presbyters are official figures, officially appointed, who have the right to respect from members of the community because they guide (serve) the flock.

Clement holds that they have been illegitimately deposed. Of course this way of thinking indicates that a legalistic attitude has begun to be adopted over holding office in a community. But the Bishop of Rome wants to raise the position of those in office above a purely functional level by creating a fundamental theological basis for it. He grounds the office of leader in an all-embracing structure of ministry sanctioned by God.[32] The argument runs as follows. Just as Christ has been sent by God and the apostles by Christ. so these last in turn 'appointed their first converts, testing them by the Spirit, to be bishops and deacons of the future believers' (I Clement 42.4). Clement sees here a kind of fulfilment of scripture, since he links the appointment of bishops and deacons to the text of Isa.60.17 LXX, which says, 'I will establish their bishops (*episkopous*) in righteousness, and their deacons (*diakonous*) in faith.' Both versions deviate from the original Tenach text, which in Hebrew runs: 'I will make your overseers peace and your taskmasters righteousness.'

We need not be surprised at such use of scripture. Anyone familiar with biblical argumentation from this time will note that here we have the same kind of haggadic use of the Bible as in so many Jewish and New Testament texts. In the same way, Judaism, for example, would ground the sabbath law which had grown up in history in a universal divine order of creation: God himself already rested on the seventh day of creation and hallowed this day. We can read such an interpretation as a particular paradigm, but must not understand it as literally historical. Paul and Matthew also 'adapt' texts on occasion, just as the rabbis did. The way in which in Romans and Galatians Paul argues that the Torah is superfluous, with reference to Abraham, is a complete *ad hoc* construction. Not a single Jewish rabbi would recognize or follow Paul's christological argument in Genesis. This may well be a legitimate reading of scripture, but if it is, it raises the question how scripture really functioned, and what that means for present-day interpretations. In my view the freedom which people in antiquity had in dealing with texts confirms that they read scripture in terms of the needs and insights of their time, as a source of inspiration and a guideline, as symbolic language in which they expressed their own history, but certainly not as a rigid mould which was binding on the future. At that time tradition was what made scripture flexible enough to meet the needs of a later time. It did not need to stop the evolution of history.

Here for the first time Clement formulates the way of thinking on which the later mainstream view of the church was to be based. And here for the first time we have the formulation of the direct line of succession from Christ to the apostles, to the bishops and to the deacons. The way in which Clement narrows the reciprocal involvement of the members of the community which we find in Paul to the obedience of the community to its leaders bears witness to the growth of a hierarchical model of thought in which those in office are to be seen as being on a different level from the '*laikoi*', the people who make up the 'ordinary' people of God.

This thought-model is clearly taking shape, but the difference between episkopoi and presbyters in this letter is still not completely clear. In certain passages it looks as if the two terms relate to the same function. Therefore I have also kept to the terms episkopoi and presbyters.

It has been pointed out that Clement is an approximate contemporary of the Pastoral Epistles, in which we can also speak of a still developing evolution in the direction of a single episcopate and a threefold ministry of leadership in the community, though this is not completely clear.

The work called 'Shepherd of Hermas', which was written in Rome around 140, also shows a similar picture. There still seems to be no monarchical episcopate, but the Shepherd does talk of the 'presbyters who are at the head of the community'. Here too we can note the beginning of a hierarchical principle.

The first texts to mention the threefold ministry, under the leadership of an episcopate which is clearly understood as monarchical, like our present-day office of bishop, are the famous letters of Bishop Ignatius of Antioch. We have his letters to the Christians of Ephesus, Magnesia, Tralles, Rome, Philadelphia and Smyrna and also a letter to Polycarp. The letters have to be dated between 110 and 130 and thus are part of the earliest Christian literature. This also contributed to their great authority in the church.

In his letters Ignatius proves to be a very intense and strict personality, even passionate, and with what one might call a mystical disposition. Encountering Christ, finding Christ, is the constant theme of his concern. As far as our subject is concerned he could be called the first great theoretician of the ministry, or more specifically of the episcopate. For his prime concern is with the episkopos. Anyone who reads his letters will note a very strong concentration of the church on the episkopos, whom from now on we may perhaps call the bishop, and also a marked theological idealization of the office. His terminology, which presents the bishop as the image of God, was to have a considerable influence on the 'ontologizing' of the church's theology of the ministry. Very much of the later church theology of the episcopate goes back to these letters.

According to Ignatius, the unity of the 'saints' in Christ is incarnated in a visible society, which needs a hierarchical order to be able to function. At the head stands the bishop. Whoever the man is, and whatever his personal qualities, in him it is not the person who is respected but the representative of God. He is the visible leader (episkopos) in place of the invisible leader, God (Magn.3.1–2). For Ignatius, too, the authority of the bishop comes from the apostles, but he points above all to the bishop's direct bond with God. The bishop is as it were the visible image of the invisible God. In the letter to the Trallians he calls him *typos tou patros* ('imprint' of the Father, 3.1). Ignatius' idea of things in the letter to the Magnesians is remarkable: Christians are called to preserve unity 'with the bishop presiding in the place of God and the presbyters in the place of the council of apostles and the deacons entrusted with the service of Jesus Christ' (6.1, cf. Trall.2.1). Thus here the representatives of the apostles are the presbyters, since the bishop has been promoted and stands in the place of God himself. Here we can note once more that, even in the case of Ignatius, such imagery cannot be understood too technically or too canonically. Like the other letters from this time, these summaries contain a good deal of rhetoric and many stylistic figures. Only later were such expressions interpreted as formulae denoting an objective reality which is to be understood ontologically. With these texts one cannot in fact even begin to discuss the question of who really represents the apostles, the bishop or the priests. Or do the deacons then represent Christ? Enough room must be left for the context in which an image functions dynamically. Ignatius applies the unity of God's work through Christ and the apostles – God, Christ, apostles, three agents – to the threefold ministry. Because of the collegiate form of the office of presbyter, he associates this with the college of the apostles; because there is only one bishop the reference to the Father fits here. Elsewhere he says that the bishop is one with the thoughts of Jesus Christ, as Jesus Christ is the thought of the Father (Eph.3.2). It is from Ignatius that an expression which later became famous in its abbreviated Latin form derives: '*Ubi episcopus, ibi ecclesia* – where the bishop is, there is the church' (Smyrn 8.2).

Around the bishop Ignatius mentions the presbyters as a 'precious spiritual crown' (Magn.3.1); they surround him as the apostles surrounded Christ. With them the bishop rules the church. However, in Ignatius the bishop is clearly different from the presbyterate. The deacons, who are also part of the threefold ministry, work with him, and they are distinct from the ordinary people of God.

Ignatius is the first unambiguous witness to a hierarchical structure of ministry on three levels. Here the idea of a church *ordo* finds an important catalyst. His letters had an enormous influence on the development of a theology of ministry which thought in terms of equality with God and Christ rather than in functional terms. However, this does not mean that at that time the churches already had this structure everywhere. As we know, Polycarp of Smyrna does not speak of a bishop in Philippi. Even Clement of Rome writes his letter to the Corinthians anonymously, and the letter is presented as a letter from the church of Rome to the church of Corinth. Ignatius, while mentioning the bishops of Ephesus, Damascus, Tralles, Philadelphia and Magnesia, does not mention the bishop of Rome in his letter to the Romans. It is also possible that there was not yet a monarchical episcopate in Smyrna, and that Smyrnaeans 8 is intended to change that. Was there still collective leadership, bishop and presbyters, as in Corinth? Be that as it may, for this period one can still point to a diversity among the churches. The church landscape in and around the letters of Ignatius is still that of a church in movement.

From the middle of the second century, Richard Hanson writes, in the literature that we posses a clear trend can be noted: there is a concern to derive everything in the church from the apostles. This is what Hanson says about the cause of this tendency: 'Around the middle of the second century the church had become fully aware of its historicity as an institution: it already had a past and had a future in front of it, and it had detached itself from its Jewish soil. Its communities, united in awareness of their solidarity, spanned almost all the territories of the Roman empire. The church was no longer seized by the dream of the parousia and the judgment at the end of the world but faced tasks, responsibilities and problems like any other institution. If the church wanted to keep its identity, it had to withstand not only the competition of attractive mystery religions and age-old cults, which were encouraged by local authorities and by the emperors; at the same time it had to make a stand against numerous Gnostic sects and schools. The Gnostic groups aimed at fusing themselves with the mainstream church and they claimed to have a more direct and more interesting access to the sources of Christian truth than, in their view, the church possessed. In this situation the church directed its gaze towards the earliest period of its history, to its "golden age", and it attributed everything that was important for its own life to the initiative and the foundation of the apostles.'[33]

This movement backwards towards the apostles took different forms. The later writings of the New Testament (the Deutero-Paulines, Catholic Epistles and Apocalypse) had already laid claim to apostolic authorship. The church's rule of faith was attributed to apostolic authority. Unwritten traditions and customs were also sometimes grounded in a famous apostle without further reflection.[34] The Creed, which was now taking shape, was attributed to the apostles, and so on. However, the most important thing was that the different communities derived their origin from an apostle, and in addition lists of bishops were composed which formed an unbroken chain with an apostle. The apostolic succession became the great argument for continuity in the church, and for example functioned very strongly in this capacity against the Gnostics, for whom individual deeper insight – which was totally unhierarchical – formed the only real bond with God and Christ.

This chapter cannot survey in detail the development in the late second century and the third century. Hegesippus, Irenaeus of Lyons, Tertullian, Clement of Alexandria, Hippolytus of Rome and Origen are the most important names in the development of the ministry in this period. This is the period in which the idea of an *ordo*, an office distinct from the people, steadily gains importance. And the consecration of those in office, more particularly the bishop, becomes an essential factor in the continuity of the church with its origin, the apostolic succession.

One name must be mentioned in this connection, that of Cyprian of Carthage (bishop from 249 to 258). In his view the bishops were directly appointed and consecrated by the apostles, and the apostles themselves were appointed and consecrated bishops by Christ. For Cyprian the apostolic succession is really a succession of consecration or, rather, of the authority which is given by consecration: 'The consecration of bishops and the structure (*ratio*) of the church is a chain of succession down the ages (*per temporum et successionum vices*), so that the church is founded on the bishops and every action of the church is guided by these guardians (*praepositos*) who were appointed' (*Ep.*33.1.1). According to Cyprian they are all bound to the apostles by a chain of consecrations.

We can see clearly the influence that this view of things had on the theology of the episcopate. It is not turning things upside down to say that Ignatius of Antioch and Cyprian of Carthage have put the essential stamp on the theology of (episcopal) ministry to the present day. It is not the purpose of this chapter to investigate whether such a view should be exclusive or is legitimate. What is important for our topic is to see that this view of things was very strongly influenced by the historical circumstances of the second and third centuries, and that while it certainly could and can be legitimate, it cannot be true in the sense that here is a historical link to an unchangeable will of Christ or the apostles. What we have here is a theological notion which the third-century church attributed to Christ and the apostles, and that is another matter.

5. The ministry becomes priestly

One last point that we need to discuss here is that of the association of the Christian ministries with the priesthood. Even Ignatius of Antioch does not yet designate the bishop and the priests with the term that was used for the priestly function, *hiereus/sacerdos*. Despite possible earlier suggestions in this direction (Didache 13/3; I Clement 40–44; Ignatius, Philad.9.1), we have to wait until Hippolytus and Tertullian (end of the second century, beginning of the third) before the idea of a Christian ministerial priesthood is clearly formulated. Hippolytus of Rome calls the bishop the *'archiereus'*, the high priest. Tertullian also speaks of the bishop as priest or high priest (*sacerdos* and *summus sacerdos*).

It is still not completely clear how the notion of a Christian ministerial priesthood developed. As is well known, the Reformation dropped it again, because it is not in the New Testament. Ehrhardt's explanation that the Christians had taken over and multiplied the Jewish office of high priest is hardly viable. Nor is the explanation that the 'sacerdotalizing' of the ministry had to do with the rise in the power of bishops probable, if only because bishops did not have much power at this time.

Various factors may have influenced this historical development. One might, for example, think of the concentration of the life of the early church on the eucharist. The concentration on what had become a cultic action grew perhaps even stronger as the expectation of the parousia diminished. The step from the notion of a Christian 'cult' to that of a Christian 'priesthood' was not, of course, a great one, above all for people who knew from the biblical tradition that cult and priesthood belonged together.

Of course the preoccupation of Christians with the Bible must also have weighted the scales. Christians were always fond of demonstrating that all parts of the Old Testament bore witness to Christ and the church. But in that case what was to be done with whole texts of the Pentateuch which meanwhile seemed to have lost their meaning? Here I am thinking of the many texts about cult and sacrifice, principally those from Exodus, Leviticus and Deuteronomy. Despite the views of Paul and Hebrews, which saw the old order of salvation and the sacrificial cult ended once and for all in Christ, this was a problem for the church of the later period. But if the precepts for the levitical priesthood could be read as a 'sketch' for the Christian priestly ministry, then the texts could again take a meaningful place within Christian Bible reading as a prefigurement of Christ and his church.

The increasing distance from Judaism must also have played a role. As long as Christianity existed within Judaism or had close connections with it, there was a very obvious barrier against regarding the Christian ministries as priestly: sociologically speaking, the term' priest' could be applied only to the official temple priests of the Jewish religion. The Jewish priesthood had been abolished with the destruction of Jerusalem in 70, and the growing notion of Christ's crucifixion as a kind of cultic sacrifice which replaced the levitical sacrifices could not make room for a sacerdotal function with the Christian church.

At the same time Hanson thinks that one important influence here must have been the pagan environment of the church. Certainly this influence played more of a role socially than cultically. Hanson says it was never the aim of Christians to imitate pagan customs or offices. But the official high priest of a city (*archiereus*) was an important figure who enjoyed prestige and honour, and was respected by the authorities. So we can imagine that when an already sizeable community in a city had good relations with the authorities, and it was asked who the leader of the group was, the answer 'the overseer' (*episkopos*) sounded rather thin. This may have led to the designation of the religious leader of the Christian community by a term which was well understood in society, the *archiereus* or high priest.[35]

The causes mentioned above all figure in the hypotheses frequently expressed about the historical origin of the notion of priesthood among the Christian communities. But once the idea was there, then logically a theology of the Christian *sacerdotium* developed. At the end of this historical survey I shall make brief mention of the views of Hippolytus and Cyprian of Cartage.

For Tertullian, the title (high) priest does not seem to be more than a new name. Hippolytus goes a step further. At the beginning of his *Elenchos*, a work directed against heresies, he refers to his own office of bishop and writes that 'we' – the bishops – are successors to the apostles. 'We partake of the same grace, high-priestly dignity and doctrine, and like them are guardians of the church' (I, preface, 6). Here it is important to note that in Hippolytus' eyes the apostles 'were clad with high-priestly dignity'. Although this may be a historically legitimate supplementation, and in this sense' guided by the Spirit', it is clear that such a view of things is certainly not in keeping with the New Testament. It even goes against explicit texts in the New Testament itself, which in Hebrews exclusively reserves the high-priestly dignity for Christ, and certainly does not regard the apostles as high priests. In a prayer before the consecration of the bishop (partly reconstructed by Dom B.Botte[36]) we read: 'May your minister . . . feed the flock, and work purely as your high priest (*archierateuein*) . . .' In the so-called *Didascalia apostolorum*, a text from Num.18.1 LXX, 'You and Aaron (in the original text, you [= Aaron] and your sons) must take the sins of the priesthood upon you', is applied to the bishop. This text again departs slightly from the Tenach.

In Cyprian of Carthage (249–58), the idea of a Christian ministerial priesthood is expressed most strongly during this period. At this time it is no longer striking that he calls bishops and presbyters priests. But his theology is striking, because he goes so much further than the New Testament and the previous century. In various of his letters he says that the bishop is sacrosanct as the levitical priest in the Torah.[37] More important as a new fact is perhaps that he connects the priesthood of the bishop closely with the eucharistic altar. In *Letter* 43,4,2 we read: 'God is one and Christ is one, and one church and one seat (*cathedra*) have been founded by the word of the Lord to Peter. Another altar cannot be erected and a new priesthood cannot be founded apart from the one altar and the one priesthood.' In Letter 63 the doctrine of the eucharistic sacrifice is made yet more profound. As sacrificial priest, in the eucharist the bishop does precisely what Christ did at the Last Supper. He offers the body and blood of Christ to God as an atoning sacrifice. For Cyprian, the celebrant becomes a cultic sacrificial priest in the Old Testament sense, who offers Christ to the Father. As a rule the celebrant was the bishop.

This survey should suffice. Writers like Ignatius of Antioch, Hippolytus of Rome and perhaps most of all Cyprian of Carthage laid the foundations for later view of ministry, priesthood and eucharist as an atoning sacrifice. Equally clearly, these views shaped a form of ministry which historically transcends that of the New Testament period, and which was also governed by various historical and religious circumstances: the growth and the awareness of the church as an institution; its separation from Judaism, which was coupled with a new hermeneutic of the Old Testament, now also regarded as a paradigm for the forms and structures within the Christian church; the quest to defend and stabilize the place of the church in the pagan world; and perhaps much else. These were expressions of attempts by the church to give the most adequate form to the message of Christ in its situation and in its time. But it is also clear that the concrete forms of the ministry cannot be connected with an explicit will of the historical Jesus, all the more so since the church itself selected what the historical Jesus had said, and already also put words on his lips which gave its interpretation of him. Luke and John provide abundant evidence of this. The general correctness of these findings of the form and redaction criticism of the Gospels can no longer be refuted.

6. Conclusion

I have attempted the impossible, and offered a survey in a nutshell: that of the development of ministries and views of ministry in the New Testament and the next two centuries. It is evident that this survey is incomplete. But that is not very important: greater completeness would only confirm the thesis of this chapter, namely that the actual growth of structural forms in the church and also the theology which is attached to the ministry are heavily determined by history. This historical survey of the development of ministry did not go more deeply into the theological models which developed in the course of its evolution. In the Catholic Church, arguments were developed of a sacramental and ontological nature to establish the specificity of the priestly office. It has not been the aim of this chapter to allude to them. I am in no way seeking to challenge the legitimacy of a particular theological development. But it is part of the express aim of this chapter to show that even a legitimate theological development is historical, time-conditioned and relative. No theology has a supra-temporal dimension. Otherwise it would be God, and fortunately it is not that. All theologies of the ministry, however profound, are the consequence of a historical development in church structure, often before the level of reflection. Tradition has at each stage presented Christ in the garb of that time, in order to keep the gospel alive.

This is really a liberating insight. It shows that the church has very great freedom over the content of its structures. At this point it enjoys the complete freedom of the children of God, and that is very good news when we think of the centuries and centuries, perhaps millennia, which the world can still expect.

Before I end, here is another comment by Paul Hoffmann: 'The church can only be understood as being different from the eschato-logical kingdom of God, precisely because of its historical determina-tion. It does not coincide with the kingdom of God. We must maintain this against any totalitarian or fanatical attempt to realize such identity with power or to force it home in an ideological way. Rather, the church is neither less nor more than a constantly new attempt to find a form of human society which fits Christian belief in the discontinuity of times and cultures. This historical nature determines its provisionality, and makes it an *ecclesia semper reformanda*, but it also gives relative justification to all the forms which have arisen in the course of church history. However, precisely because the church has this character, it also always faces the provocative question how it can preserve continuity with the original impulse from Jesus of Nazareth, to whom it owes its existence, continuity with Jesus who as a charismatic outsider and prophet put in question the religious and social conventions of his time by his message of a God of absolute and unconditional goodness. How does one remain in continuity with a Jesus who precisely by the revolutionary character of his message brought renewal, who staked his life on these new disclosures, and whose claims were definitively endorsed by God in the resurrection from the dead? The communities of the early period of the church, whose self-understanding found expression in the writings of the New Testament, were also caught up in this polarity. So one cannot distil a supra-temporal picture of the church from the New Testament and then transfer it directly to our time. The very plurality of community forms makes clear the fundamental plurality of the historical realization of the church, which precisely here also shows itself to be constantly dependent on historical factors.'[38]

Hoffmann concludes his remarkable article with the following reflections: 'The development of the ministries shows us in its way how early Christianity tried to solve specific problems of organization and authority under the influence of its contemporary environment. We must reflect that this factuality represents a solution which, while very successful in historical terms, is nevertheless historically and socially conditioned, and in turn carries with it the seeds of many problems. As well as the church form which in fact developed, our survey has showed us a multiplicity of models of the church as a community from the early Christian period, including the collegial leadership of the church. The theological legitimacy of this form was also expressed by the New Testament writers. The fact that the collegial form of community leadership could not establish itself was as much a result of historical determination as the fact that the episcopal form could. Finally, this is also true for the Pauline model of a community of brothers and sisters which later in the century was again presented by Matthew, this time in connection with Jesus, as binding on the church of all nations. Thus a look at early church history at the same time also indicates the historical conditioning of the forms of community order which came into being, and therefore also their 'provisionality'. Their plurality makes it clear that none of these forms can claim a definitive and immutable validity. For every form the decisive criterion will remain: how far and to what degree does it succeed in giving appropriate expression to the heritage of Jesus in its own historical situation?'[39]

Thus the New Testament really poses to Christian churches of all periods an abiding question: how do you give form to the message of Christ in *your* time?

I shall formulate my own conclusion with the help of some brief statements.

1. The development which runs from the New Testament terms for ministry to the threefold office and the association with the priesthood was perhaps right and completely legitimate. However, it is the fruit of a historical evolution which cannot directly be derived from an explicit will, either of Jesus or of the risen Christ.

2. The relationship between Jesus and the forms of ministry in the church is extremely open. In principle this gives the church very great freedom over the way in which it meets the concrete needs of order with the aim of building up the body of Christ. It need not say in connection with ministries that it is 'not free' to change what Jesus himself willed. For Jesus did not will anything specific in connection with later forms of ministry.

3. Different forms are possible, through all periods and all cultures, which quite legitimately and quite faithfully express the will of God as revealed in Jesus Christ. Wherever ministries serve and generate the true building up of the community of Christ in the gospel, they are the work of the Holy Spirit and are an expression of the will of the Lord. Here, however, we are speaking on a different level from that of the historical link with Jesus. To say that the evolution towards a particular form of ministry is legitimate and took place in the spirit of the gospel does not mean that at a particular moment it must therefore become the unchangeable form of ministry for all time.

4. God's revelation in Christ always remains living history. Therefore forms of ministry, too, cannot be a suprahistorical reality, untouched by the changes of time. Historical change in no way means faithlessness to the will of God or of Jesus Christ. On the contrary, here too the letter kills and the spirit gives life.

5. The gospel is the fruit of tradition and itself generates tradition. But specific traditions, however ancient and sacral, are not the purpose of

the gospel. If they become an alienating factor in church life they lose their purpose, which is to help to build up the freedom of the children of God. The apostle says: test all things, retain the good. As long as the existing forms of ministry are the best ones for helping the gospel to grow among God's people, we must preserve them. But if they become obstacles between men and women and the gospel, we may and must change them. Christ did not come to earth with the aim of establishing fixed forms of ministry or of dividing the world into a series of hierarchical levels. He came to earth to free men and women from the bonds of evil, so that they could learn to love God and their neighbours as themselves. This must also be the purpose of ministries.

III

The Parish Priest in Historical Perspective

Robrecht Boudens

1. The early and high Middle Ages

As the turbulent period of the migrations came to an end and the peoples of Western Europe had settled in the areas where they were finally to put down roots, the church, which had never lost sight of missionizing, could begin to develop and reinforce its organizational forms. Monks had brought the gospel and had founded abbeys here and there. After a number of decades a hierarchy came into being. Important cities got a bishop's seat, and when Christians became numerous or the diocese became too extended for the bishop to look after it properly, parishes came into being which were entrusted to a 'pastor' who represented the bishop and took on a number of functions there.[1] This chapter will be concerned above all with the image, the way of life and the history of these pastors.

From the beginning it should be noted that the development did not run parallel in all countries and that therefore a strict contemporaneity should not be expected. Means of communication were not as developed and frequent as they are now; the immediate result of this was that even precepts or guidelines issued from Rome did not immediately reach all places, nor were they observed everywhere. However, even in these first centuries of European Christianity, general tendencies can be noted which applied to virtually all lands.

From the fifth to the ninth century the life of the priest who was responsible for pastoral care in country parishes evolved very little. For a long time this was also to be true of the city parishes. In its main features the image of the pastor remained the same. He had to say mass, administer the sacraments, visit the sick, see that those faithful who died got a proper burial, and give a homily regularly. He was obliged to celebrate mass for his parishioners on Sundays. We find differing evidence of a 'daily' mass in the sources, which may indicate the existence of different traditions. In many places the pastor also performed the functions of a civic official. It can certainly be said that everywhere there was a close bond between the pastor and his parish. According to existing law, he was not allowed to say mass in other parishes, except when he was on a journey. Nor could he allow strangers to take part in the life of his parish, unless the strangers were travelling through or had been appointed to carry out a civic task there.[2]

From texts of synods and local councils which have survived we can see that initially priests did not wear any dress which distinguished them from ordinary people. Only in 742 was the wearing of the *casula* prescribed by Charlemagne; this was a wide over-garment which was also worn by monks, while the *sagum*, the characteristic dress of ordinary people, was forbidden.[3] More attention was paid to the distinctive life of the parish priest. Pope Celestine I reminded a number of bishops from Gaul that they had to stand out from the life of their parishioners not so much by their outer dress as by their manner of life. There is repeated reference to the canonical precepts which forbade dealings with women, the visiting of taverns and participation in hunting parties. Moreover the councils of the sixth and seventh centuries also indicate some canonical penalties which were provided for in the case of various transgressions by clergy.[4]

Such regulations and definitions suggest that the life of the clergy was not always spotless and beyond criticism. Nor can we be surprised that it was argued that priests who exercised one or another function in a particular parish should follow the custom of various episcopal churches and live in community. In this way they could provide support and reinforcement for one another and, for example, fight in the same way against superstition and pagan customs which had continued to persist. These were summed up at the synod of 742 which has already been mentioned: offerings to the dead, witchcraft, amulets, augury, magic formulae – all this was under suspicion, mixed up with invocations of martyrs and confessors.[5]

Because of the semi-Christian, semi-pagan practices of believers, catechesis was defective; this in turn was a consequence of a lack of training in the faith among the priests themselves. Anyone who was preparing for the priesthood at this time went to be taught by a pastor. In principle he had to take an examination, but a priest was only required to be able to say the Our Father and the Creed, to know how to administer the sacraments, have some idea of the regulations of canon law and the liturgy, and be capable of giving some commentary on scripture and the church fathers. The priests were also supposed to know enough Latin to understand the liturgical prayers.[6] In the preparation of his sermons the priest could seek inspiration in simplified homilies, a large number of which seem to have been in circulation in the Carolingian period.[7]

Between 1000 and 1150, and in fact deep into the thirteenth century, the picture of the pastor changed little, if at all. He remained the recognized authority in his parish and exercised his function in a seemly way. Many ordained priests who did their duty but had no outstanding qualities, good or bad, have left no trace in the sources and have not been remembered in history. But we can certainly find traces of the concern of bishops to provide their parishes with such dedicated priests.

At the request of the Archbishop of Trier, Réginon, abbot of the Rhineland abbey of Prüm, made a collection of the canonical regulations, which was used by the bishops as a guideline on their journeys to make visitations of the parishes of their dioceses.[8] From the questions that are asked there seems to have been a concern both for the priestly way of life of the pastors and the well-being of the faithful. However, it seems that in practice many abuses must have crept in and that some pastoral obligations had become a dead letter.

The bishop had to see that the pastor looked after the liturgical books and vestments carefully and kept the church itself tidy, and that the various registers were maintained. It was even more important that he did not neglect pastoral care. The bishop had to see that he visited the sick and dying, heard their confessions and administered the last sacraments to them. He had to bring communion to them personally and not have it seen to by the laity. Children had to be baptized. Was he looking after the poor, the orphans, the pilgrims? Did he sometime invite people to his table?

As visitor the bishop had also to see that worship was being provided. Did the pastor say the office at the hours provided? Did he have a clerk who could function as reader, could respond to the prayers of the mass and alternate with him in singing chants? Were the services announced by ringing the bell? Did he proclaim the word of the Lord? Could he expound epistle and gospel meaningfully?

The way of life of the parish priest was of the utmost importance. Was he suspect of illicit dealings with women? Was he a slave to drink? Was he thought always to be in and out of taverns? Was he out to stir up quarrels? Did he bear weapons in time of rebellion and disorder?[9]

The fact that these questions had to be asked means that abuses happened. Reliable scientific statistics for this period are not available, but the general impression that the documents give us is of a time in which the parish priests could perhaps be honest and dedicated, but still had not grown out of the roughness of their milieu.

Often there were tensions between priests in religious orders and diocesan priests. Many parishes had originally been established by an abbey, and in the course of time it was not always easy to determine precisely under whose jurisdiction they fell. With the rise of the Norbertines, who had incorporated pastoral care into their rule, at least the line between the parishes which were under a Premonstratensian abbey and those which were under the jurisdiction of a local bishop were drawn much more clearly. Tensions could also arise between the prince or liege-lord who had originally established a parish and the bishop who had jurisdiction over it as the church authority.

For centuries parish priests had to live in a sphere of legal tangles, but in most cases they did not have much to do with them directly.

2. Fourteenth and fifteenth centuries

The two centuries which preceded the Reformation shows us an image of the priest which was not fundamentally different from that of previous centuries, but in which certain situations had irrevocably become established.[10] The task of the priest remained the same. He had to administer baptism, and perhaps remind parents who postponed the baptism of their children of their duty. He was the minister of the eucharist and had to see that the obligation to go to mass every Easter (laid down at the Fourth Lateran Council of 1215) was fulfilled. He was usually present at marriage solemnities, and had to see that the dying were given the last sacraments in good time.

This did not involve the parish priest in much work, certainly in rural areas and even in the smaller towns. Hearing confessions and taking communion did not occupy a great deal of time. Moreover people did not go to confession and communion so often. Usually they followed the church regulation of receiving these sacraments at least once a year. By contrast, the number of blessings took up an ever more prominent place. The faithful appealed to divine support for almost everything, and the rituals contain prayers which had to ask for this support. The house had to be blessed, and the flock, the land, the harvest. When an epidemic threatened among animals or people, this danger had to be averted by prayer. Furthermore it was the task of the priest to preach regularly and to teach the children the catechism. We know from the statutes of synods that the priest also had to perform tasks for which in our day the civic authorities or the political apparatus are responsible. He had to protect children and the weak, supervise taverns and other places where there was drinking, and admonish public sinners. In various areas his presence was also required for the making of wills and other notarial acts.

On the other hand he had no pastoral care of special groups like youth organizations for girls or boys, or of social groups or associations which expect leadership or co-operation from the parochial ministry. The guilds which existed could call on a priest to say a mass, but they did not require any further attention or support.[11]

In the country, where on average the population of the parishes was small, there was therefore not too much pressure on the pastor, all the more since pastoral care did not involve much administrative work. The keeping of parish registers and registers of baptisms and deaths did not take much time. Moreover the pastor had helpers. In the larger agglomerations there were assistant priests who were also responsible for pastoral care. Moreover from the last decades of the thirteenth century another category of priests developed who had no direct involvement in the cure of souls but could offer the pastor useful help. The custom had grown up among the faithful of leaving money in their wills for masses to be said for the rest of the soul of the donor. A number of masses had to be said each day, and priests were needed for this. They were called altar priests. Sometimes they were also given the task of joining in the singing of the choir office or adding splendour to liturgical ceremonies. Sometimes they could also administer the sacraments. They did not have a large income. By contrast, the pastors and some assistant priests usually had the produce of one or more benefices and the tithes (of the fruits of the earth and the increase of cattle).[12] Moreover the parishioners usually offered their pastor an offering in kind on some occasions, for example when slaughtering an animal. The pastor might not ask for money for celebrating a mass. The difficulty was resolved by a not particularly scrupulous distinction: he did not ask for money for spiritual things, for grace, but for his work and trouble. In fact this produced a twofold category: a rich clergy who contrasted with a real priestly proletariat. The church as such may have been rich; many clergy were not.

This situation meant that quite a number of priests looked for extra income. Many had a plot of land that they worked; some practised a profession or ran a little business. Others functioned as clerks. Yet others could be branded hucksters. They had little to do with fulfilling a priestly role.

In the fourteenth and fifteen centuries the number of posts for assistant priests and benefices grew to such a degree – and with them the number of interested parties – that a paradoxical situation was created: a high number of clergy on the one hand and sparsely populated parishes on the other. In the diocese of Utrecht at the beginning of the sixteenth century, which contained around 600,000 souls, there were around 5,000 secular priests. Between 1508 and 1518 there were on average 213 ordinations a year. In a census of the population, which was estimated at around one million, the number of priests was therefore abnormally high. Moreover we must remember that some cities like Frankfurt or Montpellier had had only one parish church for a long time, while Ypres or Worms had four, Cologne sixteen and Metz twenty-six (for 25,000 inhabitants).[13] It is clear that the large number of priests led to absenteeism. Since, moreover, we know that some parishes comprised less than 100 souls and most less than 1,400, it is not difficult to understand that such a situation was to be a cause of abuses.

How was the country pastor supposed to behave?

If we investigate areas on which attention focussed during synods and councils, we can form some idea of how the church wanted priests to conduct themselves. The priest had to be simple, to avoid standing out in behaviour or clothing in any way, not to seek to be prominent, and to avoid regular visits to taverns and games of chance. Two other points are repeatedly mentioned. First of all celibacy. It is repeatedly recalled that this needed to be maintained. After the First Lateran Council (1123), the marriages of priests who had received higher ordinations was declared invalid (previously they had been regarded as illicit). Secondly, it was insisted that priests should live together in community. The aim was to avoid the solitary living of priests leading to loneliness and priests sinning by engaging in unseemly behaviour. With that aim, conferences of priests were established and country chapters held, which were to reinforce the solidarity of country deaneries. However, on this point all attempts still failed. The priests asserted their personal freedom too strongly.

The life-style and behaviour of the clergy may have differed to some degree from country to country, but there seems to have been something like a spirit of the time which proved fairly similar everywhere. An investigation of the archdiocese of Cologne has demonstrated that between 3% and 5% of the clergy came up before the judge for serious misdemeanours.[14] Taken by themselves, such excesses as have left a trace in the course of these two centuries have hardly any historical significance. However, clergy are accused of other offences so repeatedly and with so much emphasis in the literature and the sources – above all in the works of the Humanists – that it can be said without hesitation that some priests actually committed them. The fact that the regulations of the synods point in the same direction shows that they were real.

The priests were accused of being avaricious. Money was required for the performance of spiritual services and often more than the normal tariffs prescribed. Sometimes this led to simony. In all honesty it must be added that we know of quite a few priests who made money available for the foundation of study bursaries or for other good purposes.[15]

In addition there was the very widespread clerical slavery to drink, or at least to hanging around in taverns. Sometimes this was accompanied by gluttony, worldly diversions, dice or other games of chance. The habit was so deeply rooted that even after Trent the visitation accounts of many bishops were still to make mention of it. However, to generalize would be wrong and it is impossible to produce statistics. Still, it can certainly be stated that a number of priests visited taverns too readily and that some were so addicted to drink that in fact the good name of the priesthood was dragged down.

Offence was taken in yet other small respects. Some priests went hunting too often. Others neglected their prayers or spoke too irreverently and loudly in church, forgetting the holiness of the place. Yet others spoke ill of people and instigated disputes. Frequently there was a charge that clergy were backward and lacked education. But we should perhaps note that this last accusation was mostly made by Humanists, and that in their view people who had a somewhat rough appearance could easily be regarded as barbarians.[16] In the meantime, however, it seems certain that most country priests did not have a very intellectual training. Sometimes they may have been excellent pastors, but few made their mark as men of letters or as scholars. Chroniclers could poke fun at their ignorance or their lack of culture. In some cases an authentic zeal for faith could make up for their mediocre training or their weaknesses, but that was far from always being the case. Their lack of training in the faith meant that essential things were overlooked, and excessive emphasis was placed on incidentals. Sacramentals took the place of sacraments. More heed was paid to devotion to Mary and the saints than to devotion to Christ. In this 'waning of the Middle Ages'[17] a multiplication of ceremonies and devotional practices had come about and blessings began to occupy an abnormal place, so that the ordinary believer easily moved from popular belief to superstition. Huizinga states that certain actions approached witchcraft. In any case spiritual life in the Middle Ages was so overloaded that abuses and excesses were unavoidable. For a badly trained clergy and certainly for the poor priestly proletariat there was a great temptation to support any form of devotion which at the same time increased their material prosperity.[18]

On the previous pages mention has been made several times of the difficulties which commitment to celibacy brought with it. Since attention needs to be paid to this repeatedly down through history, it is worth pausing over the way in which the rule of celibacy came to be established in the Western church.

At the beginning of the fourth century we find the first traces of what later could be called a general law. Canon 33 of the local council of Elvira, in Spain, around 306, states that it is forbidden to bishops, priests and deacons to have sexual relations with their wives and thus beget children. We can see the echo here of what some church fathers taught: it is not the marriage of clergy that is forbidden, but sexual intercourse in marriage, which was a taint.[19] At the end of the same century, around 386, a council was held in Rome for the bishops of Central and Southern Italy in which (canon 9) again priests were denied the right to sexual intercourse. Here too the reason was given that their pastoral task had to occupy them to such a degree that they would no longer have any need to pay attention to the sexual.

The decision which was taken in Rome was communicated to other bishops by Pope Siricius (384–99). He insisted that they too should introduce celibacy into their dioceses. Innocent I (401–417) and Leo the Great (440–461) spoke to the same effect and a number of fifth-century councils tried to urge it on the whole church. It was still presupposed that priests might be married; however, they must live with their spouses as brother and sister.[20]

The real law of celibacy as we now know it gradually came into being between the ninth and the twelfth centuries. Leo IX (1049–1054), Gregory VII (1073–1085) and Urban II (1088–1099) enacted measures against women who were married to priests. The priests themselves were given the choice of either dissolving their marriages or ceasing to exercise priestly functions. The Second Lateran Council (1139) decreed that a marriage entered into by a priest must be regarded as invalid.

Throughout the Middle Ages the church had to urge the practice of celibacy. A low point was reached in the late Middle Ages. It may seem paradoxical, but on the one hand there are countless texts which indicate a deep respect for chastity; on the other hand in all Western countries numerous violations of celibacy can be noted. It is difficult to give a balanced judgment on the real situation of the priests, all the more so as we constantly need to reckon with regional differences. As I indicated earlier, the sources usually mention priests who failed at a moral level. The question is how widespread this failure was, and how people judged the violation of chastity. Furthermore the question is not whether there were priests who fell short in their duties, for these certainly existed, but whether living with a concubine before Trent was so common a state that people thought it normal. We find texts which would answer this last question in the affirmative, while on the other there are also texts which compel a less radical statement.

Texts which indicate a generally widespread situation occur repeatedly. R.R.Post cites one from which on the one hand it appears that the faithful were forbidden to attend mass celebrated by a *concubinarius sacerdos,* but on the other hand it also becomes clear that it was difficult to maintain this regulation very strictly, because almost everyone had a wife. This happened so repeatedly that living with a wife was regarded as a petty sin and could be tolerated.[21] Aeneas Silvio Piccolomini, later Pius II, wrote that the Friesians insisted on getting married priests 'for fear that otherwise they would pollute the bedrooms of others'. The Friesians, he wrote, judged that to live in continence went beyond the power of nature.[22] The author is contradicted by contemporaries, but there is so much other evidence connected with the Friesians that it is best to take Piccolomini seriously. Moreover it is telling that the Reformers usually motivate their action to abolish celibacy by pointing to the constant occurrence of the concubinate. In Germany suspect priests were left alone, because of the fear that otherwise too many churches would be left without pastors.[23]

The most explicit testimony that a large number of priests lived as married men in the fourteenth and fifteenth centuries can be found in the writings of the Humanists. It is possible that here they have to some degree succumbed to a general fashion or cultural phenomenon – criticism of circumstances in the church – but the failure to observe celibacy will have been serious enough to make such criticism possible. By adding up a number of facts we get the impression that the majority of clergy lived in a relationship which the church law forbade but which seemed so frequent that it was regarded as almost normal – by the authorities and by ordinary people – and certainly was not seen as a great evil.

However, we should not just generalize. There are also accounts which indicate that the failure to maintain celibacy – however widespread – was not the general rule. The fourteenth-century theologian Dionysius the Carthusian wrote that the faithful were offended when a priest lived with a woman. It would have been impossible for him to write this had the concubinate been as widespread as one might be inclined to infer from other texts. There are also texts which one might expect to mention moral transgressions and do not.

It is not easy to form an objective and balanced picture of the real state of the clergy. Depending on the documents one is looking at, one can either note that most clergy lived with a concubine or judge that the majority were not involved. Moreover we must always be aware that the situation could differ from country to country. However, it seems possible to say two things with certainty. First, a number of priests lived with their housekeepers as man and wife and this was tolerated both by the faithful and by the church and civil authorities.[24] Secondly, legislation continued to exist which condemned this situation, and it was regularly repeated, whereas transgressors were still seldom punished. As a result of this, concubinage developed into a historical phenomenon which – because of isolation and boredom – was more widespread in the country than in the city.

Beyond doubt, now and then there was a voice which called for reform. We think of people like Nicolas de Clémanges, Gerson and Pierre d'Ailly. Their calls found little response. Only when the Reformation had a large part of Europe in its grasp was the Council of Trent to be convened, which was to enact a number of reforming decrees as well as adopt doctrinaire positions. However, it was to be some generations before the life-style of the priest was to undergo a basic change.

In judging pastors from this time we must always remember that the example they were given by their bishops was anything but edifying.

3. Sixteenth to eighteenth centuries

The Council of Trent must of course be seen in its concrete historical context. It was convened for two reasons: orthodox teaching had to be established in the face of the growth of Protestantism, and regulations had to be produced which would put an end to the numerous abuses which had crept into the life of church and clergy.

As far as the priesthood was concerned,[25] one aspect above all was deepened. The priest above all had to be a pastor. The ministry of the word was neither the only nor the prime constituent element of the priesthood. With the eucharist Christ had offered a visible sacrifice and the priest was the minister of that sacrifice. It gave him his dignity, but it also presupposed that he would be mindful of this dignity. Clergy must not involve themselves in worldly things. Men and women had to be able to look up to them and imitate them. The behaviour of the priest must be regulated in such a way that 'in clothing, in gesture, in conversation, in behaviour, in talk and in all other things he should give the impression of earnestness, humility and deep piety'.[26] He had to avoid even small faults, since little shortcomings in him were more reprehensible than in others. His actions had to command the respect of all. Bishops were told that they must renew the precepts of former councils and thus urgently remind the priests of all that they had to avoid: parties, dances, games, and everything that the church regarded as being too worldly. Since some of these precepts had fallen into disuse, the bishops had to remind people urgently of them.

At the Council of Trent a good deal of attention was paid to the priestly ideal. The priest was the representative of Christ, the sacrificer of the new covenant, a man of God who lived by the gospel. He had to show maturity and moderation, have inward and outward balance and above all deep piety. The image of the priest which was outlined at Trent was that of the dedicated parish pastor, dignified and honourable, who lived by himself in a simple house where he was always accessible to the poor and the unfortunate, concerned solely for the welfare of souls and the service of the Lord.

The council fathers were aware that to implement such an image of the priest was no easy task. The country parishes were largely in the hands of rich non-resident canons or other inactive clergy, while the ministry of the pastor was *de facto* carried out by 'hirelings' of low status and little education, who usually lived in conditions of poverty and therefore, in an undignified way, sought additional employment. They wanted to be paid even for performing their priestly office: children were only baptized for payment, and absolution was not given without a penitential contribution. These abuses did not apply to all priests, but the fact that synods and individual bishops repeatedly banned them indicates that clergy did not take much note of the guidelines. Here it should be pointed out that in the sixteenth century the number of well-trained priests fell disturbingly throughout Europe. In addition to religious causes, like a general relaxation of the life of faith, there were also social causes. The country nobility, affected by the economic recession, turned bitterly on the church, which as an institution had rich incomes.

It was to change such a situation that the decision was taken in Trent in future not to allow anyone to enter priestly office unless he had had a thorough training at a seminary. It has been possible to say quite justly that the Council of Trent was worth all the trouble for the seminary decree alone.[27] The Council fathers began by pointing out that young men who were in line for the priesthood had to be trained from their youth in the *ecclesiastica disciplina* and therefore had to receive their training in a 'college' in which they would be protected against all worldly influences, an appropriate school for servants of God: *ita et hoc collegium Dei ministorum perpetuum seminarium sit.* Later a distinction was to come into being between a minor seminary (more or less corresponding to the teaching now given at a secondary school) and a major seminary (in which in addition to a theological formation scripture was also to be taught, along with the church fathers, the practice of the sacraments and the liturgy). The major seminary was also to teach everything necessary for hearing confessions. Moreover seminary life had to create the framework in which men could be trained for a serious piety: daily mass, monthly confession, regular communion, a number of pious practices.

The seminary decree was very significant for the future of the clergy. However, it was still some decades before the seminaries which were needed came into being in the different countries of Western Europe. Since it would take us too long to go into this in detail, I shall limit myself to giving the dates of the foundations of some of the seminaries. The first seminaries to be established in Italy were those of Milan and Rieti (both in 1564). Then came Imola and Ravenna (1567), Rimini and

Bologna (1568) and Velletri (1612). In France the earliest were Reims (1567), Toulouse (1590), Metz (1608), Rouen (1612), Mâcon (1617), Lyons (1618) and Langres (1619). In the southern Netherlands mention should be made of Ypres (1565), Arras (1571/1646), Bruges (1571/1591), Louvain (Collegium Regium, 1579), Douai (1586/1606), St-Omer (1638), Namur (1640) and Doornik (1666).

It was harder to develop the seminary system in German-speaking countries. This was partly because of the chaos produced by the Thirty Years' War, and partly also because cathedral chapters refused to help in their establishment. But mention can be made of Eichstätt (1564) along with Breslau (1565), Ermland (1567), Würzburg (1570), Salzburg (1577), Basel (1606), Dillingen (1614), Cologne (1615), Münster (1649) and Osnabrück (1662).

The Tridentine ideas of priesthood and the training of priests were mostly spread by the European seminaries through the so-called French school of spirituality, initially above all associated with the Oratory of Jesus. Cardinal de Bérulle (1575–1629) is usually said to be its founder. He emphasized the need of what he called *adhérence,* learning to be active with God and to be receptive to God's activity, assimilating it inwardly and developing it into an attitude to life. The priest has to realize that of himself he is nothing and certainly cannot put any hindrance in the way of what God is bringing into being in him. He must as far as possible will what God wills.

After the death of Bérulle, leadership of the Oratory was taken over by Charles de Condren (1588–1641). He dedicated his life to the reform of the clergy and the formation of holy priests. After his death, in 1641 the Oratorian M.Picoté settled in a village near Paris. With M.Olier[28] he trained a priesthood which sought to accept members who would be trained in piety and church learning. This quickly transferred to the parish of Saint-Sulpice in Paris. Without wanting to be monks, these priests observed a common rule and prayed the office together. Attention was also paid to pastoral formation. M.Olier wrote a *Directoire Spirituel du séminaire de Saint-Sulpice* for them and showed concern for the spiritual life of the seminarians.[29] He emphasized inner converse with God and often spoke to his seminarians about the exalted character of the priesthood. His *Traité des Saints Ordres* makes it clear how he imagined the ideal priest and how he saw priestly holiness. He put very marked emphasis on the life of union with Christ.[30] His view was to have a marked effect on the traditional image of the priest in the seventeenth century.

The priest has above all to be inspired by Christ the Sacrifice, and therefore pay due attention to the sacrifice of Calvary and the Blessed Sacrament, which he must venerate. Unity with Christ compels him to a deep devotion to the eucharist. The priest is 'another Christ'. He shares in the power of the sacrificial priest, and bears the priestly character as a mark in his soul. His attitude must therefore be a reflection of the attitude of Christ. Like Christ, the priest is mediator between God and man.

The magnitude of the priesthood is repeatedly emphasized. It is granted to the priest through the ministry of the sacraments to make the Holy Spirit descend on the faithful. Here is a passage from Jean Eudes to illustrate this greatness:[31]

'You, O priests, are the most noble part of the Mystical Body of the Son of God. You are the eyes, the mouth, the tongue and the heart of Jesus; or, to put it a better way, you are the eyes, the mouth, the tongue and the very heart of Jesus.

You are the eyes, for it is through you that this good shepherd constantly watches over his flock.

You are the mouth and the tongue, since it is through you that He speaks to men and that He goes further by preaching the same word and the same good message that He preached to you when he was on earth.

You are his heart, since it is through you that He gives the true life of grace to all true members of his body on earth, together with the glorious life of heaven.'[32]

In the teaching of the French school of spirituality, it was often said that the greatness of the priest exceeded all imaginable greatnesses. His dignity exceeded that of the angels and even of Mary. The priest had to love God in the name of men and offer God reparation for the evil that was practised. Only if he sacrificed himself for the souls entrusted to him could he hallow himself. Priestly holiness was participation in the suffering and resurrection of the Lord. 'The priest,' says M.Olier, 'must live as a man who has wholly died to this world and risen to a new life. He must live as an angel, lead a holy and godly life in his heart, a life that is like that of the Risen Redeemer. Like the angels he must dissociate himself from his body, for he is a child of the resurrection.'

Priests were expected to be ardent, with a constant eye to the souls that they must heal. Hence the necessity for prayer and zeal.

It makes men and women today smile when they hear that the priest must live like an angel – the priest is human; however, we must not lose sight of the fact that the school of Bérulle was a reaction to the abuses of the previous period in which the divine mission was so lost sight of.[33]

The seventeenth century was *par excellence* the century of the Counter-Reformation. Anyone who studies the accounts of episcopal visitations from this period will be struck by the many positive comments on the pastors. There were abuses in all dioceses, but in most they had become the exception.[34]

During the eighteenth century, certainly in the Romance countries of Europe, the spiritual life of priests remained fundamentally inspired by the French school of spirituality. Emphasis was put on the magnitude of the priesthood. There was no shortage of vocations, so that no parish was without a pastor. On the contrary, as also in former centuries, often a number of priests were attached to one parish. They did not live in community, but certainly in the cities formed as it were a hierarchy. One of them would function as a pastor; there were also curates and other priests attached to the parish who had some task or another. B.Plongeron calls them 'parasites', because apart from the mass with intentions they had to say for certain foundations, they had no other fixed income. They could earn a small amount, for example by carrying the cross, the baldachino or the bell when the eucharist was taken to the sick, when they worked as sacristans or joined the choir to sing the office.[35] This was the continuation of a custom which already existed in the Middle Ages.

In the country, loneliness was the enemy to be fought. At a time when means of communication were virtually non-existent, the priests had very little contact with pastors from neighbouring parishes. They enjoyed all the more the meetings which took place on special occasions like the patronal festival of the parish or the funeral of a prominent parishioner.

At the seminary it was impressed on the future clergy that later they were to impose on themselves a rule which was as similar as possible to that of the seminary. In general this advice was followed. In concrete it meant getting up early to hear confessions, meditating, saying mass, praying the office, having breakfast and after that some study. After the siesta the sick were visited, contact was made with the parishioners and administrative tasks were performed. These also included civic duties. Most priests went to bed soon after nine in the evening.

On the whole celibacy was maintained better than in previous centuries, but continued to be a problem for some clergy. Cutting polemic was written for or against compulsory celibacy. Roskovany lists more than a thousand studies and pamphlets which either defended this obligation during the eighteenth century or put it in question.[36]

The cultural phenomenon which goes under the name of the Enlightenment and which left such a strong mark on this period could not go unnoticed by the priests. The enlightened spirits were fanatical about the forces of nature and regarded pious practices as superstition. They did not deny the existence of God, but their God was a God who could be reached by reason, a cold power which perhaps lay at the origin of the world but was not further affected by the world and its inhabitants. They were indifferent to or mistrustful of the church, which held fast to revelation and believed in a providence. It is striking that a relatively large number of priests were among the original Freemasons, despite a papal ban. This can be noted in almost all countries.

Towards the end of the eighteenth century, above all in German-speaking countries, there was a call for a more rational formation of the clergy. Ignaz Heinrich von Wessenberg judged that the classical Sulpician type of priest was not up to coping with the new ideas. Their training separated the priests and future priests too much from the world, so that they could not be up with their time. Wessenberg trained the clergy according to his own model: this led to priests who looked down with some disparagement on the piety of country folk, the decorations which the peasants put up in their churches, their zeal for building Calvaries, their devotions and miraculous images, their attachment to processions and pilgrimages.[37]

4. The nineteenth century

During the nineteenth century the French school of spirituality dominated the image of the priest throughout Western Europe. Only the German-speaking countries were an exception here. In France itself the great revolution was a period of crisis. Many priests who had refused to take the oath on the Constitution of the Clergy had emigrated abroad,[38] and those who had remained lived in a situation of civic illegality and felt obliged to celebrate the mass and administer the sacraments secretly. But the French Revolution did not represent an essential break in the image of the priest. This was not least thanks to Monsieur Emery, director of the seminary of Saint-Sulpice, who was the only priest whom Napoleon respected and whom he never dared to order to close the seminary.[39] Moreover M.Emery was able to manoeuvre so skilfully that this famous centre of training for the clergy continued to remain open even during Napoleon's rule as consul and emperor. It is above all thanks to the seminary of Saint-Sulpice that the priestly type which had come into being in the French school of spirituality was maintained during the Revolution. The ideal it strove for was to continue until the Second World War.

Three books above all exercised a great influence at this time. First of all was the *Memoriale vitae sacerdotalis* of Claude Arvisenet, which originally appeared in Constance in 1794, was translated into many languages and repeatedly reprinted.[40] In writing this book – which in conception suggests the *Imitation of Christ* – the author had in mind priests who once the storm of the Revolution was past would feel the need to be strengthened in dedicated pastoral care and in union with God. In order to make the invitation more urgent, the conversation between Christ and the faithful disciple is maintained through all seventy chapters. The emphasis is constantly put on the need for the sanctification of the priest. It mentions the magnitude of the priestly calling, the need to strive for perfection, and loving fulfilment of the duties imposed by the state.

A second work is that written by G.Carron, *L'Ecclésiastique accompli*. It remained a manuscript for a long time but was published in Paris in 1823. The author was a very active priest who gave an account of how much the clergy after the French Revolution needed encouragement and interiorization. He wanted to see the life of the priest as being full of supernatural radiance, and so his book developed into a handbook of spirituality in the spirit of Saint-Sulpice. It bears witness to a solid piety, but also has a clerical aura. However, we find an authentic spiritual movement in it.[41]

Finally, mention should be made by a little work by the Sulpician C.Denise, *Thesaurus sacerdotum et clericorum*, first published in Orleans in 1754 and repeatedly reprinted in Paris, Avignon and Saint-Malo well into the century. It refers to the virtues which every priest must possess. In order to emphasize the dignity and holiness of the priesthood, numerous quotations are given from church fathers and from the Council of Trent. The whole of the third part is about the eucharist. In order to be able to offer the sacrifice of the mass worthily, it is necessary to lead a pure life. Along with Arvisenet and Carron, Denise was responsible for bringing into the nineteenth century the spiritual current which the French school of spirituality had called to life.

What can be said about the image of the nineteenth-century priest? He was supposed to strive for a holy way of life, to lead an inner life, to be intimate with the Lord. The books which he was given as a seminarian were already directed towards this, and they were later to be found in his usually slim priest's library: Sulpician in conception and inspiration. On the basis of this traditional inwardness he was to pray his breviary, celebrate the eucharist, examine his conscience and visit the Blessed Sacrament, precisely as he was taught at the seminary. The norm for his own behaviour was faithfulness to the spiritual exercises and practices which he had to perform and which regularly recurred in his life – daily, weekly or monthly. It was impressed on the priest that he was taken from among men and appointed to go ahead of them in holiness. He was a priest for ever, disappearing behind the magnitude of the eucharistic office.[42] Some bishops constantly return to this in their letters and addresses to priests and deacons.

The church held fast to the precepts of morality. Moreover in general the law of celibacy was observed well. Situations like those from the period before the Gregorian Reform or the time of the Reformation no longer occurred. Blatant cases of moral weakness were denounced by the faithful and were also subject to severe penalties. The violation of the law of celibacy was a transgression against the holiness of the priestly office. It was repeatedly pointed out that celibacy was the condition for a total love, freedom for the church, the discipleship of Christ. Offences against celibacy were regarded as far worse than, for example, shortcomings in social justice.

That does not mean that the problem did not arise. It arose, for example, especially in countries which had hardly been reached by French spirituality, if at all. At the seminary of Rottenburg a number of professors, supported by seminarians, fought actively for the abolition of celibacy. An organization was also formed to work for the abolition of this law.[43] In 1828 the lay professors of Freiburg, convinced that something of this kind must be undertaken to raise the morale and spiritual level of the clergy, presented a petition to the government to allow the marriage of priests. A considerable number of clergy and theological students signed the petition.

Around this time Johann Adam Möhler, sometimes called the father of modern theology, began his academic career in the *Theologische Quartalschrift*. One of his first articles discussed the problem of the decline in the number of priests. In it he stated that, among other things because of celibacy, the number of candidates for the priesthood would always be on the low side.[44]

There were also difficulties in Italy. In 1865 an Englishman from Florence wrote a series of letters in *The Guardian*[45] in which among other things he mentioned that an organization had been formed in Naples, the 'Società emancipatrice e di mutuo soccorso des sacerdozio italiano', with a journal, the *Emancipatore Cattolico*. A memorandum sheds light on the aim of the reform. It announced twenty-four branches in different regions of the kingdom with almost a thousand priests as members and about as many lay people. For differing reasons they supported an abolition of celibacy.

This was not a particularly large number for the whole Italian peninsula, and it should not give the impression that in Italy generally, celibacy was not maintained. There are exaggerations on both sides: the opponents making too much of an uproar, and the hierarchy and the Curia making celibacy an almost divine law and not seeing it as a church measure which moreover was observed only in the Western church.

The soutane was the sign of being taken out of the world. According to the Sulpician tradition it was also a help in delicate situations and a protection against enticements. In Catholic countries the bishops very seldom allowed priests to exchange the soutane for ordinary clothes, and only for important reasons.

If the soutane or priestly toga was the sign of being taken out of the world, it was also an expression of priestly decorum, the characteristic dress of the priestly state and a requirement of priestly fashion. In it one did not visit taverns, one did not go to the beach and did not appear in dance halls. Because of this priestly fashion, among bishops around the end of the century we find a similar reserve about clergy riding bicycles. After an absolute prohibition, in which this was seen as whim of fashion, riding a bicycle was sometimes allowed. One was given a *licentia utendi rota dicta 'bicyclette'* on condition that this permission was only used in the service of pastoral care and not outside one's own parish.[46]

It is striking that the exceptions which were allowed were always motivated by pastoral care. The priest had to show zeal in pastoral care by administering the sacraments, preaching, catechesis, visiting his parishioners, concern for the learning and spiritual soundness of those who had been entrusted to him. Being a confessor was an important task. In the nineteenth century the priests spent many hours in the confessional, above all when they were recognized as men of God. They heard confessions in parish churches, in institutes, for school-children. The confessor knew his people. The literature of all countries contains priestly figures who stood close to their people and who were loved by them. The ideal priest was hearty and jovial, lived a simple life but on the other hand enjoyed a glass of good wine and did not turn down a good meal if the occasion arose. So he could go and dine with the baron without many scruples. Ordinary people accepted this. The fact that the priest had contact with the great lord did not alienate him from the main in the street. Only towards the end of the century was there to be a change here in some industrialized areas.

The priests spoke the dialect of the people and defended this attitude, sometimes against the bishops. For example in France the episcopate called for French to be spoken because it saw many advantages in a policy of centralization. However, opposition to this developed in some regions. In French Flanders, Alsace, the Moselle, the Basque country and Provence, the catechism was passed on to children wholly or partially in their mother tongue. In quite a few cases the bishops yielded to pressure from their clergy and allowed them to preach in 'la langue vulgaire du pays', at least in some masses. In French Flanders Camille Looten played a not inconsiderable role in preserving Flemish. In the 1880s he had pressed for the retention of the vernacular in teaching the catechism but was opposed here by an overwhelming state authority. However, in 1890 Flemish catechism lessons were still being given in 75 communities of the arrondisse-ments of Dunkirk and Hazebroeck. The priest Jean-Marie Gantois followed in Looten's footsteps by defending worship in the vernacular with the same ardour.[47]

Between 1870 and 1914 many priests argued for the preservation of local traditions. Often they were pioneers in the study of local history, folklore and archaeology. As a result they got close to people, and noted down customs and usages, distinctive proverbs and ex-pressions.[48] In Belgium, so-called 'sociétés d'émulation' were set up and journals produced for the study of the local dialect and local history. Usually priests played a prominent role in these societies. Apart from individuals who revered Enlightenment ideas, in the nineteenth century the priests stood close to the people. Certainly they were popular figures in the country. They were accepted with all their peculiarities. Ordinary people knew that priests cared for them.

On the other hand, the bishops insisted that the priests should keep a certain distance from ordinary people. That did not happen out of mistrust of ordinary people, but out of a concern that the priest should avoid any form of vulgarity and not lower himself to a more earthly way of life. Willy-nilly, however, this also contributed to the rise of a 'priestly state': quite a number of people began to include the priest among the notables – those who had studied, had enjoyed a certain degree of education and knew how to behave in all circles. A *Manuel de politesse et de convenance ecclésiastiques* was a classic handbook in all seminaries.

In general it can be stated that in the nineteenth century the clergy bore witness to an active pastoral care. Priests saw to it that halls were built for the youth, homes for the elderly, parish rooms. Without seeing themselves as 'founders', they established religious congregations, or at least pious associations, which later developed into congregations. During the last decades of the century they sometimes established co-operatives, mutual societies, and savings banks for farmworkers and labourers. The average priest was neither a scholar nor a patriot but a pastor. And that is how he wanted the people to see him: as a man of God who took time to pray, to be interested in people and to go round doing good.

Perhaps the priests in the nineteenth century noticed the social phenomena too late. The developments of the time escaped them. The consequences of industrialization did not force them to rethink pastoral work, nor did they seek approaches which were more adapted to the way people lived. They had a tendency towards conservatism, although a change came here in the nineteenth century, above all in the city parishes. Before *Rerum Novarum* most clergy were hostile and polemical towards what they called 'progress', a word which had taken on pejorative connotations since the Enlightenment. They tended to label 'revolutionary' elements which usually had to be seen as the progress of civilization and culture. Towards all this they adopted a defensive attitude. This certainly applied in countries which had not yet been affected by industrialization or other social or political factors. At a local level, not a few instances can be cited of priests who saw their involvement in politics as part of their pastoral task, above all when Socialists, who were very anti-clerical, began to pose a threat to Catholic policies. The history of the church in Belgium – and not only there –

provides a telling example. The Belgian church, consciously or unconsciously, saw politics as a means of disseminating and consolidating Christianity. The correspondence of the bishops with the deans often contains political advice. They are not motivated by party politics but rather by a religious concern. Because the church wanted to maintain its influence on public life, in its eyes it was only logical for it to be able to have a role in public concerns. First the fight was taken to the liberalism that exploited the workers, and then to socialism; here there was no immediate recognition that socialism was also fighting for the rights of the workers. At the end of the century the priest looked somewhat despairingly at anything that began to resemble a factory, because in his eyes it threatened to become a hotbed of anti-clerical agitation, of protest against all that was spiritual and Christian, and to alienate the workers from what he still saw as the ideal clerical society. The parish priests saw it as their task to encourage works and organizations everywhere whose aim was to protect workers and those in need. One might think of the Conferences of St Vincent which were founded by the layman Ozanam, but strongly supported by the clergy; the Gesellenverein in Germany; and later of the Kajotters movement. Many organizations were also set up out of mistrust of socialism, which was seen as a threat to religion, and because there was insufficient recognition of its concern for the workers.

As a result of the anti-clericalism which reared its head in many countries, in the nineteenth century the priest sometimes felt oppressed, but at the same time he remained conscious of his dignity and continued to believe in his priestly ideal. He was aware that he was regarded by some people as an anachronism, but at the same time he was inwardly convinced of being a man chosen by God. In his theology he found the necessary strength to play the role in the Christian community which had been given him by sacramental post-Tridentine theology, and on this theology his spirituality was built.

Usually the theology which the nineteenth-century priests had been given during their training was very poor. As it is impossible to survey the situation in all countries in detail, I shall limit myself to the areas which originally formed part of the Papal States. The local Council of Loreto, in 1850, was dominated by a concern for the renewal of the priesthood. The situation in both the minor and the major seminaries was on the agenda. In the minor seminaries the humanities were taught. At the council an attempt was made to bring the minor seminaries up to the level of the state schools. Lessons had to be given with the clear aim of putting the young men in a position to learn theology later and to understand the office that they were to pray each day. Hardly any of the minor seminaries in practice taught Greek. Where philosophy was studied, it was limited to basic principles. Physics was non-existent. With an eye to the later priesthood, much attention was paid to religion, and the lessons always had an ecclesiastical stamp. The minor seminaries were steeped in a kind of spirit of self-defence, almost a sense of inferiority and mistrust of the real social and cultural developments.

The Modernist movement, which already began to manifest itself at the end of the nineteenth century and which strove for renewal, was to criticize this situation sharply. Romolo Murri, who himself attended minor seminary in Fermo, called the education static, alien to the world and out of keeping with the interests of the young.[49]

It is more important to make a close examination of the state of the major seminaries. In philosophy, at the provincial Council of Urbino in 1859, it was required that students should be guided above all by the teaching of Thomas Aquinas. Some decades later this was to issue in Neo-Thomism, which was taught in most of the Italian seminaries. Of course this was also the direction of the discipline and doctrine which characterized the church, above all at the beginning of the pontificate of Leo XIII.[50] Obedience to and acceptance of the magisterium was inculcated, against the spirit of liberalism and what was called 'modern progress'. Philosophy was seen as the handmaid of theology. The philosophical culture which the seminarians received seem still to be bound up with a scheme which had applied in earlier times. The priests were accused by the liberals, not wholly unjustly, of cultural indifference and of a lack of interest in learning. As a result of the traditional baggage which they had been given at the major seminary, they lacked the necessary openness and creativity to go new ways. Perrone[51]'s handbook, which was used for dogmatic theology, was thorough, but predominantly speculative, dryly presented, and dealt in unchangeable concepts. As everywhere, moral theology was predominantly developed as casuistry. Strict moralism was inculcated. P.Scavini, whose book was the authority in the seminaries, was inexorable in his plea for the maintenance of the rights and privileges of the church.[52] The broader handbook of the Redemptorist Panzuti[53] was criticized for laxity, although this author, too, was not free of long academic excursuses and did not get down to the deeper problems of moral action.

The handbooks for exegesis remained stuck in the traditional and anti-rationalistic sphere. A much-used handbook was that of Zama Mellini, *Institutiones biblicae sive dissertationes isagogicae in S.Scripturam*. It looked erudite, but there was no real exegesis in which the religious context of the sacred text was sought.[54] Church law was regarded in strictly legalistic terms. One could not trace the slightest pastoral concern. This must involuntarily have had an impact on the clergy who were formed by it. Church history was completely incidental, and the handbooks used ended at the Council of Trent.[55] The liturgy was reduced to a pedantic exposition of the rubrics during the ceremonies.[56] Clerical eloquence paid more attention to the form than to the content.

One can conclude that up to the end of the nineteenth century there was no place for real openness. Scholastic theology limited itself to speculative considerations. That meant that the future priests stood outside what was happening in society and outside scientific progress, outside the ferment of culture and outside the real problems of life.

We know that to begin with, the theology students of some seminaries (e.g. Macerata and Urbino) took the opportunity to pursue at the universities of their respective cities disciplines which were not taught at the seminary. But there was little renewal to be found in these universities. The same textbooks were used as in the seminaries, and the church authorities required a strict watch to be kept there over the purity of the doctrine. In 1860, when the Papal States ceased to exist, the theological faculties of these universities were abolished and from then on theology was taught only in the universities.

In order to train future professors, from then on each diocese was given the opportunity each year to send one of its best students to the Pius Seminary in Rome. This seminary, which was situated in the Apollinaris house of study, was established by Pius IX in 1853 with the explicit aim of raising the level of teaching in the Papal States. Attention was paid to courses in Hebrew, biblical Greek and patristics that were not taught elsewhere. One could also gain a doctorate there in theology and in canon law.

In order to stimulate the study of Thomism, academies were set up in various cities on the model of the Academia di San Tommaso which was organized in Rome in 1879 by Leo XIII. In 1900, as the result of an urgent order of the Curia, the *Summa* of St Thomas became the required textbook. A 'Roman school' of theologians formed, which thought Thomism important, and rated any other form of theological approach to the faith as subordinate to it. Less importance was attached to historical and patristic studies. The auxiliary sciences like philology and biblical archaeology were neglected in exegesis. The argument from authority was abused, and one can sense a certain disregard for the knowledge of modern culture and current problems, like evolution or Marxism. There was a degree of academic satisfaction in keeping to the scholastic method, however dry and formal it might be. The church was presented as a perfect society.

At the end of the nineteenth century and the beginning of the twentieth, with few exceptions, theological studies in the European seminaries had the characteristics of the Roman school. The Italian professors known as modernists, like Murri, Buonaiuti, Minocchi and even Vincenzo Ceresi, who was above suspicion, had commented on the closedness and immobility of seminary trainng and the one-sidedness of studies in which scientific research seemed impossible.[57] It was precisely that conservative thought which fed the so-called modernist tendencies.[58]

In the spiritual formation of the seminarians, following the mass occupied an important place, but the emphasis lay on hearing the mass, being present at the mass, rather than on an active participation. The mass was regarded as *the* source of grace. In practice, however, it did not stand much higher than other spiritual exercises, being one occasion among others for cultivating the spiritual life. Communion was seen as quite separate from the mass. On average the seminarians communicated only every two weeks; those who had received higher orders could communicate once a week. Moreover the frequency of receiving the eucharist was left to the confessors to dictate, and these saw communion more as a reward for a virtuous life than as an encouragement, strength and symbol of unity. The frequency of confession was also bound up with that of the eucharist. As far as possible it was necessary to have a regular confessor.

Meditation was another important practice which had to have a part in the daily programme of a good seminarian. Seminarians meditated for around half an hour in the morning. They dwelt on the eternal truths, the life of Christ, the duties of the spiritual state. In the evening there was an examination of consciences in which they were asked to feel disgust at the shortcomings of the past day and to resolve to improve themselves.

Particular devotions occupied a special place in the formation of the seminarians. Attention was paid above all to devotion to the eucharist:

visiting the Blessed Sacrament, veneration. There was also emphasis on Marian devotions: the rosary, the angelus, the short office of Our Lady, to which the breviary prayer was not yet linked. On Marian festivals there was an opportunity to offer a spiritual bouquet to Mary. There was also emphasis on devotions to some of the saints, like Aloysius, the patron of youth. Each room or cell of the seminary bore the name of a saint. As preparation for the liturgical festivals and in some seminaries every Friday, the way of the cross was practised. The main aim of all these different devotional practices was to encourage piety and the Christian virtues, and thus to prepare oneself for a worthy priestly life. Around the end of the century R.Murri wrote that in the formation of seminarians there was a threat that the inner vitality of the spirit would be neglected by keeping so obsessively to the performance of 'spiritual exercises'.[59]

Most European seminaries followed the trend of Catholic spirituality in Italy. Based on a degree of individualism and on personal devotion, piety began to rely heavily on the feelings. Our attention is drawn to this simply by reading the rules of a seminary. Thus it is required that seminarians must return after communication in loving gratitude, and that they must apply all their affectivity to this. Prayer to Our Lady must be warm and effervescent. In the month of May one must apply oneself to a living, warm and tender devotion to Mary. What was taught the seminarians was an affective piety, of the kind that was also to be encountered in French spirituality. In this spirituality the attention of seminarians was drawn to the dangers of particular friendships. In order to remain faithful to their celibacy, they had to be able to live out their affectivity in a love of supernatural realities. Though this piety now seems artificial, it nevertheless succeeded in forming a number of pastorally concerned figures (Don Bosco, Angelo Roncalli).

Among the forms of piety, mention should also be made of the annual retreat, a time of spiritual apartness, seen as a 'strong time' for inner life, a time of inwardness, silence and restraint, of devotion to God, of concern for personal sanctity and reflection on the magnitude of the priesthood.

During training much attention was paid to all matters of discipline. In southern Italy the seminarians were told that they must refrain from vanity in looking for novel forms of dress. To be in possession of a mirror was regarded as form of frivolity. Books which might have been brought from home had to be subjected to a thorough investigation and all works which might distract from devotion to God were confiscated.

In France the situation in the seminaries was not very different from that in Italy. Studies often also remained below standard in most French seminaries.[60] On the whole the professors themselves had not studied much, were not really specialized and were not in possession of a higher diploma. Often they lacked experience, though some of them were self-taught and were not necessarily inferior to those trained at university. Among the Sulpicians warnings were issued against an excessive zeal for study, because this might prove to be to the detriment of faith. Professors were required to be 'useful servants of the clergy, who have more need of the prayers, example and the guidance of those who are charged with forming them than of teaching, and for whom piety is far more necessary than profound and extended learning'.[61]

It was impressed on the priests who had received their training in these seminaries that once they were responsible for the pastoral care of a parish they had to remain as faithful as possible to the rhythm of their formative years. This resulted in the type of nineteenth-century parish priest described above.

Germany stands apart as far as priestly formation is concerned. Here there were three centres of academic formation and theological study. Associated with this were of course the dangers which are inherent in any investigation and any attempt at reinterpretation.

First and foremost came the school of Tübingen. Theological problems were tackled in depth in the journal the *Tübinger Theologische Quartalschrift*, which has already been mentioned. Here the significance and value of the historical method was also discovered. More attention began to be paid to the 'life' of dogma than to its metaphysics. The consequences of the fact of Christianity and of revelation in history were explored.[62]

Secondly there was the Munich Circle. Here, too, work was done on the renewal of theology and attempts were made to achieve closer contact with the laity, who seemed to be alienated from the church. They had to be got out of their feelings of inferiority. Döllinger wanted to convince them that they had the skill to oppose Protestant rationalism with equal weapons. He emphasized that they were academically free in all questions which did not directly affect dogma.[63]

In Mainz, the third centre, attention was chiefly paid not to the intellectuals but to average people: farm labourers, workers, the middle class, people of good will, pious, devoted to the church. This aim helps us to understand why much importance was attached to the formation of future priests. In contrast to Tübingen and Munich, in Mainz there was opposition to a system of training in which philosophical and theological studies could be done at state universities. The concern was to replace this system by the French pattern, which set the candidates for the priesthood apart and gave a more closed training.

Adaptation was certainly sought in Germany, after a rethinking of the theological problems and the relationship to rationalistic approaches. In fact it was the only country in Western Europe in which there was any creative thinking. That was also to influence the type of German parish priest.

5. The renewed quest for priestly identity

The movements for Catholic Action which were called into being after the pontificate of Pius XI and had been given impetus above all by Cardijn were initially propagated and supported by the clergy. The emphasis lay on action, influencing the masses, commitment to the spiritual encouragement of the various social classes. Towards the end of the inter-war period, most priests were active in one of the numerous works of the apostolate, which had been established in many forms. In order to protect the priests from an activity which would occupy them all too much, in 1937 Dom Chautard had written *L'âme de tout apostolat*, in which he emphasized that a deeply inward life was a prerequisite for a fruitful apostolate. The book was required reading in all seminaries and found its way into most priests' libraries.[64]

During these years, however, as time went on there was an increasing conviction that spiritual life and external priestly authority could not be separated. God could be found not only in prayer but just as much in all circumstances of life, provided that one was able to adopt the right attitude towards them. It is remarkable that traditional methods of apostolate were also put in question. It was asked whether the parishes and the way in which parish priests functioned could still be an adequate answer to the situation which had now developed, in which the masses were largely unchurched.

The worker priests experiment[65] which began in France and then spread to most other Western European countries was a search for a more appropriate way of bringing the priest to the people. They were no longer being reached by the traditional parochial structures. After the end of the Second World War a number of ex-prisoners of war entered a variety of seminaries. They were on the whole more mature and more developed personalities than the other seminarians and and also knew the world better as a result of their experiences in the prisoner-of-war camps. They inevitably found the training given to future priests inappropriate. A book by H.Godin and Y.Daniel entitled *La France, Pays de Mission?*, had appeared in 1943, and that too had given a negative picture of the religious situation in France. As a result, the conviction had grown that there was a need to look for new ways of getting alongside the people.[66]

Cardinal Suhard, Archbishop of Paris, was aware that the traditional relationship between priests and the faithful was no longer satisfactory. He made this quite clear in two well-known and influential pastoral letters – *Essor ou déclin de l'Eglise* (1947) and *Le Prêtre dans la Cité* (1949). Even more important is the fact that he approved two experiments aimed at bridging the gap between the church and the people of God:; the Mission de Paris, a community of priests who sought to ensure the presence of the priest among those who were no longer reached by the parochial structures, and the Mission de France. an interdiocesan seminary which was aimed at remedying the shortage of priests in certain parts of France. Most worker priests were to belong to the Mission de Paris. Their approach was not to follow the former patterns of priesthood slavishly, but to try to translate the message of the gospel into a form which could be understood by contemporary men and women.

Cardinal Suhard had indicated that adaptation to the world must not in any way mean being 'of the world' or 'making the norms of the world one's own'. In practice that did not prove so simple. Often the honourable dedication of those who offered themselves as worker priests was greater than their capacity for discernment. Their philosophical and theological training had not prepared them sufficiently for a vigorous controversy with the ideology of Marxism. Their solidarity with the workers led them to join with Communists in taking part in demonstrations for higher wages and strikes and to become members of Communist-orientated associations.

In Rome there was a fear that the worker priests were too involved in an ideal of human liberation, in so doing losing sight of their real priestly and pastoral mission. In 1953 Nuncio Marella summoned the French bishops and superiors to inform them that Rome wanted the experiment to be stopped. This measure provoked general uproar in France and in other countries in which the French experiment had been followed, all the more so since in the previous year a novel by Gilbert Cesbron, *Les saints vont en enfer*, had been published, in which the worker priests were depicted as saints. After difficult negotiations it was conceded that some priests could remain if they were prepared to accept certain conditions: they had to be of a certain age, be prepared to work only three hours a day, and to live in community with other priests.

Not all worker priests seemed ready to accept these conditions. The matter rumbled on. In 1959 the Holy Office told the bishops that Rome's decision was irrevocable. No priests might be sent as workers into the workers' world: this was incompatible with the sacral sphere of life in which they belonged. It was imperative for the integrity of the priesthood to be safeguarded. It is difficult to find this motivation satisfactory. In order to understand the motives for the abolition of the experiment we must understand it in the global context of the international situation and the long history of the Catholic Church.[67] It was the time of the Cold War. Two blocks stood over against each other. In the Communist Eastern block there was the silent church; in the West, Vatican Europe with the strict and unbending church of Pius XII, its authoritarian centralization, its Holy Office, its theological dogmatism, its unchangeable liturgy, its close-knit fabric of works, parishes, organizations, Christian trade unions and Christian democracies. But in this church there was already an apostolic quest for more openness, a missionary spirit which expressed itself in a variety of ways, a progressive wing which sensed that it was a minority. There was no real united front, but it was above all the worker priests who became the target *par excellence* for accusations. It has been said that Rome reacted against them through the establishment, the French government, the integralist Catholics. There is not much real evidence of this, only some suspicions. In any case, the hostile attitude of Action Catholique Ouvrière and the Christian trade unions is clear.

Of course it would be perverse to want to attribute the whole affair to the tension between left and right and between progressives and traditionalists. In fact the worker priests found themselves involved in an adventure for which they had not been prepared. Bishops, priests, theologians, the faithful, all reacted in their own way, on the basis of their own convictions, their own intuition, but during those years no one could have had any idea of the problems that had arisen.

In fact the church gained pastoral experience from the worker-priest experiment. For the worker priests themselves it was an unprecedented human, cultural, social and religious experience. The international political situation was its framework. Two factors complicated the situation. On the one hand there was the unbending attitude of the Holy

See and on the other the militant stubbornness of the worker priests. It was not a time of flexibility or negotiation: since the ban of the Holy Office on co-operating with Communists (1 July 1949), the systematic disbandling of the so-called Christian progressives had begun. People were far from what was later in Italy to be called *apertura a sinistra.*

But it was not the Holy See that required the abolition of the worker priests on its own initiative. The stimulus probably came above all from Action Catholique Ouvrière. In any case the Pope approved of the measure, despite the fact that three eminent cardinals travelled to Rome to argue for the experiment. The Pope could accept a degree of progressivism, but clearly only up to a certain point. In no way did he want to go further than the progressivism of Action Catholique Ouvrière. There was a line which he did not want to see crossed. However, at two points the worker-priest experiment had crossed this line. The first was connected with priestly training and the view of the priests which had been revered since Trent: the priest is taken out of the world and is appointed for spiritual matters, while the world itself is the sphere of the laity. Furthermore, movements had come into being among the laity which were inspired by the church and aimed at contributing to the re-Christianization of society.

Simply by virtue of their existence, the worker priests had revised the idea of the slow rebuilding of a Christian society by the laity. As E.Poulat puts it, there was not so much rivalry as a fundamental incompatibility between Action Catholique Ouvrière and the worker priests. By becoming workers, the priests were laicizing themselves. They were entering a sphere which was not meant for priests. They were leaving the spiritual sphere.

After Vatican II, Cardinal Veuillot, Archbishop of Paris, was to be given permission by Paul VI in 1965 to resume the experiment on his own responsibility. Worker priests are again to be found in various Western European countries, but they are no longer in the position of mediators. That they are less evident is also due to the fact that in the meantime, and outside them, many things have happened among the clergy, in the life-style of priests and in the idea which they form of their identity and responsibility. The Second Vatican Council paid further attention to the image of the priest. But that will be discussed in more detail elsewhere in this book.

From whatever perspective we view the recent period of church history, we cannot avoid the impression that over recent decades Western Europe has been facing a serious crisis over priestly identity.

However, it is good to remember that the crisis has not taken a precisely identical course in all countries, or even in all the regions of the same country. By way of example one can refer to Spain, where the proportion of priests to inhabitants has changed markedly over the last 200 years: in 1769 there was still one priest to every 141 inhabitants; in 1958 it was one priest to 1264 inhabitants.[68] We must also take into account both the internal shifts and differing historical conditions. In France during the nineteenth century the vast majority of priests came from rural areas; now that same countryside is largely de-Christianized and more vocations than before come from working-class families.[69] And all over Western Europe the number of big cities has increased, the suburbs have grown and brought their own problems, while the countryside has become increasingly depopulated. Pastoral care must take account of this, and therefore the image of the parish priest will also have to adapt to this diversification.[70]

IV

Ministry in the Church: Changing Identity

Peter Neuner

Hardly any problem in the church is being discussed as vigorously today as that of ministry in the church and the right way of exercising it. It is a quite inexhaustible topic. Should the structure of ministry be more monarchical or more democratic? What is the relationship between hierarchical and collegiate responsibility? Could women have access to the ministry? How does it relate to the numerous lay functions in the church? Above all, what will the church of the future look like if the number of ordained clergy declines dramatically? Sometimes it seems that this discussion suffers from too little attention to the basic question as compared to the many problems of detail: what really is the ordained ministry, what is its task and its significance? If there is thought about the dogmatic status of ministry, its task and its place in the church, in other words if the constants and with them the identity of ministry are clear, then it will be possible to look in a more relaxed way about the changes and variables in it.

1. The ministry and apostolate of the church

The great decisions on the question of ministry were made in the process by which the early church took form. After Easter and the sending of the Spirit the disciples strove to break through the restriction of mission to Israel and to bear Jesus' message of the kingdom of God to all the world. To the degree to which the insight became established that the return of the Lord was not imminent, that arrangements had to be made for a longer period, and that loyalty to the message of Jesus had to be maintained in an ongoing history, structures and ministries gained increasing significance.[1]

The decisive concept which served towards finding the right structures and shaping and differentiating ministries was that of the apostle.[2] The apostle was in continuity with the group of twelve which

Jesus had gathered around himself. The Gospels are to be understood as collections of reports by those who were with Jesus from the beginning as apostles and could bear witness to his resurrection. According to the Acts of the Apostles, to have been an eye-witness of the historical Jesus and a witness of the resurrection were the criteria in the election of Matthias (Acts 1.22). Acts reports that the earliest community after the resurrection 'devoted themselves to the apostles' teaching' (Acts 2.42). The apostle thus proved to be the guarantor of continuity from the historical Jesus to the risen Christ and the early church. The New Testament letters arose out of the authority which the apostles possessed in the communities as the first witnesses. And even the pseudepigraphy in the later strata of the New Testament is evidence that after the death of the apostles those who were now in authority as it were slipped into the person of the apostles and wrote to the communities what Paul and Peter in particular would have said to them in their changed situation.[3] The testimony of the apostles continued to be binding beyond their death and was brought up to date against a background of different questions.

The difficulty here is that the concept of apostle in the early church and dogmatics is not simply a New Testament term. In the New Testament the term apostle is used in very different ways, in respect of both number and content. When dogmatics speaks of the apostle, it of course refers back to the New Testament in doing so; otherwise this concept would not be a legitimate theological term.[4] Central characteristics handed down by the New Testament are maintained in it. On the other hand, a systematic overall view also means translation into a new and changed cultures and their problems. The use of the term apostle in dogma implies a development which has already taken place in the early church, in the course of which the apostolate assumed a form that proved suitable for preserving and handing down the Christian message. In the search for structures of continuity, an understanding of the apostle and apostolicity arose in the early church which served to preserve the biblical message and to translate it in a way which met the various new historical demands. The ministry took shape against a background of specific problems to which the church saw itself exposed; it was to help the church to cope with these appropriately. This understanding of the apostle became normative for any ministry in the church: it is the foundation of the identity of this ministry.

(a) The apostle as preacher

The apostles are witnesses to Jesus because they were with him from the beginning, because Jesus had called them to follow him, and they are witnesses to his resurrection. Through their testimony and their preaching they guarantee the continuity between Jesus and the church. But that does not make everyone who saw and heard the earthly Jesus an apostle: the apostolate includes a special mission. Therefore the one to whom the apostles bear witness is tangible in their own persons; through them Christ himself acts in judging and saving the world. In their message and their action they, and in them Christ himself, confront the world and the communities with authority. In the apostles it becomes clear that the preaching of the church rests on something outside us, that it is given in advance and not made. Therefore the apostolate cannot be derived from the community; it cannot be understood as delegation. The apostle stands both in the community and, as an apostle, at the same time over against it.

In their testimony the apostles penetrated new areas, thought-worlds, regions and religions and in so doing made their message universal. Thus their preaching is not just repetition but a creative process; it requires courage and sovereignty. The apostles appear in the authority of Jesus and in this authority also deal with problems which Jesus had not yet encountered. Exegesis has shown the degree to which the New Testament authors put their own statements into the mouth of Jesus and thus claimed to be giving binding instruction in his name.

(b) The apostles as founders of communities

Through the preaching of the apostles faith was disseminated, and fellowships of believers and thus communities came into being. The apostles gave detailed instructions for the ordering of community life, the course of worship, the shared service of the various charisms, the coming together of Jewish and Gentile Christians, marriage, collections and so on. They appointed disciples in the service of community leadership and strengthened the authority of those who bore responsibility in the communities. The apostles had authority in the communities which they founded and guided, which derived themselves from the authority of Christ. Apostolicity means leadership of the community.

(c) The apostles as a bond of unity between the communities

The apostles form a bond of unity between the communities; through their ministry the fellowship of these communities becomes a tangible reality. By witnessing to the Lord who appeared to them, by travelling to the communities, by sending messengers, by letters, by praying for one another, by the organization of collections for Jerusalem, this uniting bond of the apostles became concrete and could be experienced. The apostles are therefore not only individuals but a group, a college. The individual is an apostle by belonging to the community. The unity of the communities is represented by the fellowship of the college.

Here we must guard against an idealization of this unity, of the kind that is already emerging in the Acts of the Apostles.[5] The New Testament also reports tensions and controversies between the apostles. The obligation to unity did not mean that there were no controversies; their fellowship was a dynamic process and not a rigid preservation of identities. Thus the reciprocal obligation of the apostles is not to be confused with pseudo-harmony. The fellowship came into being as all understood that the very differences between them had been sent by the Lord and recognized one another's different charisms and tasks.

(d) The apostles as the abiding foundation of the church

In their preaching the apostles became the foundation of the church of all times and all places. The church understood itself to be apostolic even beyond the first generation. Here the office of apostle is unique; only the apostles could bear witness to the earthly Jesus and the risen Christ from what they had heard and seen. Their testimony is the foundation of the ongoing church: it remains fundamental and obligatory for the whole historical development of the church. The apostles as persons vanished with the first generation, but not the apostolic, because the apostolic ministry survived the persons and continued to keep their functions present. Loyalty to the confession of those who had seen and heard Jesus, an authoritative concern that the communities should have the right form and that there should be unity between them and down through history, are determined not only by the apostles of the first generation, but by all who take over their ministry. This fundamental task of the apostles is recognized by the Orthodox churches of the East, the Catholic Church and also the churches of the Reformation. With the apostolate understood in this way the church knows itself to be abidingly founded on Jesus, his preaching, his resurrection and his sending of the Spirit.

2. Ministry and succession

This systematic unfolding of the concept of apostle represented the decisive step in the development of the ministry. This was to become fruitful above all in the early Christian clashes over Gnosticism and the heretical systems which arose from its spirit. These Gnostic heresies referred to secret traditions which were alleged to have come from Jesus. They felt superior to the mainstream church and its members by virtue of these secret traditions. For anyone who had these secret traditions was supposed to be initiated into a higher form of knowledge; such a person need no longer believe like the church Christians, but had been taken up into a higher sphere of spiritual life and into an immediate communion with the Spirit. In the early Christian controversies with Gnosticism the question thus arose where the right tradition, the right spirit is alive, and how one could refute heresies which claimed to be filled with the Spirit and appealed to special traditions. In this controversy the mainstream church attached tradition to an objective criterion which could be tested by anyone, namely succession in the ministry. This argument was developed by Tertullian (died around 222)[6] and especially Irenaeus of Lyons (died around 202) in his work *Adversus haereses*.[7] In contrast to the heretics, who appealed to secret traditions which were not open to examination, Irenaeus emphasized that the right tradition was to be found where a succession in episcopal office going back to an apostle could be demonstrated. Irenaeus took over the lists of bishops from Hegesippus for this purpose. In his conception the right tradition is to be found wherever succession in episcopal office can be traced back in an unbroken chain to an apostolic foundation. For the apostles appointed disciples whose task it was to hand on the right doctrine, as is evidenced by the Pastoral Epistles in the New Testament. These in turn appointed successors who were to preserve the true faith, and so on. Now Irenaeus concludes that where there is an unbroken chain of successors in office reaching back to an apostle, there is a guarantee of the right apostolic tradition, for it is the essence of the episcopal office to preserve tradition faithfully and hand it on. In succession in office, succession in ministry, there is a tradition which can be controlled and thus a guarantee of apostolicity, in contrast to the secret doctrines, illuminations or alleged traditions of the Gnostics, which cannot be controlled.

The understanding of ministry was enriched by the idea of succession in the controversy with Gnosticism. This succession is not an end in itself, but serves to preserve the tradition and hand it on. The handing down of the true message does not take place automatically, but rather has a personal focus: it needs particular organs and persons as its vehicle. Tradition comes about through people who hand it down, and these are the successors of the apostles. Because what the apostles have seen and heard is fundamental for the church of all time, they need successors to hand on their testimony, which remains fundamental to the community of believers. For the testimony to origins is not only the beginning but the abiding norm for all later development of the church; it has a binding content and is not just a first stage which can be superseded.[8]

Here the church as a whole stands in the succession of the apostles, because it believes and bears witness to the teaching of the apostles. It is apostolic as a whole because it is founded on the teaching of the apostles, and to the degree that it remains so and hands down their testimony without a break, because it orientates its life and practice on what the apostles presented and lived out fundamentally for the church of all times.[9] For this apostolicity of the church as a whole to be guaranteed, among other things it also needs a succession in office. Within the framework of discipleship of the whole church generally there is also the special discipleship in the apostolic ministry. The church as a whole and its ministry in particular have a reciprocal relationship in their apostolicity. On the one hand it is illegitimate to limit the apostolic character of the church to succession in office, as though only those who succeeded one another in office were the vehicles of apostolicity, or even apostolicity were identical with succession to office. On the other hand, however, succession in office is a necessary sign that the church as a whole remains in apostolic discipleship and succession. 'The Catholic view is that continuity in the episcopal office is an essential sign of and means to the identity of the apostolic faith. It is an essential sign – i.e. only a *sign*, not the substance, and only *a* sign, not the unique sign and criterion; in other words it is not *ipso facto* a sure guarantee. It is an *essential* sign – and that also means an indispensable sign for the full form of the apostolic succession and the church.'[10] Joseph Ratzinger expressed this notion as follows: 'Succession is the form of the tradition, and tradition is the content of the succession.'[11] The tradition takes place in the form of succession to office, and tradition, the teaching of the apostles, is its content, its substance. Succession to office is at the service of tradition, the preservation of apostolic doctrine as this was preached and maintained fundamentally and once for all by the apostles for the church. The chain of succession to office is the form in which the tradition is handed on.

Already in the early church the problem arose that the chain of succession was not of itself sufficient to guarantee the true faith. For soon even those in office were opposed to one another, one denying that the other had the true faith, although in all cases their office could be derived from an apostolic foundation. So succession is not a guarantee for the future which works automatically. Additional criteria were needed for distinguishing right tradition from heresy. In the early church there were essentially three possible solutions here. In the formation of the canon the tradition was tied back to origins: the true church is to be found where the message of the New Testament has been maintained unfalsified, and only there. In this sense, for example, the apostolic message is also rightly recognized through scientific exegesis of scripture and the origin is preserved by the critical function of exegesis and the history of dogma. Thus the first criterion is accord with scripture. According to Irenaeus there are many churches which go back to apostolic foundations; it would be too much to demonstrate the continuity of all of them. Therefore it is enough to agree with the church of Rome because, according to Irenaeus' argument, this is particularly qualified since at its origin stand not just one apostle but two, Peter and Paul, and because their tombs are in Rome.[12] Here true tradition is associated with the church in Roman and accord with it. A third solution is the institution of synods and councils: the right tradition is where the bishops represent the faith of their particular communities and arrive at a common statement of faith. The individual bishop can err, but the college of bishops cannot. This last notion at first proved to be a power in history: the true church is alive in the council; there the tradition is unbroken. In the Western tradition this conviction became associated with the idea of Rome; the college is only the college of bishops when it acts and speaks in unity with the Bishop of Rome.[13] It is not the individual succession of bishops that guarantees orthodoxy, but the place of the bishop within the college of which the Bishop of Rome is a constituent part. These criteria were meant to guarantee that the church remained in the true message, that the *consensus ecclesiae*, the common faith, was taught and lived out in a way which was both diachronic, i.e.

lasting through history, and synchronic, i.e. taught and lived out in every phase of the church.

3. The tasks of the ministry

From this historical reflection on the foundation of the ministry in the apostolate which was developed in early Christianity it is possible now to bring together some tasks which the ministry has to fulfil and which accrue to it according to the faith of the early church.

(a) Service to apostolicity

The ministry serves the apostolicity of the church tradition, and it is there to guarantee this tradition and to keep it alive. It is at the service of fidelity to the message, which has been preached once and for all. The ministry has to preserve apostolic teaching, to see that it is not replaced and overlaid by an alien teaching which is opposed to it. Those who hold office in the church are first of all obliged to preserve the apostolic tradition.

Thus confrontation is also part of ministry.[14] Those in office are not just representatives of the community, but also speak and act in the name of Christ and are responsible before him. They can and if need be also must say to the community things which do not flatter it and which it does not want to hear.

(b) Salvation beyond human control

The apostles also hand down what they themselves have received, what has been given to them. The apostle is not the religious genius who needs no holy scripture, no dogma and no confessional statement because he is capable of producing this himself.[15] Those in office do not seek to make something of themselves, but faithfully to hand on what has been said to them. This is a consequence of the message of justification. Christian faith does not primarily consist in doing something, achieving something, inventing something, but in receiving a gift, accepting something gratefully. Salvation is not our work but is given to us; it comes to us from outside. This *extra nos* is also visible in the minister who acts in the name of Christ and the way in which the ministry is handed down in ordination.

(c) The service of transmission

The ministry has the task of guaranteeing the unity of the church through history. But faithfulness and identity in no way mean merely holding fast to immutable statements, for tradition is a living process. Thus the ministry itself took shape in the process of translating the biblical message into an ongoing history in the Graeco-Hellenistic world. Here what had already been said and what was already known was not simply handed down and repeated without a break. In the encounter with Hellenism, Christianity was challenged by new questions and problems with which the earliest community had not yet been confronted and to which Jesus himself had not yet given an answer. These questions were new and the answer was given to them in faithfulness to the tradition in a creative process.[16] The development of dogma followed the motto *fides quaerens intellectum*: in faith it was possible to formulate a correct answer to new questions in loyalty to tradition. Hellenization was the most far-reaching process of inculturation that the Christian message had undergone hitherto. The process of translation which was achieved here of course had a price, and did not go through without friction. But it would be wrong and one-sided to call for an inculturation of Christianity in non-European cultures and at the same time repudiate the Hellenization of Christianity as the fall of early Christianity. And it would be just as false and one-sided to regard Hellenization in the formation of dogma and the structures of the early church as normative and at the same time *a priori* to reject present concerns for inculturation in a world which does not think, or no longer thinks, in Hellenistic terms. The tradition which the ministry has to serve thus proves to be a dynamic process, not a mere repetition of something that is always the same.

(d) The authority of the ministry

Those in office are leaders of the community and as such have authority. It is their task to accept new members into the community, in other words to administer the sacraments of initiation. Certainly the early church recognized baptism by heretics, and declared baptism by lay people and even the unbaptized as valid. This was particularly important for times of schism and persecution. However, it does not seem sensible today to begin from this emergency situation and question the general connection between the ministry and the sacraments of initiation, baptism and confirmation. The fact that even baptism by those who do not hold office is valid does not mean that the basic link between ministerial leadership of the community and the administration of the sacraments should be abolished in normal cases as well.

The ministry has to guarantee the faithful transmission of preaching by appointing new ministers and initiating them into the task of proclaiming what has been handed down to them. Ministers have to ordain and appoint colleagues who ensure that the word of God does not fall silent and that the sacraments are administered.

(e) The foundation of unity

Just as the ministry is obligated to preserve the unity of the church through history, so it is obligated to preserve unity in a particular age. As leader of the community, the minister is at the service of unity in the local church; the unity of the local churches in the universal church is guaranteed and expressed through the fellowship of ministers. The church, the *una sancta catholica et apostolica Ecclesia* of the creed, comes about through the openness of the local churches to one another, through their taking responsibility for one another.[17] Here the ministers have an important function in that they bind the local churches which they represent in communion with the other local churches and their ministers. For this reason, according to the faith of the early church the celebration of the eucharist is under the leadership of the minister, since in the eucharist the synchronic and diachronic unity of the Christian church is designated and realized: the unity of all the communities which assemble at the eucharist in memory of the Lord, and also their unity with the saints who have lived at all items as models of faith. This unity in space and time is represented by the minister, who thus proves to be the genuine president at the celebration of the Lord's Supper.

(f) Ministry as service

Ministry is a relational concept. One can talk about ministry only in terms of the church; ministry exists within the context of the church and must be understood in the light of the church. At the Second Vatican Council this was expressed by designating the ministry as service. A service can be defined only in the light of that which it has to serve, for the sake of which it is there. That means that the ministry is defined in terms of the church, and not the church in terms of the ministry. The starting point and framework of the doctrine of the ministry is the church as mystery and as people of God. In the early church Augustine formulated these notions in classic words which were also quoted by the Council: 'When I am frightened by what I am to you, then I am consoled by what I am with you. To you I am the bishop, with you I am a Christian. The first is an office, the second a grace; the first a danger, the second salvation.'[18] However, it does not follow from the statement that the office is defined in terms of what it has to serve, that office could be understood as delegation by the community, as if the community were merely to transfer the authority accruing to it to an individual. It is part of the structure of the church that it also includes the confrontation expressed in the ministry.

The fact that office is defined here in terms of its task, especially as a ministry of word and sacrament, and not primarily in ontological terms, does not contradict what Vatican II says. The Constitution on the Church states that the special priesthood is distinct from the universal priesthood of all the baptized 'essentially and not only in degree'.[19] The next sentences make it clear how the tern 'essentially' must be understood. It means that those in office shape and lead the priestly people, that they perform the eucharistic sacrifice and offer it in the name of the whole people. These are utterly functional descriptions. Thus according to the Council the essence of the office consists in the tasks of preaching and the administration of the sacraments. The authority of the one in office is not a third element alongside this, but is precisely this ministry of word and sacrament.

According to what the Council says, this office does not differ from the universal priesthood of all baptized 'in degree'. The minister is not a Christian to a greater degree than any other believer. As far as being a Christian is concerned, there is no difference between the two. The specific character of being in office is the task of serving the people of God to whom the person concerned is appointed.

Like baptism and confirmation, ordination also bestows a sacramental, inalienable character. This means first of all that these sacraments cannot be repeated. They are given once and for all. The doctrine of the sacramental character came into being in the early church when baptized Christians who had lapsed from the faith in times of persecution converted again. Did their reception back into the church require baptism to be administered again? The decision of the early church was that it did not. Baptism holds once and for all; it puts an inalienable stamp on people and therefore needs no repetition. This conception of sacramental character was subsequently applied to other sacraments, which were similarly not repeated: confirmation and ordination to the priesthood. So this doctrine does not mean a superiority of the ordained minister to the laity or a transformation of essence which is to be understood ontologically; it indicates the fact that ordination to ministry is not repeated. Anyone who changes ministry and takes on a new ministry does not need to be ordained again. To this degree ordination differs from investiture, appointment to a specific pastoral ministry. Thus in principle ministry is to be understood as something for life, and not as a 'job'. The task which is handed on and received and the promise of grace stamp the person as a whole.[20]

4. The ministry and ministries

Against the background of these constants in church ministry the problem now arises of the legitimacy and limitations of changes in it. The basis for multiplicity and change[21] already exists in the fact that ministry is exercised in the form of individual concrete ministries or offices. According to the Second Vatican Council, from antiquity the offices have been those of bishop, priest and deacon.[22] The link made between these offfices offers a way of approaching the phenomenon of change.

(a) Historical concretions

The way in which church ministry became structured in early Christianity was as episcopal ministry. All the features which were depicted as constants and constituents of ministry pertained only to the bishops. In the early church the bishops are the ministers *par excellence*. For theologians who feel especially obligated to early undivided Christianity, the episcopal ministry is *the* ministry. Thus for example in the first half of the nineteenth century the Tübingen theologian Johann Adam Möhler wrote virtually a hymn of praise to the bishop. He described him as the visible union of the faithful in a place, the personal embodiment of the love of the faithful for one another. According to this notion the bishop is the manifestation and the living centre of the Christian striving for unity; he is the love of Christians for one another which has become conscious of itself, the means of maintaining this love and realizing it.[23]

What Möhler was formulating here was of course not simply a description of the status of bishops and the way in which they exercised office in his time. Rather, he wanted to engage in a theological reflection on what church ministry is, and only at a secondary level did this result in something like an ideal for bishops. Möhler's description of the original constitution of the church also implied a criticism of church order as he himself experienced it. For in contrast to this conception, in the nineteenth century the bishops were usually treated in a very miserly way by theology. In the course of the increasing concentration of all church responsibility and authority on the Pope alone, during the second millennium the theological status of bishops faded increasingly into the background. As a consequence of the overcoming of Gallicanism and conciliarism, the office of bishop itself was further evacuated and seemed to have been absorbed into the papal primacy. Thus Möhler's almost hymnic description of the office of bishop in the early church was not least also the criticism of a development in which this office seemed to have been increasingly sacrificed to the central power of the papacy. It is no coincidence that half a century after Möhler, the critics of the First Vatican Council gave the impression that with the universal authority of the Pope, which the Council called truly episcopal, in the Vatican church the office of bishop had ceased to exist and had been taken up into the papacy. For if the Pope has full episcopal authority in every diocese, then the bishop no longer possesses this authority. Thus, according to the criticism of the Old Catholics and the Orthodox, there were no longer any bishops in the Roman church, but only papal delegates, Vatican emissaries. By this definition of the primacy the church had abolished the episcopate as the early church understood it.[24] Thank God that this criticism of the council was not confirmed by the subsequent effect and interpretation of the Vatican definition. Taken by themselves the texts of the definition would have been open to such a maximalist interpretation.

In the course of the concentration of all church authority solely on the Pope, the episcopal office was also devalued theologically. In mediaeval sacramental theology the consecration of bishops no longer appears as a sacrament, but only a sacramental, which reduced the office of bishop to an administrative function that might possibly be endowed with secular power; it hardly continued to appear as a spiritual office appointed for the salvation of souls. According to the dominant interpretation, the bishops of the imperial church had a twofold authority: the authority bestowed by their consecration and the authority of their jurisdiction. As this interpretation ran, spiritual authority is bestowed by ordination to the priesthood (and not consecration as bishop), and jurisdiction by the transference of the authority of office which – depending on the standpoint – was seen as deriving from the Pope or the emperor. Both authorities could also diverge, and possibly even be bestowed on different persons. In that case, alongside the bishop as the instrument of jurisdiction there was the consecrated bishop who had to perform spiritual acts but had no jurisdiction.

In this conception, the consecration of bishops logically did not appear as a sacrament, but as the transference of administrative authority. Sacramental ordination and thus the office were regarded completely in terms of power to celebrate the eucharist, and this was bestowed in ordination to the priesthood. It transferred the one and undivided office to which only a few competences, especially those of confirmation and ordination, remained attached; they were first enabled by consecration to the episcopate. Consecration as bishop appeared as a non-sacramental institution to jurisdiction, as a legal act.

In this view, which was widespread. if not dominant, in the theology of the second millennium, and which was advanced up to the Second Vatican Council, church office was regarded in terms of the priest, whose was now *the* ministry. At the centre of ministry now stood authority to offer the sacrifice of the mass and forgive sins, and here bishops and priests did not differ. This is the essence and task of the ministry in the theology of the second millennium. Granted, the distinction between bishop, priest and deacon was attributed to divine institution, but the paradigm of the minister was now the priest and no longer, as in the early church, the bishop.

(b) The view of the Second Vatican Council

As is well known, the Second Vatican Council referred back to the early church and in so doing considerably revalued the office of bishop. Supplementing the statements of Vatican I, it is now said of the episcopal office that it is by divine right that bishops 'personally exercise . . . proper, ordinary and immediate power' and are therefore not 'to be regarded as vicars of the Roman Pontiff'.[25] But above all the Council teaches that 'the fullness of the sacrament of Orders is conferred by episcopal consecration'.[26] It is the source of both the jurisdictional and the sacramental authority of the bishop. He has his office not only in the sacramental sphere but also in the sphere of jurisdiction by virtue of ordination, which bestows a *sacra potestas*. Through episcopal consecration bishops stand in succession to the apostles. Episcopal authority as a whole has a sacramental origin and must therefore be exercised with spiritual means. To interpret it as a claim to social power would be to misinterpret or abuse it. In secular categories it has to be said that the bishops were the great 'gainers' at the council, and their office was markedly elevated by comparison with pre-conciliar teaching. The church's ministry is now generally understood and interpreted in terms of the office of bishop.

By contrast, the Council treated the priests in a very miserly way. Whereas previously they had been seen as *the* ministers of the church, now their office was derived from that of the bishop. 'While not having the supreme degree of the pontifical office, and notwithstanding the fact that they depend on the bishops in the exercise of their own proper power, the priests are for all that associated with them by reasons of their sacerdotal dignity.'[27] In the decree on the ministry and life of priests it is said that their ministry is that of 'co-workers of the episcopal order', that it participates in this authority. The apostolic ministry, which in the full sense is only exercised by the bishops, was 'handed over in a subordinate degree to priests'.[28]

Whereas before the Council it was difficult to make a theological evaluation of the special character of the bishop as opposed to the priest, since then the problem has been to provide a basis for the special status of the priest. There is no dispute that the consecration of bishops and ordination of priests is one and the same sacrament. The bishops exercise the apostolic ministry, and the priests have a part in it. Here the Council leaves it to theology to define this 'participation' more closely. This presents problems to dogmatics, since the idea that a sacrament can be given in different degrees is not a simple one. Sacramental teaching was always concerned to prescribe the elements that have to be guaranteed for a sacrament to be administered validly and permissibly. How can one assess a valid and licit administration in terms of content? The Council left the task of thinking this out to the theologians, and in so doing accepted a degree of vagueness, regarding this as acceptable. However, in other respects, too, the priestly ministry was clearly limited by the Council and developments after the Council. Traditionally, many priests had derived their ministry from the threefold ministry of Christ and the church, the priestly, royal and prophetic ministry. Now, to their astonishment, the Council attributed precisely this threefold ministry to the laity. The laity were in fact defined as 'the faithful who by Baptism are incorporated into Christ, are placed in the People of God, and in their own way share the priestly, prophetic and kingly office of Christ, and to the best of their ability carry on the mission of the whole Christian people in the Church and in the world'.[29] In the Decree on the Laity they are even called 'true apostles'[30] who 'are assigned to the apostolate by the Lord himself'.[31] This urgently raises the question: what is still left ecclesiologically for the priests between the bishops who have been promoted and the laity who have been promoted? And in any case they have to share this space, which has already become very narrow, with deacons, the distinctiveness of whose status has been rediscovered. It has often been noted that in the end the Council was a burden on priests. At least one of the reasons for the post-conciliar crisis in the ministry is the ecclesiological displacement of the priests in the texts of Vatican II.

Following the Council, a series of vocations arose in the church, comprising a number of tasks and ministries which had traditionally been exercised by priests and had been reserved for them. They are based on a passage in the Constitution on the Church, which states: 'Besides this apostolate which belongs to absolutely every Christian, the laity can be called in different ways to more immediate co-operation in the apostolate of the hierarchy, like those men and women who helped the apostle Paul in the Gospel, labouring much in the Lord (cf. Phil.4.3; Rom.16.3ff.). They have, moreover, the capacity of being appointed by the hierarchy to some ecclesiastical offices with a view to a spiritual end.'[32] So whereas there is a general authority to the church's apostolate which accrues to every Christian and is derived from baptism and confirmation, the Council also recognizes a special commissioning in the framework of the ministry which takes place through the hierarchy and on the basis of a delegation, which as a rule is conferred by ordination. Further reflection on the understanding of the ministry has been sparked off in the theological interpretation of this commission. What does it say about the ministry, that many of its functions have in the meantime been taken over by so-called 'lay people'?

(c) Ministerial functions in 'lay hands'?

These vocations which have recently come into being have loosened the traditional difference between priest and lay person in practice and for the church public. The Council itself rediscovered the deacon. He on the one hand belongs to the clergy, since he is ordained, but on the other as a rule he lives with a family and has a secular job. This is a decisive breakthrough in the practice of putting the clergy in the sphere of the church and the laity in the secular sphere. Alongside it, the profession of pastoral assistants, which soon became open to women, developed out of a specific emergency. Pastoral workers are not ordained, and thus are laity in the traditional sense; but on the other hand, in fact they are caught up willy-nilly in tasks which priests had performed before them. Thus the pastoral worker often appears as a substitute priest, as a quasi-curate who does all the things that the curate used to do, apart from celebrating the mass and administering the sacrament of penance. The tremendous decline in the number of priestly ordinations and thus above all of younger priests, and the equally rapid rise in the number of theological students, mark the key points in the development. In the introduction of pastoral assistants, the combination of ecclesial existence as a lay person and appointment to ministerial tasks traditionally performed by the clergy seems to have blurred the distinction between clergy and laity.

In this discussion, the official church has been very concerned to bring out the difference between the ordained ministry and the laity; the image of the priest is to be emphasized as clearly as possible. The 1977 statement by the German Conference of Bishops 'On the Ordering of Pastoral Ministries' was above all concerned with this question.[33] The text was dominated by the idea of drawing boundaries. The role of pastoral workers was here exclusively derived from the lay status bestowed on them by baptism and confirmation. As such they were competent to serve in the world, but their influence in the church was clearly to be suppressed. Their lay status was emphasized to the point of a statement that 'the pastoral vocation of the laity begins immediately with their service to the world' (no.4.2). There was a concern to avoid the impression that here was a 'ministry without ordination'. Therefore in future the particular work of pastoral workers was to be seen as support for the ministry of those holding office in the church; in no way might they be entrusted with 'all pastoral work in the community or tasks in the general sphere of fundamental ministries on their own responsibility, excepting only those functions for which ordination is necessary' (no.4.2). In order not to affect the image of the priest and probably also to reinforce celibacy, there was a concern to bind the laity as far as possible to service of the world, granting them every freedom there but reserving the office bestowed by ordination as far as possible for the church sphere.

The theological interpretations of these newly created lay offices presented in particular at the end of the 1970s differed widely.[34] Gisbert Greshake emphasized above all the profile of the priest. He defended celibacy and bound the pastoral workers to service in the world but could not conceal his deep scepticism about the coming development. In the end, the problem was an acute crisis over ministry within the church with a dramatic decline in ordinations and a rapid increase in resignations. It was clear that the traditional concept of pastoral care could not be maintained in the long run, with all the resultant consequences. Hermann Josef Pottmeyer, the fundamental theologian at Bochum, was concerned above all to give the pastoral assistants a profile as laity, not to disparage the position which they were then in practice already occupying in many dioceses, but in order not to raise hopes which in the long run would prove unreal. He was driven by the anxiety that controversies over the correct understanding of the ministry and the meaning of celibacy would be a burden to young people and could well lead them to bitter disappointments.

Karl Rahner reacted in a different way. Already before the Council, in discussions of the lay apostolate he had argued that where this was exercised as a main occupation it should be understood as an office and that those who exercised it should in some cases be understood as clergy. When the post of pastoral assistant came into being, he raised the question whether this function, which is a ministry of preaching, diakonia and (at any rate in part) also the sacraments and thus is a pastoral ministry, cannot or must not be recognized as sacramental. In the end it is bestowed by the church, which is understood as the fundamental sacrament; it is an important function in the church, and serves to convey salvation and build up communities. In 1977 Karl Rahner raised the question, 'Why should the bestowing of an office of a permanent nature not be regarded as sacramental or (at least if the church wants this) why cannot it be regarded as sacramental in principle?'[35]

Stimulated by these reflections of Rahner's, in 1977, in a lecture to the Catholic Academy in Bavaria, Peter Hünermann made the proposal that the post of pastoral assistant should be incorporated into orders as an office. The most important argument for this was that since antiquity church office had been bestowed in different stages, some of which go back to an appointment merely by the church. Traditionally there were the four lower orders, and then the sub-diaconate, diaconate, ordination to the priesthood and consecration as bishop. Of these various stages the last three – the diaconate, priestly ordination and the consecration of bishops – were derived from divine appointment and thus understood as sacraments. As a result of the Council of Trent, the *ordo* by divine institution was transferred to these three stages. The lower orders, too, were related to the *ordo*; they represented a preliminary form, though they had been introduced by the church and could not be attributed to divine institution. The Second Vatican Council abolished the lower forms including the sub-diaconate, or at least interpreted them in quite a different way. Of the three sacramental levels, Vatican II says only that these have been practised in this form in the church 'since antiquity'. The concrete shape of the church's ministry thus underwent a clear change; it took place in the course of history and went through stages which have been clearly derived from church institution. Evidently the church has the authority to give concrete order and function to ministry as an essential function in its life.

Against the background of these reflections on the history of dogma, Hünermann now raises the question whether one cannot suppose that the bishops have 'divided the *ordo* anew by the creation of the institution of pastoral assistants'?[36] The church has the obligation to make its ministry so concrete that it can fulfil its commission in a particular historical situation. It certainly does not have the right to dispose of its ministry, since this is a given, one of the constants. But as history shows, it certainly does have the authority and even the duty to shape the ministry in such a way that it becomes effective as ministry. In the concrete shaping of the ministry, from a dogmatic perspective the variables are obviously greater than is often assumed. History shows that the starting point for new reflections on ministry usually lay in church practice. First of all, in response to concrete demands, a structure came into being which theology then had to reflect on and if possible to legitimate. Hünermann asked: is not this precisely what is happening again in the introduction of the office of pastoral assistants? In an emergency and to guarantee functions which could no longer be performed by ministers in the traditional sense, the bishops have divided up the ministry anew. Theology now has the obligation to follow this process critically and to interpret what has been happening in it. Why should it not be possible to implement this interpretation in terms of an incorporation of the functions of pastoral assistants, men and women, into the ministry? Why should this office not have a part in the sacramental foundation of the *ordo* in a wider sense, and participate in it?

Since this discussion, which took place in 1977, silence has fallen on this topic. None of the suggestions made by Rahner and Hünermann were taken up, and the lay character of pastoral assistants was emphasized. Moreover new reflection on the laity, which came to a climax in the 1987 Synod of Bishops, was carried on under the slogan 'Against a clericalization of the laity and a laicization of the clergy'. Here it was in danger of defining laity and clergy in mutually exclusive terms, a position which Vatican II had already superseded in its reflections on the people of God as the reality which embraces both. So pastoral assistants were again kept to their lay status, and the main effort was to distance them as far as possible from anything pertaining to church office. Unless it was unavoidable, ministerial functions were to be carried out if possible by a team of laity, not by an individual 'minister', so that the public was not given the impression that something like a ministerial office without ordination had been bestowed on a resource person for the community.

By contrast, in striking tension with this theoretical position, meanwhile, in practice 'so-called' laity have taken over very important functions in the church, indeed within the framework of the structure of its ministry. Today functions which are among the tasks of the ordained ministry are performed by people who have not been ordained. Moreover as a rule the appropriate church mission and authority is transferred to them in the *missio canonica*. According to current canon law 'laity' and others can be entrusted with the following tasks: preaching except for the homily (c.766), leading the ministry of the word (with sermon), administrating baptism (c.230§3), assisting at marriage (c.1142), administering sacramentals (c.1168), and church funerals. In addition, c.517§2 quite generally raises the possibility that a priest may nominally 'supervise pastoral care', whereas 'a deacon or some other person who is not a priest or a community of persons' in fact exercises it.[37] In the official liturgical books which express the life and self-understanding of the church in a special way, it is provided that so-called 'lay people' shall direct the following liturgical celebrations: worship for catechumens, baptisms, Sunday services in parishes without a priest (if need be with the distribution of communion), ceremonies of betrothal (with the blessing of rings), marriages and funerals. 'Lay' people can be charged with distributing communion outside the mass, communion of the sick and the viaticum. They lead the liturgical hours, penitential services and separate liturgies of the word, and eucharistic devotions with the exposition of the sacrament. The liturgical books provide for a series of blessings of things and persons by the 'laity', like the imposition of ashes on Ash Wednesday, the procession of palms on Palm Sunday, the washing of feet on Maundy Thursday and the Veneration of the Cross on Good Friday.[38]

Meanwhile these possibilities are becoming practices not only in the mission areas for which they were originally intended but also among us, because already the emergency often allows no other choice. At the same time there is an increasing tendency to combine several communities in a federation and appoint one priest to them. Moreover many dioceses are beginning to appoint lay people as resource persons in the communities and to entrust them with ministerial tasks. The designations and the legal structure differ. In Limburg and Bamberg such people are called 'reference persons' and in Linz 'pastoral assistants'. The Pastoral Forum in Munich pleaded for the appointment of 'pastoral officials'. In Speyer 'pastoral team leaders' are appointed and then 'overall responsibility' in a parish is transferred to them, whereas the priest nominated in accordance with c 517§2 takes on an often very fictitious 'ultimate responsibility' which in any case does not connect with the tasks of the pastoral assistant. In general, in the meantime 517§2 has been applied on a broad front in order to be able to guarantee the functions of the church through people who have not been ordained.

It is obvious that this practice is not in harmony with the official position about the lay nature of pastoral assistants, both men and women. Such a difference will prove harmful in the long run. The understanding of the sacraments and the interpretation of the church must be fundamentally affected if the sacramental understanding of the ministry is separated widely from the concrete exercise of ministry, and if those who are sacramentally ordained no longer lead the communities but only perform ritual actions from outside, while the actual leadership of the community is transferred in terms of jurisdiction but no longer has sacramental roots. Here dogmatic obscurities are arising because a modification of the rule of celibacy, which would pose no problems to theology, at present seems to be ruled out for disciplinary and legal reasons. If this happens, the prevailing practice should not just be accepted with a more or less good or bad conscience, but there should also be consistent theological reflection, and those who de facto perform ministerial tasks in the church should also be allowed participation in this ministry which is to be deemed sacramental. 'The church formerly had offices which have now ceased to exist, and today it is developing new offices which will presumably shape and change its future picture in a decisive way.'[39] The fact that since antiquity the sacramental office has been handed down at several levels, that only bishops hold it completely, and that priests and deacons hold it to some degree, may doubtless pose a theological problem, but would also make it possible to incorporate the pastoral workers in this official structure of the church in a gradated way. It is manifest that they do not have this office in full, but that also applies to the priesthood and the diaconate. This difficulty would in any case not be peculiar to the ministry of pastoral workers; the church has been able to get on quite well with them so far – better than with so-called 'laity' who theoretically have to be denied most of what they are asked to do in practice.

V

Leadership in a Voluntary Movement

Jan Kerkhofs

Very gradually, but already by the end of the second century,[1] the increasing inculturation of Christianity into Western society led to leadership in the church taking over many, if not most, characteristics of the secular – and very sacral – social order. Above all, in due course it took over those of feudalism.[2] The Orthodox churches and the churches of the Reformation also developed in this way. Not only were there 'princes of the church' (we might think of the Papal States and the many prince bishoprics), but church dignitaries had a place of their own in the parliaments which came into being. The interweaving of church and political structure (later states) became tradition. In many places the parish priests were among the notables of town and village. For many, a church office meant elevation to a higher class of the social hierarchy. Higher learning was a prerogative of the clergy. Church law and civil law were interwoven. In certain countries the church owned a third of the land. In the meantime the separation of church and state has increased or been completed in most Western countries. Even where Christianity is still the official state religion, the ties with the state are becoming progressively looser (Great Britain, Scandinavia). 'Christendom' is dissolving into a pluralistic democratic society. The far-reaching consequences of this for the formation of church leadership are becoming clear. In the many countries in which 'confessing believers' as opposed to 'Christians' form a minority,[3] in sociological terms a faith community must increasingly be classed more as a voluntary movement. Voluntary movements have their own characteristics. One joins them or leaves them by virtue of one's own convictions. The leaders are chosen or replaced by different agreed systems. Terms of office are limited but usually renewable. Other than in senior citizens' associations, candidates are looked for who are between thirty and fifty-five years of age, certainly for posts with greater responsibility. Except in men's clubs and women's associations, in principle no distinction is made between men and women. Arbitration procedures are provided for in case of conflicts. In international networks, decentralization and subsidiarity are important characteristics by which it is possible to play an active part in local situations and changes. A clear and limited set of goals[4] is maintained which can be adapted though consultation and well-defined decision-forming. Now that churches are forming voluntary organizations, and even see themselves challenged to become a voluntary movement, if they are to play a dynamic role, it is important to examine leadership in the church from this perspective.[5] The church is in fact also (though not exclusively) a human institution. Those who exercise leadership in it are also (though not exclusively) volunteers; and although many are 'called' – certainly the priests – those who are 'called' are also volunteers. In ecclesiological terms there is of course no such thing as a subjective 'calling'. This chapter will limit itself primarily to a sociological perspective.

1. The membership

We are born in a particular country and with a particular nationality. All citizenship with its rights and duties is built on this. For all other forms of affiliation to a group there is free right of association, and Western Europeans have a free choice here. They can change from one party, profession, school system, professional association, to another. Anyone who belongs to a voluntary organization can leave it provided that certain obligations are met. One can join on condition that one fulfils a number of criteria. It is even possible to belong to a variety of voluntary organizations at the same time.

This mobility, on the basis of free choice, has also become established in connection with the churches. Up to the French Revolution and often long afterwards, it was in practice impossible. The increase in pluralism and a positive attitude of toleration left more scope for ideas here as a result of a wide-ranging weakening of social control and the disappearance of the restrictions imposed by civil law which had characterized the period of *cuius regio eius religio*. Catholics, Protestants and Orthodox change churches (for example because women are or are not admitted to the ministry or because of a specific item of faith or form of authority). Christians leave their churches, as is happening by the million, or remain 'Christians' out of tradition without being 'believers'. After conversion, non-believers join the voluntary movement of the 'faith community'. In the past there were heavy social and ecclesiastical sanctions against these various forms of movement. At one time a death penalty was imposed for such practices – persecution or at least social excommunication. Now to be able to change churches is part of the right to religious freedom. This freedom of choice has even penetrated to many Christian families: their homogeneity has been weakened, if it has not already been lost. Relatives and children can belong to different churches or to none at all. Moreover people can leave churches and then return later. This mobility is a characteristic of free associations and – as far as the church is concerned – of the quest of many people for their identity

Of course one becomes a member of a voluntary association for very different reasons: in the hope of material or intellectual advantage, for relaxation, because one is in search of social relationships, or for political motives. For the churches, the desire to belong to a faith community which is regarded as a meaningful group event is of course the decisive factor.[6]

In what has been said so far, one common characteristic is striking: membership is not automatic; at least intrinsically, it is not an inherited tradition, nor is it an absolute social obligation. One joins because one more or less explicitly wants to. So one is not at best a name on a sheet of paper, nor does one remain a member as a result of social control. Studies indicate that in certain communities there are votes for a 'Christian party' in a secret ballot by some who do not dare to practise, while in other communities members of the church secretly vote for an anti-clerical group. This whole rapidly developing progress has major consequences for church members and volunteers. From a definitive and static membership there is an evolution towards a silent exodus among some groups and increasing commitment on the part of others.[7] The institutional church is thus very gradually becoming a 'movement' among other movements. The church is not a system to which everyone belongs in principle, parallel to the state.[8] People opt for it out of conviction, out of a need for security and interpersonal support.[9]

2. Shared responsibility

Anyone who joins a voluntary movement will be affected by it. The chapter of the Benedictine order is a model here, perhaps the forerunner of democracy in communities and parliament.[10] The more educated people are, the more they want account to be taken of their views in spheres which involve them. This also explains why political democracy established itself best as a constitutional form in countries with a good educational system which was accessible to all. But also outside politics, too, a process of democratization has set in above all in the second half of the twentieth century: in business life, in education, in welfare, in concern for the environment – for both men and women.

At the same time, the shadow sides of democracy are also visible. The segmentation of the whole of life leads to government becoming a matter for specialists; capability and the concentration of power go hand in hand, so that the very complex democratic system can lead to oligarchical forms of government, alienated from the grass roots. In addition the welfare state has led to many people opting for 'bread and circuses' rather than the burden of responsibility during their increased leisure time, and passively leaving the function of government to others.[11] Populism is then a natural consequence, with a cult of personalities and stars, and with the uncontrollable influence of pressure groups operating behind the scenes and the corruption attaching to them. Most people still want a say when the interests of their own group are involved; then they want to gain advantages by more or less vigorous expressions of protest. Then a sense of the common good – at a local, national or European level – ebbs away. Experts therefore indicate the need for a caring society,[12] among other things by better training for responsibility from school and youth movements onwards, and by giving people real and viable responsibility down to the lowest level (which means the indirect exercise of power). Obviously this leads to decentralization and an adaptation of the subsidiarity principle, also guaranteed by law. The need for open government grows in parallel to this. Here voluntary organizations are forced from within to allow some leeway everywhere, precisely because volunteers are involved.

However, this process will not produce results as long as qualified people are disheartened or are insufficiently supported in taking real responsibility. In a constantly changing society there is still a great need for individuals who have not only balance but vision, for creative and prophetic figures who can play their part in groups, who help to pioneer ways of getting out of the inevitable impasses and who can control conflicts. In a society which is involved in an unprecedented degree of increasingly rapid change as a result of computerization, in which international trends influence local decisions with increasing rapidity and questions are constantly asked about the real meaning of 'customs', this form of leadership has become indispensable everywhere, and certainly in voluntary organizations. In addition, sensitivity to the need for co-existence between one's own precious views and the omnipresent multi-cultural society is more and more a requirement.

Without an intensification of the dialogue between all members of society and between all forms of leadership (e.g. administrative, cultural, socio-economic and prophetic), social dynamics get stuck.[13] This then results in frustrations, indifference, civic flag-waving and dangerous forms of intolerance and polarization.

All that has been said so far can be applied to complex social systems, like the churches – and of course to a multi-national and multi-cultural entity like the Catholic Church. This is all the more the case, since churches belong to the category of voluntary organizations in which everything depends on the interests, the creativity and the responsibility of members. But the central hierarch in a faith community is the Spirit of Jesus with its great difference in gifts.[14] The Second Vatican Council – perhaps for the first time in history – seems to have been clearly aware of this. Synodicalism was recognized at all levels, among other things by the provision of means of participation. However, anyone who follows the still brief development of the bodies created for this purpose has to note that they seem to be far less efficient than was originally hoped, above all at the higher level of national synods and Roman synods of bishops.[15] Not only theologians, but also bishops, recognize that they suffer from a spirit of restoration, with a return to a pre-conciliar mentality and the practices that go with it. The 'movement' which often continues, for example at a diocesan level or lower, as indicated by some French and German diocesan synods, is usually curbed at a higher level or at least suspected, if not treated with suspicion (cf. for example the reactions to *Ordinatio Sacerdotalis*). This has consequences: discouragement, a growing number of 'Christians without a church'[16] and, in wider circles, distrust of the church. The 'reception' of the Council has got stuck.[17] The fact that information can no longer be controlled by the authorities – the Index of forbidden books has disappeared almost silently – accelerates this process of loss of face in even qualified media. This whole development is increasingly leading to a shift of dynamic groups and their leaders to what one can call in sociological terms the 'periphery' of the official church: to base communities, alternative celebrations, critical movements and parallel religious publications. Many still dedicated laity, religious and priests are moving out in this direction. For a long time these groups have been gathering Christians who still have hope, but are disillusioned. For many people, however, above all in the rising generation, this is becoming a silent exodus: the distance between the possibilities inside and outside the church is becoming too great.[18] Even the great Catholic women's organizations are no longer growing, with all the consequences that will have for passing on the faith to the next generation. In the meantime many people involved in church government (bishops, priests, responsible lay workers, religious superiors) feel that they are between the devil and the deep blue sea and are facing severe conflicts of conscience over their ambiguous loyalty. Certain bishops then try with difficulty to row against the stream. Others give way, but informally support more pluralism and hope for a more open climate within the church. Yet others opt to achieve greater unity by systematically tightening things up and by excluding those who think differently among the faithful and even among fellow bishops, to do away with excessively turbulent polarization. This disorientates the less well-trained or well-informed faithful, and they seek salvation in more or less responsible special devotions. Most young people are uninterested bystanders or look for other ways of fulfilling their religious needs.

The synods and the surveys still indicate abundantly clearly that those who are most committed, the active volunteers, want to have more of a say and a further implementation not only of the letter but also of the spirit of the Second Vatican Council.[19]

3. Paid officers and volunteers

A voluntary group is primarily built on the conviction and high-mindedness of its members. But it cannot exist without structures. As soon as it becomes at all large, it needs a more or less extensive body of paid officials. Volunteer movements inevitably become voluntary organizations (with all the advantages and disadvantages). We see that not only with the Red Cross, Amnesty International, Greenpeace and Pax Christi, but also with the great women's movements and youth movements. Often the paid officials were originally ordinary volunteers who guaranteed the handing on of the 'spirit' of the movement. Larger organizations need real professionals who are sometimes attracted from outside. However, the efficiency of their skills in no way replaces the dynamic of the distinctive inspiration of the movement. Therefore paid officers always need to maintain the spirit of volunteers in their work. To the degree that they act as paid officials they become a danger to the volunteer movement. Then ideals are narrowed to become a means for something else, like earning a living or political power. As a result, the fixed framework becomes alienated from the real questions and wishes of the grass roots or begins to manipulate the members instead of motivating them. Furthermore, volunteers often put in almost as much work as part-time officers, just as part-time officers can devote a considerable amount of their spare time to the movement. The formal distinction between these categories then becomes blurred, giving rise to problems about hierarchy and payment. It is therefore necessary to give a precise account of the rights and duties of 'voluntary paid officers' and ordinary volunteers to ensure smooth working. The church began as a volunteer movement with hardly any structure and no full-time officers. Peter certainly continued to be a fisherman for some time, and Paul earned his living for a long period. It is nowhere said that those who are appointed elders must give up their work. That is also the way in which the great religious orders began. Their expansion made an order necessary, to the point of recognizing official leaders and an increasing degree of uniformity and centralization, with its positive and negative consequences and the need for periodical reform. However, the churches are not ordinary voluntary movements. Not only do they have a great variety of sometimes very varied aims, more after the fashion of a holding company (we might think of catechesis, liturgy, care of the sick, teaching, help in development, the organization of pilgrimages, building bridges between churches), but they also constantly touch on the key questions from which human beings seek meaning. For this last, central task they are 'under' a fundamental 'charter', Holy Scripture, and they recognize that they are guided by the Holy Spirit, active in a living tradition with a government to order it.

As an age-old volunteer movement, the churches are influenced historically to a marked degree by their setting in successive cultures. This setting has not only the advantage of enabling a concrete presence in a model of society which is socio-culturally determined but also the disadvantage of causing entanglement in a time-conditioned framework. The movement can be trapped in the organization. Thus many church structures and traditions also bear the burden of a past Byzantine, feudal, monarchical social order. All the churches got entangled with the existing model of the state and to a more or less important degree became part of it; as a result they acquired a semi-official political status (we might think of the many forms of link between church and state; the prince-bishoprics, sometimes more than a thousand years old; the Papal States; the councils and synods led or influenced by princes; the double and thus ambiguous function of the nuncios; concordats, church tax and so on). Thus often the 'volunteers' become a corps of civic officials. What should have been a 'vocation' became a 'profession'. The effect of this is still being felt, even in a secularized and democratic Europe. Many people are finding this time-lag a burden.

In the meantime the crisis over the ministry has led to a revaluation of the voluntary status of both priests and laity.[20] Because of it, people are rapidly becoming aware that the churches are supported by paid and unpaid volunteers. Of course this leads to questions about the competences of the two groups and the boundaries between them, above all as the competences are constantly shifting and church law here is inevitably lagging behind. At the same time, in addition to the old structures of parish, deanery and diocese, a complex of new structures has grown up beyond these territorial divisions: catechesis, instruction, welfare work and numerous movements have their own frameworks and officials which are developing into parallel hierarchies. The shortage of priests means that the presence of the official traditional professionals – the ordained priests – here has markedly diminished or disappeared completely. Thus new church sectors are coming into being with relative autonomy, comparable to some degree with the exemption of the old religious orders. In these new sectors, the church as a movement is often stronger than in the old structures of the church as an institution or organization. But in this institution, too, the place of volunteers has grown considerably. The age-difference between the older priests and the younger laity, who are often better trained, adds the challenge of tension between generations. Church government is thus being confronted with a new and complex situation. The recruitment basis of volunteers has changed in many places, above all over the last fifty years. Formerly, many more unmarried women were ready to offer their services, not least in order to fill their leisure-time meaningfully (moreover in the nineteenth century many worked in the numerous small diocesan congregations). A large number of them, including married women volunteers, belonged to the middle class. As a result of the levelling out of the social classes on the one hand and the rapid rise in the employment of women between eighteen and fifty on the other, the potential here has declined seriously. It is now above all those over fifty who have the necessary time. In the meantime thousands of small village communities have closed, thus reducing the supplementary pastoral contribution of the sisters. As a result there is more and more dependence on lay volunteers drawn from among the middle-aged.

The increase in scale in regional pastoral work, above all in the rural areas, where the amalgamation of parishes with a shortage of priests is taking place most rapidly, puts greater demands on volunteers, who now sometimes have to travel considerable distances for their tasks, for example attending meetings, whereas formerly people lived close to the village church. Moreover surveys indicate that many volunteers prefer to commit themselves to a well-defined task and for a limited period (not least because of the mobility of modern families). It also happens that communities get stuck by taking the easiest way out, for example keeping older people too long in a particular office, or above all by relying too much on them, thus giving the impression that the church is an old people's club. Similarly, surveys also indicate that certain volunteers are over-worked and that a large number feel insufficiently trained to take on pastoral tasks, above all where these involve preaching and leadership. These individual examples are enough to deflate the illusion that a church can be formed almost exclusively of volunteers.

Such a group of volunteers requires a firm framework of paid officers. In their case a number of factors come into play which need to be taken into account: meeting family commitments, the fact that part-timers are not regarded in the same way as full-timers, spending more money on pastoral work. The paid officers need to be preserved from clericalization: they need support and training for teamwork, and at the same time they must not be demotivated by not having any say. Local politics poses a special problem. Many faith communities polarize around views about society, church and belief. Where a priest can sometimes still stand authoritatively as a guardian of unity, this is very much trickier for a salaried lay officer, above all where personal party-political preferences can introduce tension. Where different parishes are amalgamated under one priest or a team of priests, a responsible local lay person is usually indispensable as a point of reference. Volunteers who have a good deal of time are not always the most suitable people for this task, in which social qualities have a priority. Quite often no suitable parishioner can be found to be a reference person (although older teachers are often skilled at this). If recourse is had to a pastoral worker, a pastoral assistant or a deacon, the problem of payment becomes inescapable. This brief summary of factors shows the degree to which the transition from a church of predominantly professional celibate priests to a church of laity, volunteers and professionals, puts considerable demands on the staffing policy above all of large dioceses.[21] In a number of countries the function of deacons is therefore being revalued: the dean is becoming more of a regional head of personnel and an animator than a pastor tied to one parish. The dean is also close enough to volunteers and paid lay workers to make possible warm interpersonal relationships, which are becoming increasingly important.

Investigations in all countries are showing that many priests are not prepared to work in teams with laity, whether professionals or volunteers, above all if these are women.[22] They are too clerical, or have not assimilated the emancipation of women. In that case the training of clergy, sometimes including the bishops, is a prerequisite of a good future development which does not frustrate the most creative volunteers. Volunteers need to have enough room for experimentation to develop their own initiative and to contribute to the inculturation of the gospel in a modern milieu.

The rapid decrease in the number of clergy and their ageing inevitably raises the question of what volunteers, given the right training, can be selected to become part-time or full-time professionals. One cannot completely rely on lay theologians with an academic training, not only for financial reasons, but also because they may not be suited to pastoral work. There is a need to be able to make timely plans in a very rapidly changing situation. It therefore seems desirable to make solid prognoses at more than a diocesan level – as is already happening in many places – and also to make the faithful aware of the situation and the constraints which it imposes. In too many places eyes are still closed to the realities, despite the warnings of many synods.

In the meantime, in addition to the classical structures, 'self-help groups'[23] have also come into being all over the church, not only to meet material needs but also in order to enable growth towards a contemporary form of training in faith and experience (base communities, Bible circles, prayer groups). *De facto* personal parishes are being established on top of the territorial parishes. Here volunteers do almost everything. Existing structures should not *a priori* think that there is dangerous competition here, or attempt a strategy of recuperation. The possibility of free circulation to other such groups will become necessary, and will need episcopal control in order to avoid disastrous alienation or sectarian deviations. So in some places the general supervision is entrusted to a bishop, as for example in Spain.[24] Of course it is probable that some of these church self-help groups will want one or more of their members to be recognized by the authorities as a fully-qualified president, even in the sacraments and the liturgy. We can also note that in more and more movements the priests (chaplains, spiritual advisers) are being replaced by laity, men or women. In the long run the question of sacramental competence is also being raised.

The growing number of volunteers in the churches will have an impact on the traditional paid officers, the priests. Above all younger ones see themselves less as a 'separate' class or a social cadre and more as volunteers – although they may be paid and professional – which moreover they are and remain by virtue of their calling. At the same time a particular tradition of 'tolerance', of a climate of solidarity and the involvement of all pastoral workers, not just the priests, seems to be developing. There is ongoing reflection and evaluation. By preserving a distinct, renewed identity, the priest will gain significance as a fellow-believer in a church of brothers and sisters. Perhaps this is the main positive feature of the present phase of transition with its unavoidable atmosphere of crisis.

4. Adult leadership

The time when a child could become emperor lies far behind us. Moreover princes now have only a symbolic function. Secular leadership in politics, economics and culture at present requires a very long period of initiation. Outside small family businesses hardly anyone now has final responsibility before he or she is thirty years old, and for medium-sized enterprises, leaders are usually chosen from people between the ages of thirty-five and fifty.[25] In selection, scientifically established psychological criteria are increasingly taken into account; here 'natural' qualities of leadership are of course important, certainly in connection with posts like those of managing director or president of a governing body. Age does not automatically bring promotion to higher responsibility. In some big organizations no one holds a top post beyond the age of fifty-five; then one becomes an advisor. The ultimate norm remains being capable of exercising a degree of leadership.

In a complex organization – which can also include smaller groups – leadership is increasingly, though not exclusively, exercised by a team. No one is in fact sufficiently skilled to provide a balanced and purposeful solution to complicated problems without a great deal of discussion and the contribution of a variety of specialisms. This team leadership certainly calls for the acceptance of one or another form of *primus inter pares*.

All this of course applies to most voluntary organizations and movements, above all where these have a varied range of people among their members and have to combine different purposes, as for example do cultural associations. The governing councils above all have a pivotal function here.

What has been said above can easily be applied to churches. We no longer have bishops or cardinals who are still children, as in the Middle Ages. The minor seminaries or juvenates which children or minors entered are things of the past, at least in north-west Europe. This does not mean that immature young men have stopped applying to seminaries and religious institutions; indeed often – because of the limited number of candidates – such people are accepted too readily. But even here changes are increasingly taking place. Those who enter seminaries from a secularized world in which the institutional church is looked on with suspicion or indifference, above all by the youngest age-groups, are usually older than candidates used to be before and shortly after the Second World War.[26] Furthermore, in Central Europe persecution put high demands on the candidates. However, the dramatic development is that perhaps greater adulthood is not a major factor in explaining the reduction in the number of candidates: clearer demands in matters of belief, a better insight into the consequences of committing oneself to a lifelong celibate life, the limited possibilities of having a say in the church, a somewhat precarious material position in an aggressively consumerist society, the challenge of an irrevocable and definite decision, no longer compensated for by a higher position on the social ladder, are so many barriers in the process of selection.

One important aspect must not be forgotten in this context. Whereas earlier many very gifted young people applied to become priests (in a number of countries, many belonged to the first quartile of those who succeeded in secondary education), the level has irrevocably declined. The pressure of public opinion, the loss of the social prestige which in most milieus was associated with the ministry, the enormous spread of higher education and so on, are so many factors which explain the shift in quality. In the meantime society has become much more complicated, and often makes much higher demands at an intellectual, ethical and psychological level on those who by virtue of their profession have to deal with questions of meaning. Soundings indicate that many more creative people may opt to become lay theologians rather than priests. Of course in the long run this has consequences for the quality of the higher echelons of the church, where leaders have to be selected from within a narrowing group. It also means that more recourse has to be had to lay people as professors in theological faculties – a phenomenon which used to be unknown.

Whereas in the course of history the all-important thing was to find good 'administrators' who in addition to the religious and above all liturgical care of a static society could also serve to form a kind of ethical policy-making body (one might think of the Emperor-sexton Joseph II), and were honoured for this by the state, now the prophetic and creative aspect is becoming ever more important. A voluntary movement constantly requires initiative, a flexible way of dealing with language and symbols, an understanding of problem areas which have not arisen before, and the marked differentiation and individualization of its members. Repeating the customary is no longer enough today. At the same time, however, for many believers the institutional church remains a safe house from which certainty and trust in tradition is expected rather than movement and renewal. As a result, leadership very much comes under the pressure of the tension between past and future. Some leaders are so gifted that they can sustain this all through their lives. Most need constant training, a sabbatical period for reorientation, and the support of inspired younger members of a team. A considerable number seem to be burnt out around the age of fifty. This last category is growing and increasingly requiring a structured and humane approach, not least for the well-being of the implicit faith community. This whole problem is too complex to be dealt with in the space of a short section.[27] However, a systematic approach is needed if the tension which is arising in many places between older priests – those inspired by Vatican II – and younger ones who sometimes dream of a stricter clerical identity is not to increase and have emancipated lay believers among its victims.

5. The demolition of sexism

With relatively few exceptions, leadership in Europe always used to be men's business. This continued to be the case at a political, university, industrial and cultural level until after the Second World War. Waging war was also men's business, often blessed by male princes of the church. Few women had access to higher education, and only individuals were given any public responsibility. Around the end of the twentieth century this situation has completely changed. In most Western universities there are as many female as male students. Teaching and administration are predominantly in the hands of women, as too are most institutions for social welfare. Women ministers can be found everywhere. The number of important female employers is constantly increasing. What once were exclusively male clubs are opening their doors. Legislation rejects any discrimination on grounds of sex.

In the meantime women, including Catholic women, have organized themselves into very important organizations. In Flanders alone, the three major Christian women's organizations comprise more than half a million members. Charitable work, whether Christian or not, to a large degree depends on women volunteers. The same is true of all catechetical work.

However, for many people the church seems to be the last bastion of male supremacy, although the facts in part tell against this image. There are three times more female religious than male religious. Female superiors are usually in charge of far more women and responsible for more institutions than are male religious. Women form the great majority of practising Catholics and the 'faithful'. In some countries women head the highest national organizations for laity and are members of the bishop's council.

Of course they clearly have no place at the level of priesthood and jurisdiction. They are even being excluded from the two new 'ministries' which *Ministeria Quaedam* (1972) envisaged. Not a single woman was allowed a say in the Roman synods on catechesis (1977), the family (1980), the laity (1987) or the religious life (1994). This anomaly is repeatedly pointed out by spokesmen in national and Roman synods. The reaction in broad circles to the papal brief *Ordinatio Sacerdotalis* (June 1994) shows how sensitive the issue has become. However, the polarization, first in the Swedish Lutheran church and then in the Church of England, shows how difficult it is to take account of a minority even in a democratically structured church. And here we are still talking about national churches in the West. However, acting as if women in the church are no problem also seems quite impossible. The heart of the matter here lies more in the jurisdictional sphere (the right to have a say and participate in decisions) than in the sacramental sphere (ordination). Of course women can also have a say in ordination, for example by stimulating serious theological study of ordination. In the meantime, reflection on the place of women in the church has long been started in base communities.

6. Terms of office

In feudal society, in which civic authority was also legitimated with 'divine origin' and was often confirmed by a semi-sacramental 'anointing', the leaders – on the basis of honorific titles or after election by an oligarchy – were usually nominated for life. In reality their period of office could be limited by a high mortality because of sickness or through assassinations.

In the twentieth century, universal suffrage gradually came to be established, and this resulted in limited terms of office. Norms of convenience and the need for control have led to new formulae for nomination and removal from office. Presidents, university rectors and chairs of almost all governing bodies are in principle elected for a limited period. Procedures for deposition are provided for in cases of misconduct during terms of office. Anyone who is thought accepable can be re-nominated or given another senior post. The main reason for these restrictions is that they offer protection against the abuse of power and against rigidity. In addition there is a concern to avoid a particular generation monopolizing decision-making power for too long because of increased expectation of life.

The most important volunteer movements have incorporated these limitations of terms of office into their statutes, usually in order to guarantee the dynamic aspect of the 'movement'.

A symbolic, relatively important, but timid adaptation of this shift of perspective took place for the Catholic Church during and just after the Second Vatican Council. Cardinal Suenens was able to persuade Paul VI that bishops should offer their resignations at the age of seventy-five (he had first envisaged seventy, and a draft text even mentions sixty-five, but he rightly expected great resistance to this[28]). Once cardinals have reached the age of eighty they may no longer take part in a conclave for the election of a Pope. In principle the prefects of the Roman congregations need to have their function renewed every five years. In a number of dioceses it is proposed that parish priests should accept the possibility of retirement at the age of seventy, despite the shortage of priests. In many abbeys the term of office of the abbot is limited (to twelve years or less). In most religious institutions, superiors are replaced every six years by nomination or election. Clear terms of office are laid down for the presidency of pastoral councils. At the time of the council and in various Roman episcopal synods, a number of bishops asked for a time limit to their office (up to e.g. twelve years).

It will probably continue to be impossible in so complex a system as that of the Catholic Church, in which very different secular traditions of exercising office have to be taken into account, to lay down general regulations for age restrictions apart from those mentioned. However, the question cannot be completely evaded either. The problem touches on a delicate question in the theological tradition, namely the permanent character of the priesthood now that, certainly in the Western world, the time of static social systems is over. This applies all the more to the churches, given that many of the most committed are aware that the church is very much a voluntary movement.

Loyalty to one's own conscience, responsibility to others, but also the objective demands of the task, the experience of being 'burnt out', the excessive stress, a permanent crisis of faith, of ethical behaviour or the emotions, come into conflict with the obligation to accept a task for the whole of life and to fulfil it obediently. Many younger people who feel that they have indeed been called to a church ministry and are suited to it, recognize that in addition to compulsory celibacy, the lifelong duration of an ordained ministry deters them. In some churches, like the Anglican and Orthodox churches, older married persons on the verge of retirement are still called to accept an ordained ministry part-time for the ten or fifteen years of active life that they still see before them. However, there is above all a great shortage of younger pastors, and pastors for young people. In certain pastoral councils it is being asked whether pastors of around thirty could be called for a possibly limited time, and even be given ordination, including priesthood.. The more seriously the contribution of the faith community and suitability are taken, the more difficult it will be to avoid this kind of question, though the church has little or no experience of it.

Of course objections will be raised from the perspective of an authentic or supposed tradition: a priest for eternity, eternal character, the indissolubility of marriage as a parallel to the sacramental and celibate priesthood, and so on. But how deep does the saving significance of these features go, and which of them is part of the unchangeable tradition? From the previous chapter it will be clear that theologically there are fewer limits than is usually thought.

7. Financial difficulties

For most voluntary movements the financing of paid officers is a constant concern. Appeals are made for contributions from members, from foundations, sometimes also subsidies which are provided by the state for particular initiatives, above all cultural ones.

The history of the financing of what can disrespectfully be called 'church personnel' has still to be written. For centuries this financing was closely bound up with feudalism. Later the states provided systems for this which were usually complicated; quite often they made church ministers too dependent on the political government. In some countries this resulted in systems of church tax, levied in conjunction with the authorities. The advantages and disadvantages of this are now being discussed.[29] The difficulty of reorganizing church finance after the relative separation of church and state in Spain and Italy and after the liberation of Central Europe illustrates the complexity of the problem both for what Yves Congar has called the 'poor and serving church' after Vatican II and for secular states. In a number of countries like the Netherlands and France (and the USA), financing is based above all on contributions from the faithful.[30] These vary markedly depending on national traditions (they are low in France and high in the Netherlands). For all citizens, the state at most guarantees a minimum income and a minimum pension.

The decline in the number of the faithful and practising Catholics and the progressive secularization of states automatically results in a reduction in the traditional means of finance, though not everywhere. Fewer priests in theory means lower expenses. However, a church which wants to evangelize and go against the stream must be able to invest in new forms of commitment. It was quite clear from the first chapter that entrusting tasks to lay officers was hampered by the limited financial means. No such pastoral work is possible without a fixed framework of professionals. It therefore seems urgently necessary to pay more attention to this aspect and to look towards the future. This is all the more necessary where in a number of countries the religious institutes were often very generous patrons of initiatives towards renewal. The ageing within them, which also means ongoing care of the old, may soon exhaust this source of finance.

It is possible that as the faithful come to have more of a say and, although these will be less numerous, form nuclei of more committed Christians, they will want to contribute substantially more. If this is to happen, there will be a need for clear information not only about needs but also about the application of resources, at every level.

8. The challenging dialectic of movement and organization

As it grows larger, every movement inevitably also becomes an organization. In this way it defends itself against the chaos of space and undermining through time. Organizations, above all as soon as they become international and multi-cultural, inevitably develop towards uniformity and centralization unless strong counter-forces are built into their structures (as for example in federal state structures).

In keeping with the aim of its founder, the church needs to remain a movement of 'followers of the Way' (Acts 9.2), for which unity needs to be a constant concern. Dynamism and cohesion are both features of the Christian project. Both are seen as fruits of the Spirit. In its many forms, the ministry has the task of realizing both.

History teaches that this ideal has remained almost impossible to reach. In the *World Christian Encyclopedia*,[31] D.Barrett describes around 21,000 autonomous Christian confessions. In his book *Provisional Churches*,[32] C.Duquoc offers a theological reflection on this: all churches point to the kingdom of God, but no one church can completely identify itself with the kingdom. One of the main reasons for this difference remains the multiplicity of cultures in which the message of the gospel has taken form and which have put their own emphases on it.[33] Taught by a dramatic past that is still a burden on evangelization, the ecumenical movement therefore seeks to reconcile two tasks: growth towards more unity, with more respect for diversity. Encouraging this tension is a condition for inculturation in the non-Western world. If an organization is not exported, the movement will not put down real roots. However, the challenge is no less great for Europe, the homeland of the three great Christian traditions, Roman Catholic, Orthodox and Reformation, all three characterized by a particular cultural seed-bed. All three are called to take part in an exodus from the tradition of 'Christendom' and be present as movements in a secularized society. All three are prevented from becoming relevant movements to a greater or lesser degree by their organization and traditions. In all three it is above all the ministers who often experience painfully how the wine of the gospel bursts old skins.

In fact, despite the renewal of countless parishes, many of those in office and many faithful can see how the organization is holding the movement in a strait-jacket. A number then seek a way out in one of the numerous new movements.[34] Some of these are markedly charismatic, and others are explicitly on the way to something new, beyond Vatican

II, or are returning to a pre-conciliar style. Some display ingredients of all three. It is striking that many of them have organized their own forms of training for their leaders, including priests, alongside the dioceses or on their periphery – to some extent on the model of the older religious orders. In addition, every country has a large number of very different Christian base communities, often linked flexibly by networks. Many of them have come into being out of dissatisfaction over the lack of movement in the church. They, too, have their own style of leadership, which is more informal, with or without priests. Some of these movements or base groups are explicitly ecumenical; by contrast, others reject any serious dialogue with Christians of other churches.

For any church, certainly for the Roman Catholic Church, the question of the relationship between the existing structures and these new forms of faith movement is a difficult task. Defining the place of the ordained priesthood here sometimes becomes very difficult. In some movements there is a call for priests of the pre-conciliar type, in others for a radically new model and in yet others for every kind of intermediate form. The combination of adequate unity and adequate diversity has immediate consequences within and between the churches. It puts enormous demands – also sociologically – not only on church leaders but just as much on the faithful, who see that the old structures are tottering but have no vision of a new alternative which can grow harmoniously. A number take the advice of Gamaliel, when he says, 'If this plan or this undertaking is of men, it will fail; but if it is of God, you will not be able to overthrow them' (Acts 5.38–39). As a result, all come up against the limtiations on room for experiment, or confusion and evolution towards wild growth and sectarianism. It is a pity that the European Synod of 1991 did not go deeper[35] into this dialectic of movement and organization.[36] It still affects both the whole ecumenical question and the attempt within the European Catholic Church to find new forms of group and models of government.

The question of a new form for all offices and ministries doubtless needs to be made more precise in this context. How is movement to be given priority over organization? What form of organization can support this movement flexibly? What leadership is needed for it? A 'revival' of pastoral councils and synods (diocesan, national and European) is certainly a necessary way. But real prophecy from individual laity, religious, priests and bishops is equally a prerequisite. At all events, those in office need to see that the church remains a movement, that the organization serves this movement and that in all its sections the church puts itself under the constantly new call of the Spirit of Jesus in furthering the kingdom of God, and that it constantly attracts volunteers for contemporary faith communities.

VI

Where Now? Possible Scenarios

Jan Kerkhofs and Paul-Michael Zulehner

The previous chapters have described with inevitable brevity the urgency and complexity of finding answers for a Europe which is poor in priests, and also the perspectives which exegesis, history, sociology and theology can open up. It is also becoming clear that the period of two *societates perfectae*, church and state, standing alongside each other, is over and that the faith communities are taking the form of voluntary associations in the midst of others in a pluralistic and multi-religious society.

Of course the situation in other continents is moving in a similar direction (USA, Canada, Australia) or is already many years further advanced (Latin America and large parts of Asia and Africa). As the existing model of priest and parish has been exported from the Latin Western European church, the finding of solutions in Europe can also be an inspiration elsewhere.

This chapter seeks to offer scenarios. None of them is *a priori* convincing. All have advantages and disadvantages. New formulae will cause crises, according to some more serious than continuing in the present crisis. The view of pastoral theology as to what a faith community now needs to be may well be the decisive factor. Whatever course is followed, the old adage *'sacramenta propter homines'*, the sacraments are there for people, needs to be followed, and not vice versa.

1. The redistribution of available priests

From the beginning of the church, with Paul's apostolic journeys, the sending out of priests to areas where there are none or too few has been an expression of the universal and shared responsibility of the churches for one another. In this way Christianity spread to Asia, North Africa and northern Europe (the sending of the Benedictines to England by

Pope Gregory and the mission to north-west Europe by the Irish monks) and, at the time of the discoveries and colonialism, to the other continents. After Vatican II, from 1967 on Fidei Donum priests were sent above all to Africa and Latin America, usually for limited periods. The Pro Mundi Vita foundation (1960–1991) was initially intended for sending European priests to Brazil. But the shortage of priests increased in Europe as well. So in 1960 Coadjutor-Archbishop F.Jachym of Vienna and Mgr J.Deleport established a European seminary for priests in Maastricht,[1] with the aim, among other things, of getting priests for Germany, Austria, France and Scandinavia from the Netherlands and Scandinavia. The drop in vocations led to the closing of this seminary.

In 1991 the Roman Congregation for Catholic Education in Seminaries and Institutes of Studies published a document on possible redistribution of the priestly potential.[2] Because the Holy See excludes the ordination of *viri probati*, the document proposes as possible solutions: the promotion of Fidei Donum priests (in Latin America there are around 2,500, around 1,000 of whom come from Spain), an urgent appeal to the Western religious congregations to work in parishes, and the promotion of the permanent diaconate and non-ordained ministers (e.g. catechists). The document urges the long-term encouragement of vocations of celibate men (through new seminaries and seminaries for diocesan priest missionaries). In fact its appeal is addressed above all to Europe and North America, where 38.8% of Catholics and 73.1% of clergy are.[3] Given the facts in the previous chapters, such a strategy seems to have little chance of success – with perhaps, for the moment, Poland as to some degree an exception.[4] Some Western European bishops, for example, draw on Polish priests, as does Cardinal A.Simonis (of Utrecht) in the Netherlands, but this policy is opposed by Bishop H.Ernst of Breda, who doubts the possibility of the pastoral 'inculturation' of these foreign priests. In Walloon Brabant (Belgium), recourse is had to African priests studying at the Catholic University of Louvain.[5] Of course a structural problem cannot be solved with such stop-gaps. Moreover these priests who have been provisionally imported are not prepared to devote themselves to a completely different cultural milieu, in contrast to members of the great missionary institutions in the past.

2. More intensive promotion of the shared responsibility of the laity

The African churches, like those of Indonesia, are to a large degree supported by thousands of catechists, who look after countless 'mission posts' in the absence of priests. In Latin America, sisters are responsible for hundreds of parishes, and there too a large number of base communities are led by 'celebrants of the word' or other responsible persons.[6] What until recently was very much the exception in Europe now seems quite customary here. We saw how more and more lay people have been recruited. This recruitment puts new demands on priests and laity.

Priests are more involved than they ever used to be in the training of these lay people. Sometimes they have had to change over, for example as seminary professors, from the training of future priests, male and celibate, to the training and support of men and women, sometimes married, with or without children. This has made new methods necessary, and even a revision of the content of courses, without any tradition to go by. As a result of these major changes in their task, on the basis of their experience, a number of teachers have even begun to ask questions about the theology of the ministry, about the possibility of different forms of training and sometimes also about the recruitment of women. Priests engaged in pastoral work in the parishes have also increasingly found themselves in a new situation. Instead of being in fact in sole charge as they were – above all when Latin was the liturgical language – now they are becoming members of pastoral teams with usually younger lay people who have brought with them a tradition of involvement and democratic government. Moreover the rapid evolution of higher education after the Second World War meant that many lay people had also become much more mature in knowledge of the substance of Christianity, in both theology and spirituality. Furthermore, quite a few older priests felt threatened in their identity (tasks more and more being put in the hands of lay workers), though others rejoiced at the development. This beyond doubt contributed to a degree of polarization within the priesthood itself, as is evidenced not only by the splitting off of the followers of Archbishop Lefèbvre, but also by the rise of groups of priests who do not go that far, but give a minimal interpretation to the conciliar texts about the laity. In addition, above all women who are engaged in pastoral work sometimes have difficulty in gaining recognition as full colleagues from this kind of priest. Presumably the collaboration of priests and laity is going better in most places (there are no representative studies for Europe, but dozens of smaller investigations point in this direction), among other reasons because in many countries future priests (or deacons) are given theological and pastoral training alongside lay people.

Of course a whole series of new problems are arising here. To mention just some of them: where laity who are employed full-time work permanently with priests, the question arises why they cannot be members of the council of priests. Quite a number of lay people with university training are more intelligent and dynamic than their priestly colleagues and yet – with very rare exceptions – they are given little encouragement to take part in the government of the church. The tension becomes even greater when lay people are *de facto* leaders in a parish, whereas by canon law the ultimate responsibility is put in the hands of a priest.[7] Of course this has been the case in Latin America for centuries, and since the last century also in the missionized parts of Africa, but in Europe people have not got used to the fact that those who actually lead the parish are not the ones who are finally responsible. Thus pastoral work itself leads very rapidly to the question whether it is not time to move away from the theological tradition that the president of the faith community also should be president at the eucharist.

Conversely, the priest who is responsible for several parishes runs the risk of turning into a mere administrator of the sacraments. In the old Western world, where people want church funerals more than church weddings and even more than baptisms,[8] the priest is becoming closely identified with being present at the departure from this life of people who have little belief, if any at all.[9] No wonder that elderly priests then get depressed. Priests are also seeing how the task of preaching – the sacrament of the Word – is increasingly becoming the domain of the laity. As the practice of going to confession has declined very markedly in large parts of Europe and has virtually disappeared among the younger generations, even of practising Catholics, the result is that apart from taking funerals, the task of the priest is focussed on baptism, the eucharist and marriages. In the meantime in many faith communities the question is increasingly being asked why responsible lay people may not baptize and take marriages; they often know the families better than the priests, and as younger people are closer to the way they think. The result could be that the role of the priest became limited to the celebration of the eucharist and the co-ordination of pastoral work in the parishes for which he had ultimate responsibility.

Of course many of these questions could also be answered within the present system, at least as long as a substantial group of priests remains available. According to canon law, in certain circumstances it is possible for lay people to be given permission to baptize children, and to take marriages and funerals without the eucharist.[10] In many so-called Third World countries such a practice is quite usual. By the distribution of tasks within a regional team of priests, priests can specialize in working with particular groups (young people, the sick) or in particular tasks (catechesis, training in the liturgy). Younger and part-time deacons can arrange the co-ordination of pastoral work and supervise the recruitment and appointment of the laity. If this pastoral option becomes established, in training and teaching far more skills in social communication will be needed than before. This could stimulate a smoother collaboration between priests and laity (including women) and help to put an end to the clericalism of the clergy and the 'lay clericalism' of some committed laity. In this way laity and priests can experience one another more as members of the same people of God with the earliest Christian ideal of brotherhood and sisterhood.[11] At the same time pastoral work can come to life more: the priest is less the one who is separated, a kind of monk in the world, and the laity bring their experience to the point of preparing a contemporary liturgy and a living homily. This development also opens up perspectives for contributions by theologically trained women about the Bible.[12]

However, this ideal, too, has its limitations. First of all, it presupposes a minimal presence of younger and qualified priests. In more and more places this is not the case. Secondly, full-time laity need to receive an adequate salary, higher than priests receive in many countries, since they have families to support, even if they can live in an empty clergy house (as is already the case here and there).

Of course the real problem lies deeper. As soon as it becomes the rule that a lay person or a team of lay people leads the local community in everyday life, three questions arise. First the definition of their competence in terms of local responsibility as compared with that of the priest-moderator who is ultimately responsible (canon 517§2). In a number of places the faithful see the person with local responsibility as the real community leader and do not understand that he is not an ordinary 'pastor' ordained for the task. Moreover lay pastoral workers in hospitals who are asked to anoint the sick or celebrate a eucharist have the same experience. Secondly, there is the theological anomaly, already mentioned above, of the president of the community who cannot preside

at the eucharist. Should the present-day situation continue for generations, then many communities will follow a 'Protestant' model: the
equilibrium between the sacrament of the word and the sacrament of
the eucharist will be broken and there will be a one-sided emphasis on
the word. Attempts to salvage the identity of the priest can sacrifice the
sacramental identity of the faith community in a subtle way. Finally there
remains the problem of the durability of the function of the lay
community leader. How long will laity be ready to burden themselves
with leading a community and will this be accepted by family and
community? A celibate priest can move elsewhere, but that is far less
easy for a lay person. In principle the latter will thus be appointed for a
particular place and a limited period – perhaps to be extended.

The problems discussed above have been well summed up on the
basis of French experience in a striking article by B.Sesboüé.[13] He
makes nine points, which can be listed briefly as follows: 1. the parish
communities get used to leadership by a non-ordained minister; 2. the
faithful feel not only the absence of eucharist and confession but also
that of the priest when there is a death; 3. the ministry of the word is
detached from the sacramental ministry; 4. there is a break between
preparation for the sacraments and the administration of them; 5. tasks
which are normally those of ordained ministers are entrusted to people
who are not ordained; 6. para-sacramental actions come into being, for
example in connection with anointing the sick and confession; 7. it is
difficult to avoid the clericalization of lay leaders, because socially and
psychologically they belong to the 'clergy'; 8. the best laity are too much
in demand for pastoral work and are less available for commitment
outside; 9. the laity who are most often appointed are women, with the
result that the pressure to ordain them is increasing. Sesboüé finds all
these tensions healthy; in this way life can compel the institution
gradually to make new, more responsible, pastoral decisions. He sees
only two possibilities: either substantially to reduce the administration
of the sacraments and stop entrusting all kinds of pastoral tasks to the
laity, or to endorse these new ministers and leaders by an ordination.

Thus the frequent recruitment of lay people seems to create as many
problems as it solves within the existing church order.[14] And yet in
Europe and elsewhere this recruitment is a matter of life and death.[15]

There are a number of studies about whether parishioners are ready
or not to accept as responsible persons those in a parish who can replace
the priest-pastor (legally always under the direction of a priest from
outside the parish). Thus a study from Austria[16] shows that in 1980

52% and in 1990 58% claimed to be in agreement with the following statement: 'Many people are now saying, "As far as I'm concerned anyone who has the necessary skills and commitment is acceptable."' The following graph indicates who would not be accepted.

Graph 1. Those who are Rejected as Replacements for the Pastor

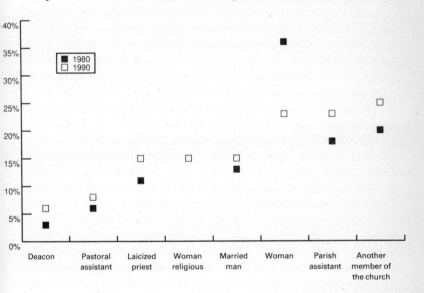

3. An increase in the number of deacons

It was certainly not the aim of the Council to introduce the permanent diaconate in order to make up for the shortage or priests, although some council fathers saw a possible interim stage here on the way to the ordination of *viri probati* (well-tried married men) to the priesthood. As the German bishops recognize, only a priest can replace a priest.[17]

However, under the pressure of the shortage of priests, in more and more places deacons are being burdened with the actual leadership of the parish – after all, they are 'ordained'. Even the document issued by the Congregation for Seminaries mentioned above seems to see a way here, at least for the Third World churches.

However, figures indicate that the number of deacons is increasing much more slowly than that of lay people with pastoral training, among other things because the figure of the deacon is too vague.[18] He can do little more than a lay person can (viz., read the gospel and preach at the eucharist – thus if there is already a priest present). Most deacons are neither recruited for their gifts in leadership nor in most cases trained to preach the word. If they are full-time, they are confronted with the same financial problems as lay workers. Young deacons who are widowers may not remarry. Moreover women are still completely excluded. From a theological perspective deacons have a distinctive task in the church and this lies in the area of *diakonia*, charitable work, not primarily in the liturgy. It is bad theology to hold out the prospect of the diaconate to men who, because of the obligation to celibacy, cannot offer themselves for the priesthood and thus receive a surrogate priesthood. Furthermore, deacons with a full-time job often have little time to take on all the non-specific priestly tasks of a pastor. It may also happen that in a world in which mobility is a requirement in so many professions, or where their families require it, they have to move house at times which are highly inconvenient for pastoral work. In fact the diaconate as a solution to the shortage of priests is leading into an impasse.

4. The regrouping of parishes

In many parts of Europe the country parishes have been so depopulated by emigration that they can no longer form viable faith communities, above all when in addition an exodus from the church has reduced churchgoing to tiny percentages of the population. Different approaches have been tried to ensure a responsible pastoral presence, from the fusing of many mini-parishes into one parish with a centrally situated church building to the maintaining of existing parish nuclei, federated around one parish with a priest or team of priests. This happens in many French, German, Spanish and Belgian parishes. Thus for example Charny in France (with 1,600 inhabitants), which is the capital of a canton in the Yonne, is the centre of a parish of 14 communities (with a total population of 5,000). In the majority of French dioceses, as in numerous places in Catalonia, the ADAP formula ('Assemblées Dominicales en l'Absence de Prêtres', or 'Assemblées Dominicales en l'Attente du Prêtre') i.e. Sunday celebrations in the absence (or while awaiting the appointment) of a priest, or ADAL ('Assemblées Dominicales Animées par des Laïcs'), Sunday celebrations held by lay people, have been introduced for a number of smaller parishes.[19] According to the studies of M.Brulin, by far the majority of parishes in which alternating Sunday celebrations in the absence of a priest take place are very small.[20] Except where the faith community is really too small, most dioceses, as an emergency solution, choose the solution of decentralization along with the usual abolition of the smallest places of worship. Experience teaches that in this last instance attendance declines even further; the population and their leaders get the impression that the church, too, is leaving these impoverished country communities in the lurch and is neglecting the older people who find it difficult to move. Furthermore the laity then feel less motivated to commit themselves.

The strategy of regrouping parishes is being systematically implemented in many places.[21] Here are some illustrations. The decrees of the diocesan synod of Dijon in 1992 divided the diocese into five pastoral zones totalling 18 deaneries in all. These deaneries comprise 65 parochial groupings. Each parochial grouping brings together several villages, communities or parts of a town. The terminology has not yet settled down. The preference is to leave all the structures flexible so as to prevent these structures from causing paralysis if the dynamic forces in the diocese diminish further. Central contacts are appointed in the villages who see that needs and initiatives get through to the diocese. The diocese of Sens-Auxerre reorganized its parishes in 1984: their number declined from 510 to 110. The diocese of Limoges has just 32 parishes. The diocese of Digne in the Basses-Alpes provides a model which has almost become classic. In 1959 it had 84,335 inhabitants distributed over 6 'archiprêtrés', 34 deaneries and 323 parishes. Of the 34 deaneries, 4 were without resident deans, 10 without dependent parishes and 10 others with only one dependent parish. Of the 323 parishes, there were 65 with and 258 without a resident pastor. This completely worn-out structure was abolished and more than 100 parishes were done away with. In 1964 the diocese of Reims had 720 parishes and 391 priests, and in 1994 – for 600,000 inhabitants – 87 parishes and 608 places of worship were involved in the regrouping. In 1972 the archdiocese of Munich-Freising (at the time comprising 2.1 million Catholics with 943 active priests, two-thirds of them in pastoral care) decided to regroup the parishes into 184 parish federations.[22]

Of course the ADAP require a good selection of local reference persons, responsible for a small pastoral team. Most dioceses have made their own rules here. Thus Bishop J.P.Jaeger of Nancy and Toul describes the statutes of his diocese as follows.[23] Referring to *Christi Fideles Laici* (the Roman Synod of Bishops, 1990) and to canon 145 of the Code of Canon Law, the *nota* defines the status of the 'pastoral animators'. They can be given responsibilities as diocesan representatives in a movement, or in pastoral work in schools and hospitals, always in collaboration with a priest. They can look after a parish without a resident priest (c.517§2) for a limited period, under the supervision of a priest moderator. Above all, the *nota* says, they can become pastoral animators for a task relating to a whole deanery. In that case they will work in a deanery team of priests. The animator is officially appointed to this team in a mission letter by the bishop and this appointment can be marked by a liturgical celebration. The pastoral animator can either be a volunteer or salaried. A table lays down the salaries of part-time or full-time animators, the contribution of the diocese being reduced in proportion to the population of a deanery, which also contributes pro rata on this basis. Before an animator is appointed, there is a wide consultation about actual needs and financial means through the pastoral system of the deanery. Then a candidate is proposed: this is the responsibility of the deans and an episcopal vicar. This candidature is judged to be at diocesan level, and if the candidate accepts the conditions laid down, he or she is called and sent by the bishop. Then may follow a contract of employment with the diocese. The person who is called needs already to be involved in pastoral work in a faith community and to be taking part in its sacramental life. The appointment also presupposes that the animator wants to develop his or her spiritual life, and is willing to bear witness to the faith and also to support others in doing this. An appointment can possibly imply some restraint over certain public functions in order to avoid confusion. Of course all this presupposes both appropriate preparation and continued training, and the capacity to work within a system and to accept support and evaluation. The tasks entrusted to the animator can be taken on in dialogue with all those involved. Each deanery has a fund which pays the expenses of the pastoral animator.

The option for a kind of confederation of parishes does not prevent there also being some caution about taking the all-too-easy step towards the ADAP solution. Thus Archbishop R.Bouchex[24] of Avignon prefers the reorganization of eucharistic celebrations to encouraging ADAP. The latter remains a solution for an emergency, like a sudden illness or the unexpected absence of the pastor and the impossibility of finding another priest. The archbishop says that the parishioners must not be content with an ADAP or begin to think that communion without a full eucharist is an ordinary pattern. They must remain aware that the absence of a priest is a sign of poverty. There may be communion at an ADAP, but the bond with the pastor must always be indicated. The ADAP must not give the impression of being an ordinary celebration of the eucharist, and sometimes it is necessary to point out the shortage of priests and the need for vocations. Furthermore the ADAP presupposes a faith community which is sufficiently alive and has a number of lay volunteers. ADAP are not suitable for small parishes: here there is a danger that the preparation and animation will always fall to the same person, and this leads to weariness and discouragement. For all these reasons it is better – if possible – to reorganize the celebrations of the eucharist: one mass on a Saturday afternoon and no more than two masses on Sunday morning. Then no mass will be celebrated every Sunday in all parishes, entrusted to one pastor. Certainly there is always a mass in the central parish church. Where no mass is possible, as many of the parishioners as possible are to be invited to go to the same church in a neighbouring parish where mass is being celebrated; care needs to be taken that old people are given a lift there. Thus every parish community remains more or less homogeneous. The pastoral councils see that no parish goes a whole year without a local celebration of the eucharist. Two festivals need special attention: Easter Week, when it is best to hold one celebration in the central parish for everyone, and Christmas, when there should be as many celebrations as possible in all parishes of a certain size, if need be with the help of another priest. Finally, the archbishop points out that each parish needs to be a nucleus of spiritual life. Therefore the parish church must see that it is open at regular times for prayer meetings in which children, too, can take part and learn to pray, and special attention needs to be paid to the sick and the elderly.

Of course this whole development calls for new reflection on the significance and the shape of parishes. For example, at the 1988 diocesan synod of the diocese of Le Mans, with reference to canons 374 and 515 it was decided to regroup the country parishes which did not seem viable and use the term 'parish' from then on of a group of parishes. The village churches remain the normal places for weddings and funerals on condition that they are maintained and that the celebrations are prepared by the residents of the villages. A diocesan commission was entrusted with the regrouping. The same synodical resolution also indicated the possibility of establishing a kind of personal parish for people who form a faith community on a non-territorial basis. Here the pastoral councils of the deaneries have to sort the wheat from the chaff.[25]

The French conference of bishops discussed these problems in 1990.[26] The record contains above all statements, questions and suggestions. Some speak of 'the end of a parochial civilization'. All emphasize the great difference between situations (some country areas become tourist centres at weekends or during vacations). The main criteria remain the viability, including the missionary élan, of a faith community and a foreseeable durability. Nothing is possible unless it is promoted by local and regional pastoral teams. Nor is the challenge limited to the country. Bishop F.Frétellière of Créteil points this out after a description of his diocese. It is one of the smallest in France (245 square kilometres), but comprises 1.3 million inhabitants in 79 parishes (8 of between 1,700 and 5,000 inhabitants; 17 of between 5,000 and 10,000 inhabitants; 33 of between 10,000 and 20,000 inhabitants; 11 of between 20,000 and 25,000 inhabitants; 10 with more than 25,000 inhabitants, the largest of which has 35,000). He has 150 priests below the age of seventy-five (a third of whom are religious priests or secular priests employed elsewhere), with an average age of sixty. There are 10 seminarians. The term 'restructuring' is never used. In fifteen places all parishes are entrusted to one priestly team under the leadership of one pastor. The priests celebrate the eucharist in turn in the different parish churches – something which many parishioners find difficult and which also does not help the formation of local pastoral teams.

A number or priests have problems over being involved in a team ministry, and some suffer from their appointment *in solidum* because that prevents them from being pastors themselves. Therefore there is a move towards a more personalized strategy: one priest is assigned to each parish church, though he is not the pastor. Even where new churches are built for demographic reasons, clergy work in a team without a particular priest being appointed 'pastor'. As far as possible an attempt is made to maintain the existing places of worship. It is recognized that sometimes small parishes are regrouped too quickly; the less active faithful become disorientated; moreover, as a result of immigration large numbers of new residents may arrive unexpectedly. Therefore there is a search for sensitive solutions, in the forefront of which is collaboration between priests and with laity. At all events it continues to be very important that places of worship are still recognizable (with the ringing of bells!) and that small, accessible places for prayer remain open. At the same time rooms for meetings are to be provided, in which religious or a married couple, both pastoral animators, can be found. One problem which has still to be solved is the way in which the important decisions can be taken in a team. Should they be taken only by the pastor moderator, or with the other priests, and with the laity and the sisters?

In the final synthesis Bishop J.Rozier of Poitiers points out that the parish remains an entity of great symbolic significance – also for those in authority in the community – by reason of its social and cultural functions. But its present-day form remains unclear. Must every Catholic belong to a parish? How far can the 'modern nomad' belong to different faith communities? And what is to be done locally with the many foreigners in a multi-lingual Europe?[27] The bishop argues that in no way must the sacramental dimension (baptism, confirmation, eucharist) and the place of the priest and the bishop be lost. Every parish must continue to be a mission. At the same time it is important to remain open to further development, and here both the top and the base of the dioceses need to interact. 'It is the diocese which makes the parishes and not vice versa.' In general it can be noted that the traditional parishes are developing in the direction of larger 'pastoral units' (in some dioceses from 700 parishes to 70 'pastoral units'), but the local communities remain, with the adaptation of church buildings, clergy houses – the latter are quite often lived in by lay animators – and parish centres, and structures for catechesis, liturgy, care of the sick and so on. Priests are increasingly been given responsibility *in solidum*. The anxiety about 'priestly identity' is real, but continues to raise questions, as does the identity of the deacon. The term 'pastoral' broadens out into 'ecclesial'. There is a quest for a firmer terminology (and theology) for the many kinds of lay animators. Training must be more a matter of guidance on the spot with room for creativity. In his statement Bishop Rozier makes two important remarks. One is about the time factor: 'Time, with many lags and tensions, will without doubt lead to a better balance and more or less permanent procedures and compromises. But it may also bring out the shortcomings of our present constructions. One sign of their quality will be whether they attract young men to the possibility of a priestly ministry or put them off' (159). Another comment is about the need for clear rules. It is important to be clear about responsibility and the resolution of tensions and conflicts; thus, for example, the direction of a parish cannot depend on the 'style' of a new pastor who tries to undo the decisions of the pastoral team and the previous pastor.[28]

5. Splitting the one priestly ministry into series of 'ordained' tasks

Up to the Second Vatican Council four 'lower orders' and the subdiaconate were recognized in the church. These were regarded as ordained ministries and not just as services, in the sense of *Ministeria quaedam*, which made it possible to give male laity the 'appointed ministries' of lector and acolyte. This last solution did not enjoy any success. But these models indicate that offices and ministries in the church can be multiple, and can be introduced and abolished. For example, by a liturgical appointment (ordination), it should be possible to give lay hospital pastors the possibility of administering unction to the sick in addition to baptizing and taking funerals, and also to authorize them to preside at services of reconciliation – which are not *per se* identical with confessions.[29] Time and again the suggestion is made in various places that for certain faith communities there should be a small team of trained lay people authorized to administer the sacraments through an appropriate liturgy (ordination) and possibly for a limited time. Thus at the end of 1993 the student pastors of Germany, Austria and Switzerland proposed at their congress in the Schöntal monastery (near Heilbronn) a 'relative ordination' by virtue of which male and female pastors should administer sacraments in the communities entrusted to them which are normally reserved to deacons or priests. In Brazil, Bishop T.Cloïn of Barra de Bahia, for many years secretary of the conference of Brazilian senior religious superiors, seriously considered ordaining a team of married men in his far-flung diocese, in which priests were very scarce, for a particular parish and for a limited period.[30]

Except in this last case, which is quite clearly concerned with priests, a new kind of 'presbyterium', the suggestions made briefly above about splitting the ministry raise delicate questions. A much-noted report by W.Kasper, Bishop of Rottenburg, at the time of the assembly of the German bishops in the spring of 1994,[31] suggested that there should not be too hasty acceptance of the bogey man of the 'clericalization of the laity' in order to reject the two developments. Granted, he pointed to the dangers of attacking the basic sacramental structure of the church and of a crisis of identity among priests and laity, Kasper himself recognizes the impasse and leaves unanswered his own question ('do we not have to ordain those who *de facto* lead the community and are competent to do so?), though he says that it is better to avoid unrealistic discussions and exhaust all the possibilities of canon law which are at present available.[32] In the meantime, the number of laity who are in fact leading communities is constantly increasing and the number of priests is declining. This bring us to the problem of the ordination of *viri probati*.

6. The ordination of *viri probati*[33]

Already before Vatican II and outside Europe there was talk of the possibility of ordaining *viri probati*. This term is understood to denote married men, with stable marriages, adequately trained and prepared to be ordained priests by the bishop. The topic was removed from the agenda of the Second Vatican Council by Paul VI.[34] Afterwards such ordination was asked for at a number of synods,[35] by bishops,[36] councils of priests[37] and theologians.[38] After a divided and unclear vote, the Roman synod of 1971 gave negative advice to Paul VI. The maintaining of compulsory celibacy in the Latin church was also confirmed in the 1990 synod. John Paul II, while recognizing that celibacy is not essential, has constantly emphasized the appropriateness of maintaining it. The topic has also been discussed regularly outside Europe. According to most surveys, which have not, however, been carried out in all European countries, an increasing majority, even of Catholics who practise regularly, would prefer the ordination of *viri probati*.[39] Of course a pastoral decision does not depend in the first instance on majorities and minorities, but the *sensus fidelium* can also be expressed in it. The central norm remains the safeguarding of what is essential for pastoral care, as described e.g. in canon 213 of the Code of Canon Law, which confirms the right of the faithful to the word of God and the sacraments. Traditionally it has been recognized that a faith community has a right to the eucharist and that the leader of a faith community must normally also preside at the eucharist.

The whole problem has been clearly summed up in a text from the joint synod of the German dioceses (1972–1975). This states: 'There are different standpoints on this question . . . It is not easy to make a decision on it because freely chosen celibacy is a high value for the priesthood and for the church as a whole. On the other hand, when the well-being of the church is seriously at risk, all standpoints, however important, must fall into the background if they are not necessary on the basis of an obligatory doctrine of faith (*iure divino*). Therefore it is generally recognized that an extraordinary pastoral emergency can require the ordination of married men whose marriage and profession has been tested.'[40] This text goes on to say: 'Therefore the bishops must ask: is there such an emergency in Germany or will there be one in the near future? What concrete models can be developed in order to ensure an ordered ministry for the well-being of the communities?'[41]

The German Catholic adult catechism also goes into this and states: 'That the present shortage of priests . . . is a symptom of a deeper and wider crisis and not cannot be remedied just by simply changing a law. In the last instance is it not clear that at present that not only celibacy but also marriage itself and the family are in deep crisis? The two are . . . very closely connected.'[42]

Here we want to approach this complicated problem in as matter-of-fact a way as possible.

A first question is how a faith community is defined. Whereas in the first centuries a faith community amounted to a house church often of barely 100 people, now – in Europe as well – there are parishes of 30,000 and more. In our present-day society one can hardly argue that every house church or every base community has the right to a president who is a priest.[43] A faith community must normally be sufficiently large and vital to be able to have its own priest[44] and support him, at least in part, except where a community is being started in a missionary context. Some argue that a community which does not produce a celibate priest is not vital enough to have the right to a priest. On the basis of the tradition of both the Western and the Eastern churches this view is unacceptable. Of course the ideal extent of a faith community depends on many contextual factors. Some suggest between 2,000 and 10,000 faithful. However, here account is seldom taken of actual practice or the needs of a renewed evangelization. It is certain that a real shortage of priests, which many bishops recognize in their dioceses, is quite possible.[45]

No one will deny that the scenario of the ordination of *viri probati* has disadvantages as well as advantages. To take the advantages first. A number of parishes would again have local priests, an important factor both for maintaining the faith, which also according to many studies is closely bound up with sacramental practice, and for the animation of pastoral teams. Far more than in former periods of history suitable candidates are available among pastoral workers, deacons and lay theologians. Present-day priests could again be encouraged by the prospect of successors, rather than having to regard themselves as the 'last of the Mohicans'. Married priests are often closer to the everyday reality of families, though they need not necessarily be the only ones who are, and can speak with more experience of the ups and downs of married life, bringing up children, problems with jobs. This can be a plus for the inculturation of the gospel in secularized society through language and symbolism. Married priests can also help to overcome the tension between clergy and laity which still arises.[46] As far as their livelihood is concerned, in countries with church tax and traditionally high contributions from the faithful, they pose few financial problems to the parish. As already happens in the case of laity active as pastoral workers, certain facilities can be offered, like making a clergy house available as a home. Often the task of a priest, above all if it is performed in a team, can possibly be combined with a part-time job.[47] The early retirement age in secular jobs also opens up prospects for candidates to the priesthood. Everywhere inspiration can be drawn from the experience of ministers in other churches.

Of course in recruitment, in addition to the qualities which are required of celibate priests (adequate training, solid faith, a serious spiritual life, the capacity to be leader of a team), other more specific conditions arise, including the agreement of the partner and if possible her real spiritual support, a stable marriage and acceptance of the situation by older children. In addition to this Karl Rahner gave as a criterion that a candidate should once have been able to win over a pagan to the faith. One repeatedly hears the possibility of divorce being raised. This danger is a real one, as is clear from the experience of the Reformation churches.[48] However, it must honestly be recognized that in the last thirty years the number of priests who have left the church has been substantial,[49] and that in some European countries the number of priests with a relationship not approved by the church is presumably quite large.[50] It therefore seems desirable in the case of the ordination of *viri probati*, from the beginning to set a sufficiently high age as the norm, though this immediately raises the question how one can then appoint younger candidates for pastoral work among young people (with the delicate suggestion of reflection on the possibility of 'temporary ordinations'[51]).

Questions can also be asked about the limited mobility of married priests. However, this aspect should not be exaggerated. Many workers, too, have to move house more frequently than before because of the demands of their job. If a person in addition is ordained into a team, and for a particular faith community, then the question of a temporary ordination arises again. If one takes into account here that the candidate needs to have shown that he has played a positive part in a particular faith community over a longer period and is judged favourably by the pastoral team, he will usually be a 'presbyter' (an older man) and less likely to move house.[52]

However, it would be naive to see the ordination of *viri probati* as an easy magic formula. First of all, it is by no means certain that the number of good candidates will increase markedly.[53] Even suitable and motivated faithful come up against a number of obstacles built into the present ministry. The two main ones seem to be: 1. the very fact, at least according to established tradition, of having to commit oneself for life; and 2. the uncertainty about the possibility of having a say in the church and about 'legal safeguards' in it (the discussion of human rights in the church proves a sensitive topic in many places).

There are no fewer problems for the church authorities themselves. First, the candidates, at least psychologically, cannot be regarded as being any less 'professional personnel' than the celibate priests. They presumably remain deeply aware that they are deliberately volunteering and are not offering themselves in order to 'earn their living' in the church, like those employed in other professions. Secondly, the church authorities are aware that a solid spirituality is extremely important. All the studies indicate that believers expect first and foremost spiritual support and guidance from their priests.[54] If a married priest is to maintain this year in, year out, which can represent a heavy burden in a predominantly indifferent, if not agnostic society, it is important for his spouse to offer him real support. While it is already difficult to make a good forecast about the future quality of the spiritual life of a celibate priest, this seems even more tricky when it comes to assessing a couple. That is one more reason for choosing older candidates who with their spouses bear witness to a stable and deeply spiritual life.

Secondly, the church authorities will have to take account of the fact that not just married couples, but families, are involved. Experience with married deacons and pastoral workers is instructive here: not least if their pastoral work is to maintain its quality, these need to be able to devote sufficient time to their families and to protect them from overwhelming demands from the parishioners. If this does not happen, the stress undermines pastoral work and married priests encounter the same problems as many celibate priests. Therefore this raises the question of the availability of the priest. If, for example, he has to be in church every weekend, the very time when – especially where both partners are working – all members of the family tend to have a more intensive family life, alienation and tensions are inevitable. It is therefore impossible to avoid the question whether a 'presbytery' model is not the best solution for married priests: they are ordained into a team so that each can reckon on 'free weekends', as is the case with the caring professions. This implies envisaging teams first in the larger parishes, e.g. in urban areas (where married priests are also likely to be accepted more quickly), while in smaller country parishes use is made of older men who only work part-time or are already retired.[55]

To this list of problems must be added the challenge which is posed to celibate priests. They will have to learn to work with married colleagues. Experience with married deacons in the parishes shows that this collaboration sometimes requires a long period of adjustment on both sides: some deacons are more clerical than the priests, and some priests feel threatened by the deacons who invade their territory. Celibate priests can regard married priests as second-class. Then there is the danger of two classes of priests, where status and authority are determined not by suitability but by whether or not the priest is married. Even more tricky is the effect on the celibacy of celibate priests. A number will inevitably be caused a crisis. The faithful will support some of those who want to marry or in fact do so. Priests who have left to marry will urgently ask to be allowed to exercise their ministry again. Hidden relationships will be made public more readily. Whatever happens, a transitional crisis will be inevitable, and a serious effort will have to be made in the dioceses to 'discern the spirits' honestly by good spiritual guidance.

After absorption into the body of priests there remains absorption into the faith community itself. Surveys show that a majority of faithful in a number of Western European countries are positive about married priests – there have been hardly any surveys in Central Europe – but presumably this is not the case for other countries. Certainly there are those who are opposed to it everywhere. Here and there a rebellion occurs within the church, as that in the Church of England and the Church in Wales over the ordination of women, which is a very real one. Changes in present-day practice will thus require a long period of appropriate education. The ordination of clergy who have come over to the Roman Catholic Church from the churches of the Reformation has taken place without many problems.[56] It will certainly not be possible to limit the ordination of Catholic *viri probati* to exceptional cases, and this will provoke different reactions. Moreover, most faithful are hardly aware, if at all, that this practice has already existed for centuries in the Catholic churches of the Eastern rite.

Some writers suggest that a beginning should be made in some countries and that developments should be evaluated after a certain time. But the fact that the same situation prevails almost everywhere, that the modern media will immediately ensure that information is transmitted world-wide and that even if a change should be limited to Europe, it will be taken up in an accelerating process in all other parts of the world, makes this option difficult, perhaps utopian. Moreover in many non-Western countries the situation is far more serious than in Europe and sometimes has been for centuries, as in the region of the Andes. In the end the decision probably has to be made that for an intervention with such far-reaching pastoral consequences perhaps only an ecumenical council can decide on a new orientation. Until this has really been accepted, thorough dialogue at the basic levels of all dioceses is indispensable.

If a regional or an ecumenical council is to open up new ways, finally there remains the question of the chances of recruiting celibate priests. In theory, of course, it can be argued that the charism of celibacy does not cease to exist as the result of a decision made in connection with a new pastoral situation. However, no one knows how many priests today have chosen celibacy voluntarily, or more out of necessity because they have, or thought that they had, above all a vocation to the priesthood. It is highly probable that the influence of Vatican II's revaluation of marriage and the awareness of the great, though perhaps exaggerated, significance of sexuality will cause the number of candidates for a celibate priesthood to continue to decline.[57] Without doubt, this will lead to authentic celibacy 'for the sake of the kingdom of God' being lived out and recognized with less ambiguity, and also have a positive effect on religious life.[58] However, the genuinely chosen celibate existence of a diocesan priest must continue to be a viable option. For a number of such priests, the support of communities of diocesan priests will be welcome. In a diocese they will be able to form the nucleus of the animation, though always in conjunction with the most capable priests and pastoral workers, men and women. In special cases and under definite conditions a move from celibate to married priests can be considered; in general, however, it is said that this possibility could put heavy and unfair burdens on pastoral conversations between celibate priests and women.

There remains the question of the selection of bishops. Two courses are possible in theory: either to follow the practice of the churches of the Reformation, most of which have married bishops (which makes a wider choice possible), or to follow the practice of the Orthodox churches, in which only unmarried men – often monks – or widowers are elected bishop.[59] Of course it can be objected that here, too, new ways need to be taken by a church on the way towards ecumenism. At all events, great care is necessary here, and *a priori* it makes no sense to take all possible steps at the same time. Moreover, we cannot lay down everything for coming centuries now, and perhaps many faith communities will be so small that the pattern of the first centuries with married bishops[60] will prove the only suitable one. For the present, the practice of the Orthodox churches seems likely, on condition that the bishops do not allow themselves to be manipulated by the state or by their extended family, and that sufficient suitable candidates are found from among the celibate priests.

Some would naturally conclude from what has been said above that whatever ways are taken (from maintaining the *status quo* to far-reaching changes), the problems will increase rather than decrease. This seems probable, but the facts seem to rule out maintaining the *status quo*. Either married priests for local faith communities are rejected and with this the *de facto* sacramental character of the Catholic Church with all the consequences, or present practice is changed and married men are ordained, again with all the consequences. There is something dramatic about this dilemma.[61] The experience of the churches of the Reformation teaches, finally, that the abolition of compulsory celibacy is not automatically a solution to the shortage of priests.[62]

7. The ordination of women

The list of scenarios would remain incomplete without including here the possibility of the ordination of women to the priesthood. Notwithstanding the instruction *Inter Insigniores* of the Congregation for the Doctrine of Faith (1976) and John Paul II's apostolic brief *Ordinatio Sacerdotalis* (1994), which excludes the priestly ordination of women, discussion continues in the church. The possibility of ordaining women to the diaconate has been taken up in various quarters, e.g. by Cardinal C.Martini of Milan and Bishop A.Luystermann of Gent. The German conference of bishops had made a positive statement about it at an earlier stage.[63] The literature on the diaconate and priesthood of women is now almost too extensive to survey.[64]

This is not the place to go into the theological implications of the ordination of women to the priesthood.[65] But it is necessary to take seriously the fact that many tens of thousands of women (religious and lay) are involved full time in catechesis, liturgy and pastoral work.

The opinion of the faithful on the matter is developing all the time. Thus for example in the report of the bishops of England and Wales to the 1987 synod we read:

'Many pointed out that women were that part of the laity who did most of the work in the parish. However, women should be adequately represented on decision making bodies and be seen to be taking leadership roles. Equal partnership between men and women in the Church and greater participation by women should be actively encouraged. Many felt worried that the church was lagging behind society whereas it should really be leading the way in an area of justice such as this. Many groups said that a married clergy would be able to relate better to women and some women spoke of their experience with certain priests who they perceived as not taking them seriously and keeping them at a distance. On the whole, when women's ordination to the priesthood was mentioned, it was more likely to be supported than opposed.'[66]

Here we may note that since any real authority in the church requires ordination and only males can be ordained, women are institutionally excluded from the structure of church government. Most surveys in Europe indicate that there is a positive attitude towards women who take on the leadership of a parish without a priest. Different national synods or pastoral councils have argued for the ordination of women to the diaconate (West Germany, Switzerland, Flanders, the Netherlands, Austria). The same is true of a number of diocesan synods, for example in France and Germany (Munich). Readiness to accept a woman as priest increased in Austria from 64% in 1980 to 79% in 1990. In Wallonia (Belgium), 56% of those involved in pastoral work have a positive attitude (36% are negative).

Of course experiences in Great Britain, where the ordination of women as priests in the Church of England (1994) has led to great tensions with a minority, counsel great caution. There were also tensions initially in the Swedish Lutheran Church, though now it seems that even senior Catholic clergy in Sweden and Denmark are speaking positively of experiences with women priests in the sister church. No one can predict how opinion among European Catholics will develop further, or what standpoints a church government which is clearly divided within will take in the future. It is clear that the possibility of the ordination of women to the priesthood in the Catholic Church would have world-wide implications and is hardly conceivable without a general council later. This is not the case with the ordination of deacons.

Whether these ordinations could be an answer to the shortage of priests is not obvious. In various countries the readiness of women to commit themselves full time in the present model of the church is stagnating. A number of competent women hesitate to take on a task for which it is difficult to find men, whether celibate or not. The present needs will not be met by ordaining women deacon any more than it will be met by ordaining men to this ministry. But there have never been so many theologically trained women available as there are at present. Many want to take pastoral responsibility, though a large number have little inclination to copy the existing male model and involve themselves definitively in the present church system. Once again it is becoming clear that the thorough renewal of the faith community at every level is a prime requisite for filling the ranks of the church.

8. A key question: What priests for what communities?

Bishop J.Homeyer of Hildesheim has rightly emphasized this central aspect. it is above all important to overcome the shortage of communities and not just the shortage of priests. In this perspective he mentions two negative fundamental decisions: 'First, in order to be the church in a new way we must not begin with structural measures. So we must not begin – as I am constantly saying in my diocese – by abolishing parishes in order to cope with the shortage of personnel. In that case we would maintain as many communities as we have priests, but otherwise nothing would be changed – except for a possible (but doubtful) reduction in the burdens on priests. The second fundamental decision is that we must not begin by transferring to full-time lay workers all the tasks which can no longer be performed by priests. In that way it could seem that all we need to renew the church is a sufficient number of full-time workers who would then take over most of what the priest has done hitherto – but this would change nothing in the communities. In this way the charisms which are present among the faithful would again be blocked.'[67] A counter-question can make this clear: if there were again enough celibate priests, what would then remain of all the new courses which are now being adopted?

Thus the orientation sketched out presupposes an intense process of increasing awareness: communities must be challenged to greater creativity,[68] and the faithful need to think it worthwhile to see themselves all as volunteers for whom involvement and training go hand in hand. The small local faith community must feel itself really responsible for its vitality, both within and in its relations with the outside world, and be encouraged to take concrete decisions in these areas. Everyone needs to recognize that the spirit is working at the basic level even now. Only in this way will the gospel be able to take on new forms in postmodern culture, in a new language and with new symbols. Then old priests, too, will have hope for the future and younger men and women will find it worthwhile to join in.

9. A sketch of the future

All these reflections call for a high degree of patience among the faithful. But the more church members become aware of themselves, the less patient they will be prepared to be with a church government which is increasingly said to be unwilling to take up the possibilities known from church history.

Given the mass of such historical knowledge of pastoral work and the fact that patience is wearing thin, we might develop the following scenario for the future:

1. *Starting point.* The starting point will be provided by Christian faithful who for a long time have had to live in a place without a pastor. Because they want to continue, these communities will shape the basic features of their lives as a community of believers on their own initiative and responsibility, in other words with the help of those gifts which they have received from God (I Cor.1.27).[69]

2. *Pastoral leadership.* Pastoral teams will be formed for the most important areas of community life (liturgy, preaching, charitable work). One person will be responsible for each team.

The leaders of individual pastoral teams will together form the pastoral leadership team of the community. They will choose from their number a person whom this leadership team finds competent. The pastoral team will take over 'pastoral leadership of the community'.

Normally these tasks will be honorary, but possibly a paid post can be envisaged.

3. *Spiritual ministry*. This viable community with its pastoral leadership will be aware that it is associated with the living tradition of the gospel (diachronic unity) and in communion with the other Christian communities of the one church (synchronic unity). It will also know that the action of Christ 'in person' is made visible in the community in the ministerial preaching of the word and the celebration of the sacraments (first of all baptism). Nor will there be any dispute in this community that these elements of a fully established community are concentrated in the 'spiritual office'. In their conviction, it will be an obligation of that office to ensure unity in space and time, and to present Christ in reliable symbolism as the centre of church life in word, sacrament and eucharistic celebration. Each church member is in any case involved in this concern for unity, and in an everyday fashion is made capable of being a representative of Christ.

As has been said in connection with the 'pastoral leadership of the community' which already exists without a priest, the person in office exercises the 'symbolic ministerial leadership of the community'. This person makes it clear that the community is not inventing itself but rather owes itself to the action of God in Christ through the Holy Spirit. However, the ordination of some does not imply the subordination of others.

By virtue of this knowledge of the need for such a spiritual office, this community which has achieved maturity will also be aware of its responsibility for this office towards the wider world. Therefore it will propose to the bishop a small number of people (women and men) from its ranks (or from elsewhere) and ask him to make this group a presbytery and endow it with the necessary spiritual authority (*ordo*). Here the spiritual authority of the office need not be assigned only to an assembled group, but can be divided differently depending on the pastoral task: everyone working in pastoral care of the sick will receive authority to administer the sacraments of penitence and the sick; those who work with young couples will receive authority to marry them. Finally, sufficient will be given authority to baptize and celebrate the eucharist.

4. *A challenge to the church authorities*. Of course some bishops will say that they are not in a position to give their official approval and the desired spiritual authority to the presbytery because the people proposed include married men or women.

But in that case in future surprising developments could take place. Some communities would show understanding towards the bishop and continue to wait patiently. But other communities – supported by an organization for communities without a local priest – will one day begin:
– to celebrate the eucharist in accordance with Jesus' command 'Do this in memory of me', even if this celebration does not fully correspond to the ordinances of a sacramental celebration of the eucharist;
– they will anoint the sick, even if they do not claim that this is the full form of the unction of the sick;
– they will pray for forgiveness with those who want to reorder their life and confess their sins, even if this does not amount to the express form of the sacrament of penance.

Some bishops will then attempt to catch up with this development which anticipates present possibilities by changing church law. In this way they will regain the possibility of shaping developments from within. But others who are not well disposed to these developments will risk being detached from a development which will not be prepared to be classed as 'no longer Catholic'.

Perhaps such a realistic scenario for tomorrow may encourage the church authorities today to go on the offensive in making use of the many untried possibilities for renewing the communities and thus also the ministry of the church today.

Notes

1. The Shortage of Priests in Europe

1. The facts are always published two years after the year in question, e.g. those for 1992 in 1994.

2. E.g. P.Ester, L.Hallman and R.de Moor (eds.), *The Individualizing Society. Value Change in Europe and North America*, Tilburg 1993; P.M.Zulehner and H.Denz, *Wie Europa lebt und glaubt*, Europäische Wertestudie, Düsseldorf 1993.

3. In 1998–89 the province of Brussels comprised 970,346 inhabitants, 5,959,051 Flemish and 3,209,319 Walloon (including 66,610 from the German language-area).

4. According to the European Values Study weekly practice among Belgians in Brussels in 1990 was under 17%; in practice 60% never go to church, only 54% say they believe in God, and 34% in a life after death; more than 53% say that they have little or no confidence in the church.

5. The situation is changing rapidly. According to the secretariat of the German conference of bishops, in 1994 of 13,327 parishes and quasi-parishes 66% had a resident priest and 34% did not.

6. Source: *Berufung: Zur Pastoral der geistlichen Berufe. Christen haben eine Mission*, Heft 32, 1994, Informationszentrum Berufe der Kirche, Freiburg.

7. Schweizerisches Pastoralsozoiologisches Institut, *Kirchliches Personal/ Personnel ecclésiastique, 1986–1990*, Sankt Gallen 1993.

8. R.Weibel, 'Wenn die Ausnahme Regel wird', *Schweizerische Kirchenzeitung* 4, 1994, 50–4.

9. P.González, *Faire parles les chiffres. Analyse de la situation socio-pastoral de l'Eglise Catholique dans le canton de Vaud*, Faculté de Théologie de Fribourg, 1994. Of the 519 priests (1974), 415 were younger than sixty-five, of the 377 (1994) only 206.

10. *Profile of Religious in Ireland*, CMRS, Dublin 1990.

11. On the occasion of the assembly of the National Conference of Priests (Birmingham, September 1992), a specialist remarked that this development is 'an event of truly historic proportions'. He added: 'The Church in England and Wales is not at the edge of a precipice, we have already fallen over the edge and are hurtling into the unknown.'

12. In 5 dioceses by 15% and in three by more than 20%.

13. M.Brulin, 'Les Assemblées Dominicales en l'Absence de Prêtre.

Situation Française en 1987. Les Résultats d'une enquête nationale', *La Maison-Dieu* 175, 1988, 111–67.

14. J.Gelineau, 'Un visage renouvelé de l'Eglise. Quand les prêtres se font rares', *Études* 364, 1986, 819–32. See also the dossier 'Les Clercs', in *Actualités religieuses dans Le Monde*, 15 September 1993, 24–39.

15. Estadisticas de la Iglesia Catolica 1992, Madrid 1993.

16. According to a note by Professor V.Sastre.

17. M.E.Gandolfi and A.Filippi, 'Parrochie senza prete. Problema d'oggi problema di domani', *Il Regno, Attualità*, XXVII, no.685, 1992, 382–90.

18. For example, Parma has 71 parishes with less than 100 inhabitants, 75 with 101–250, 54 with 251–500, 39 with 501–1,000, making a total of 239 parishes with less than 1,000 inhabitants as compared to 72 with more than 1,000 inhabitants. However, in the mountain areas, tourists need to be taken into consideration; for example Bolzano (with 59 parishes without a resident pastor, 90 with less than 500 and 80 with between 501 and 1,000) receives more than 3.5 million tourists annually (1989).

19. See R.Gubert (ed.), *Persistenze e Mutamenti dei Valori degli Italiani nel Contesto Europeo,* Trent 1992.

20. I am grateful to Prof.W.Zdaniewicz, SAC, Warsaw, for these figures.

21. Between 1979 and 1993 the population of Poland increased from 35 to 38.3 million.

22. *Kosciól Katolicki w Polsce, 1918–1990,* Rocznik Statystyczny, Warsaw 1991 (ed. L.Adamczuk and W.Zdaniewicz), 129–33.

23. *The Position of the Church in Czechoslovakia,* Pro Mundi Vita, Special Note no.28, 1973; *Les croyants tchécoslovaques et la lutte idéologique,* Pro Mundi Vita, Dossiers Europe-Amérique du Nord 17, 1982.

24. Z.Bohac, *Pfarrermangel. Bericht über die Situation der Seelsorge in der böhmischen Kirchenprovinz,* Prague 1991 (MS).

25. P.Kolác, 'L'Église tchèque, quatre ans après', *Études* 381, 1994, 79–89.

26. E.Andraš, *Die Kirche in Ungarn,* Pro Mundi Vita: Dossiers, 1984/2 (special edition).

27. A.Maté-Tóth, *Pfarrmangel. Fallstudie in der ungarischen Diözese Szeged-Csanad* 1991, Szeged 1991 (pro ms).

28. *Christ in der Gegenwart* 24, 1994.

29. *Christ in der Gegenwart* 35, 1993.

30. This note was prepared in 1994 for the present publication by the Greek Orthodox sociologist Dr G.Moustákis.

31. A.Bäckström, *In God's Service. A Study of the Clerical Profile in the Diocese of Strägnäs,* Uppsala 1992.

32. H.Heind (ed.), *The Evangelical Lutheran Church in Finland 1988–1991,* Research Institute of the Lutheran Church in Finland, Tampere, 44, 1993.

33. Because of the great variety of churches in Great Britain, as is also the case with the Landeskirchen in Germany, it is impossible to give a coherent picture of these two countries. Between 1975 and 1980 the parochial clergy of

the Church of England declined from 12,000 to 9,000. After a brief increase in 1980 the number of candidates for the priesthood declined further. In 1985 there were 9,529 priests for 13,295 parishes. Recourse is made to 'part-time priests' and the employment of older volunteers with an appropriate training. In 1931, more than 50% of the clergy had responsiblity for parishes with less than 1000 inhabitants, in 1988 only 9%. Around 1985 the Evangelical Church in Germany had a maximum of 11,000 theological students. Since then the number has constantly declined (7,500 in West and 1,000 in East Germany). The motives for becoming a pastor seem to be changing: people want to get a paid job quickly. Only a minority has been given a really religious upbringing at home. In France, too, 15% of places available in the Reformed Church remain unoccupied (see also 'Eglises protestantes: une situation nuancée', in D.Hervieu-Léger and F.Champion, *Vers un nouveau christianisme?*, Paris 1985, 70–5.

34. See e.g. A.Vandenhoeck, *Pastorale diensten voor leken in West-Duitsland*, licentiate thesis for the faculty of religion in the Catholic University of Louvain, 1991.

35. M.Gartmann, *'Laien'-theologen in der Gemeindepastoral. Notstandsmassnahme oder Beruf mit Zukunft?*, Düsseldorf 1981.

36. 'Kerkelijke Statistiek van het R.K.Kerkgenootschap, 1985–1990', *Kerkelijke Documentatie* 121.20, 1992, 7,14–15.

37. According to a KASKI study (1987), it seems that of a total of 850,000 weekend churchgoers more than 200,000 do more than just go to church, and are also actively involved in church life. Around 55% of the active churchgoers are women. The greatest percentage of active members is in the smaller parishes and among the 50–64 age-group (*Informatiebulletin* 121.16, 1988, 25–7).

38. 'Resolution of the Special Synod of the Dutch Bishops', in *Archief van de Kerken*, 1980, 223–36; R.Huysmans, 'Sondersynode der niederländischen Bischöfe in Rom 1980', *Theologische Praktische Quartalschrift* 129, 1981, 379–84.

39. Thus in the diocese of Haarlem it is forecast that in the year 2000 75 priests and 90 pastoral workers will be available for pastoral care (as compared with 125 priests and 75 pastoral workers in 1995).

40. R.Michiels and W.van Soom (eds.), *Pastoraal Ambt in een priesterarme Kerk*, Louvain 1990.

41. J.Somer-Gotteland, 'Les équipes "Anime"', *Lumen Vitae* 36, 1981, 457–66.

42. Thus France has around 220,000 lay volunteers (in catechetics alone). More than 1,000 are paid as pastors in official teaching. The situation differs from diocese to diocese: Lyons has 150 paid staff (most part-time), Nanterre 40, Rennes 24 and Verdun 2 (*La Croix*, 13 June 1992).

II. *Ministries in the New Testament and the Early Church*

1. Tenach does not have the connotation of 'old' (and thus *passé*). The Old Testament is not *passé* for Christians either. Tenach is an acronym derived from

the Hebrew names of the great blocks of text which make up the Hebrew Bible: Torah – Nebiim – Kethubim, or Law – Prophets – Writings. The acronym TeNaCH has been formed from the letters T, N, K (pronounced CH at the end of a word) to denote the whole of Hebrew scripture. The word is used only for the Hebrew canon and not for the Greek translation, the Septuagint (LXX), which has more books.

2. As an illustration, reference might be made to the periodical laying on of hands by the king, who was thought to be able to cure people of certain diseases. The picture of Louis XIV as a miracle worker in the church of Saint-Riquier, France, is one of many testimonies to this view. The garments and ritual objects displayed in the Jewel House in the Tower of London also make it clear how sacral (even sacramental) the anointing of a king was thought to be. The link with the Bible is also shown by the legend connected with the Stone of Scone which lies under the coronation throne in Westminster Abbey; it is said to be the stone on which Jacob rested in Bethel (Gen.28.11).

3. Well-known examples of anti-royalism are Gideon's refusal to be made king in Judg.8.22–23; Jotham's fable in Judg.9.7–15; I Sam.10.17–27; perhaps even I Kings 1–2, etc. One might also think of the tense relationship between prophecy and kingship, with the sometimes very fierce criticism of the kings by the prophets.

4. The relationship between tenth-century recollections and the sixth-century Deuteronomistic or even later re-reading and re-working is a problem which is still controversial. Cf. A.Caquot and P.de Robert, *Les Livres de Samuel*, Geneva 1994, 15–19 and bibliography; K.Whitelam, 'King and Kingship', in *Anchor Dictionary of the Bible*, New York 1992, 40–28. Since A.Alt it has been accepted almost as a matter of course that the actual origin of the kingship in Israel must be sought in a charismatic emergence of Saul in a military context – the fight against the Philistines and the Ammonites – and that initially it was not meant to be dynastic.

5. One example of insight into necessary change is the curve of population growth in the world. The turbulent 1994 Cairo Conference makes this illustration a topical one. By scientific extrapolation one can more or less calculate the curve of growth in world population from antiquity to the present day. We can draw this curve precisely for the last century. In many discussions of contraception the number of people the world can support plays a role. Now there are 6 billion people on earth and the arguments often go like this. In theory the world can support 20, 30 . . . billion people, provided that we have sufficient food (which in itself already presents terrible problems in the sphere of providing this in practice). Now these calculations are for a relatively short period, say, for the next 50 or 100 years. But if the birth-rate continues to rise with the same curve, and the calculations are made over 150, 200, 500 years, then the figures become so ridiculously large that it is quite clear that something may be done because something must be done. And of course that influences the view people take of contraception.

6. J.Roloff, 'Amt/Ämter/Amtsverständnis, IV. Im Neuen Testament', *TRE* 2, 1978, 509. For my comments generally I am indebted to the whole article 'Amt/Ämter/Amtsverständnis', ibid., 500–622, and above all to the articles by D.Thomas (Old Testament, 501–4), C.Thoma (Judaism, 504–9), J.Roloff (New Testament, 509–33), R.P.C.Hanson (Early Church, 533–52).

7. The most important passages for the use of *leitourgia*, *time* and *arche* in connection with ministry are: Luke 1.23; 12.11; 20.20; Rom.8.38; 13.6–7; I Cor.15.24; Eph.1.21; 3.10; 6.12; Col.1.16; 2.10,15; Titus 3.1; Heb.1.7; 3.3; 5.4; 8.2,6; 10.11f.; Jude 6; for the terms connected with priesthood see e.g. Luke 1.9; Acts 14.13; Heb.2.17; 5.6; 7.5; I Peter 2.5,9. In order not to burden the notes unnecessarily, I shall mention here all the basic material consulted for this lexicographical study. The information can be found under the key words discussed. A van den Born (ed.), *Bijbels Woordenboek*, Roermond ³1969; G.Kittel and G.Friedrich (ed.), *Theological Dictionary of the New Testament* (10 vols.), Grand Rapids 1964ff.; H.Balzer and G.Schnieder, *Exegetisches Wörterbuch zum Neuen Testament* (3 vols.), Stuttgart 1980–1983; W.F.Arndt and F.W.Gingrich, *Greek-English Dictionary of the New Testament*, Chicago 1957; H.G.Liddell and R.Scott, *A Greek-English Lexicon*, Oxford 1961; R.Morgenthaler, *Statistik des neutestamentlichen Wortschatzes*, Zurich ⁴1992; see also the *TRE* article by J.Roloff mentioned in n.3 above, and E.Schweizer, 'Ministry in the Early Church', *ABD* IV, 1992, 835–42. For the Old Testament I consulted as a basis J.Botterweck and H.Ringgren, *Theological Dictionary of the Old Testament*, Grand Rapids 1975ff.; L.Köhler and W.Baumgartner, *Hebräisches und Aramäisches Lexikon zum Alten Testament*, Leiden ³1967–1990; E.Jenni and C.Westermann, *Theologisches Wörterbuch zum Alten Testament* (2 vols.), Munich and Zurich 1971–1976. The concordance used was H.Bachmann and W.A.-Slaby (eds.), *Computer-Konkordanz zum Novum Testamentum Graece von Nestle-Aland 26. und zum Greek New Testament 3.*, Berlin 1980; the Greek text was Nestle-Aland, 27th edition, and the edition of the Vulgate that of A.Colunga and L.Turrado, Madrid 1977.

8. Or 79 times, if one omits Mark 3.14 ('whom he named apostles'), the textual basis of which is uncertain, as an interpolation from Luke 6.13. It is probable that this is an interpolation, but the text is confirmed in the major manuscripts, like Sinaiticus and Vaticanus, and thus as far as textual criticism is concerned is probably correct.

9. Heb.3.1; I Peter 1.1; II Peter 1.1; 3.2; Jude 17; Rev.2.2; 18.20; 21.14.

10. Given the limitations of space I shall not examine the secular and extra-biblical significance of *apostolos*. The lexicographical tools of Greek give us enough information here. K.H.Rengstorf has extensively illustrated the historical and cultural background of the word in Kittel's *Theological Dictionary of the New Testament*, 1, 398–447.

11. See e.g. John 5.36; 6.29,57; 8.42; 10.36; 17.18, 21,23,25.

12. J.A.Bühner, in *Exegetisches Wörterbuch zum Neuen Testament*, ed. H.Balz and G.Schneider, I, 344.

13. Contemporary textual criticism reads the name of the second person as Junia, the wife of Andronicus. This means that Paul also called women apostles. Earlier Junias was regarded as a man. Be this as it may, they did not belong to the Twelve, and yet were called apostles.

14. We can note one exception to the rule, in Luke 11.49. In a reaction against the scribes Jesus says: 'Therefore also the Wisdom of God said, "I will send them prophets and apostles, some of whom they will kill and persecute."' It is, however, possible that Luke is alluding to the Twelve, in which case the text should not be understood in general terms but as a *vaticinium ex eventu* of the persecution and martyr death of Jesus' own disciples. But this is uncertain.

15. The authenticity of this text as an authentic logion of Jesus is doubted. If the saying does not come from Jesus himself, then it belonged to the earliest prophetic-eschatological interpretation in the preaching of earliest Christianity that we can reach, and comes from Q. Cf. F.Neirynck, *Q-Synopsis. The Double Tradition Passages in Greek*, Louvain 1988, 62; Burton Mack, *The Book of Q*, New York 1993, 118. Official interpretations are then in any case later. For the origin of the Twelve cf. W.Trilling, 'Zur Entstehung des Zwölferkreises. Eine Geschichtskritische Überlieferung', in *Die Kirche des Anfangs*, Erfurt 1977, 201–22. Trilling himself leaves open the question whether the Twelve originate from before or after Easter. But if it should prove that the Twelve come from the period after Easter, this works as an *a fortiori* argument about church ministries and tells against associating exclusive masculinity in them with the will of Jesus.

16. Here it should not be forgotten that both the intertestamental literature and the Qumran litrature indicate that the symbolism of the assembly of the twelve tribes of Israel had an important place in the pattern of eschatological expectation at this time. The genre of the testaments of patriarchs, of which fragments have been found in Qumran along with verses which were known earlier (4Q537, 538, 539; 1Q21; 4Q213, 214; 4Q 540, 541, 215), and a fragmentary description of the New Jerusalem (2Q24; 4Q554; 5Q555; 4Q15; 11Q18 1–24), provide interesting comparative material.

17. E.Schillebeeckx, *Ministry. A Case for Change*, London and New York 1980, 48.

18. For the brotherly structure of the Matthaean community see W.Trilling, 'Amt und Amtsverständis bei Matthäus', in *Mélanges Bibliques* (FS B.Rigaux), Gembloux 1970, 29–44, also in *Studien zur Jesusüberlieferung*, SBAB 1, Stuttgart 1988, 77–92.

19. For an attractive discussion of this point see R.E.Brown, *The Community of the Beloved Disciple*, New York 1970, 34ff. The preaching of Jesus in Samaria and the conversion of a whole Samaritan village are in conflict with Jesus' command to the missionaries in Matt.10.5: 'Enter no town of the Samaritans.' This prohibition is much more likely to be historical than John's conception. Luke 9.52–55 reports that the Samaritans were very hostile, and according to Acts 8.1–25 the mission in Samaria began only some time after the origin of the church. It is therefore thought that John 4 is not a factual acount but that the

evangelist in a formal theological story attributes the (offensive?) mission among the Samaritans proleptically to Jesus.

20. See Paul Hoffmann, 'Priestertum und Amt im Neuen Testament. Eine kritische Bestandsaufnahme', in *Priesterkirche*, Düsseldorf 1987, 12–61: 31. Also in *Studien zur Jesusüberlieferung* (n.18).

21. Ibid., 32f.

22. Statistics: *diakonos* occurs 29 times in the New Testament; the distribution of occurrences is: 18 in Paul along with Ephesians and Colossians, 3 in I Timothy, 3 in Matthew, 2 in Mark, 3 in John (there are 7 occurrences in the LXX). Cf. Morgenthaler, *Statistik* (n.7), s.v. *Diakonein* occurs 36 times in the New Testament; the distribution is: Matthew 6, Mark 5, Luke 8, John 3, Acts 2, Paul 4, I Timothy 2, II Timothy 1, Titus 1, Hebrews 1, I Peter 3. *Diakonia* occurs 33 times in the New Testament; the distribution is Luke 1; Acts 8; Paul 19 (12 in II Corinthians); I Timothy 2; II Timothy 1; Titus 1; Hebrews 1; I Peter 3.

23. The phrase is not 'their women' – in which 'their' would refer to the male deacons – but 'the women'. A word is said about the wives of deacons in v.12, in precisely the same way as for the episkopoi: they must be husbands of one wife. Whereas there are no further specific comments about the wives of the episkopoi, it looks as if something specific is said in v.11 about the women, because they exercise a similar function to male deacons. In the same interpretation it then seems quite probable that there were no women episkopoi, so that nothing is said about them.

24. Statistics: *presbyteros* occurs 65 times in the New Testament; distribution of occurrences is: Matthew 12, Mark 7, Luke 5, Acts 18 , I Timothy 4, Titus 1, Hebrews 1, James 1, I Peter 2, II John 1, III John 1, Revelation 12 (there are about 150 occurrences in the LXX). The term does not occur in Paul and the Gospel of John. The word *presbyterion*, as the assembly of presbyers, occurs once, in I Tim.4.14.

25. See e.g. G.Bornkamm, in *TDNT* VI, 651–83.

26. It is interesting to note that Paul makes a distinction between apostles, prophets and teachers. For him the tasks and gifts are not yet fused in one figure for considerations of office, as was to happen with the figure of the bishop in later ideas.

27. Note that the word *presbyteros* in I Tim.5.1 still indicates only the age: *presbyteros* is an older man.

28. Statistics: *episkopos* occurs 5 times in the New Testament; once each in Acts, Philemon, I Timothy, Titus and I Peter. The term *episkope* occurs 4 times in the New Testament, once each in Luke, Acts, I Timothy and I Peter.

29. Cf. Beyer, *TDNT II*, 595–622.

30. 'Haggadic' comes from the Jewish term haggada. Haggada is a typical form of narrative Jewish exegesis which is characteristic of the non-legal texts of the Jewish tradition, more particularly the Talmud. Haggada is characterized by the very free reinterpretation and even the rewriting of biblical texts. We also

find examples of haggadic interpretation of scripture in the New Testament, for example in the infancy narrative of Matthew and Galatians.

31. For a convenient translation of the Apostolic Fathers and Ignatius see *Early Christian Writings*, Penguin Books, Harmondsworth [2]1987.

32. Hoffmann, 'Priestertum und Amt' (n.20), 47. Cf. Roloff, *TRE* 2, 527f.

33. R.P.C.Hanson, in *TRE* 2, 536.

34. Hanson gives the 'Quartodeciman dispute' over the date of Easter as an example.

35. Ibid.,540; I am also indebted to Hanson for his suggestion of other possible causes.

36. B.Botte, *Hippolyte de Rome. La Tradition Apostolique d'après les anciennes versions*, SC 11bis, Paris 1968, 44.

37. E.g. Cyprian, *Letters* 3,1, 1–2; 4,4,3; 59,4,1; 73,8,1, etc.

38. Hoffmann, 'Priestertum und Amt' (n.20), 12f.

39. Ibid., 59f.

III. The Parish Priest in Historical Perspective

1. E.de Moreau has written an interesting article on the origin of parishes in the Low Countries: 'Comment naquirent nos plus anciennes paroisses en Belgique', *NRT* 65, 1958, 926–46.

2. For the whole question see G.Bardy (ed.), *Prêtres d'hier et d'aujourd'hui*, Paris 1954.

3. MGH, Capitul.I, 24–26.

4. C.Vogel, *La discipline pénitentielle en Gaule des origines à la fin du 7e siècle*, Strasbourg 1952.

5. MGH, Capitul.I, 24–26.

6. E.Vydouval, 'Les examens du clergé paroissial a l'époque carolingienne', *RHE* 14, 1913, 81–96.

7. R.Laprat, 'Le sacerdoce chrétien du 6e au 9e siècle', in Bardy, *Prêtres d'hier et d'aujourd'hui* (n.2), 63–111.

8. Migne, PL CXXV, 777–92.

9. J.-F.Lemarignier, 'La sacerdoce et la société chrétienne de la fin du IXe au milieu du XIIe siècle', in Bardy, *Prêtres d'hier et d'aujourd'hui* (n.2), 113–52.

10. G.Lebras, 'Le clergé dans les derniers siècles du moyen-âge', in Bardy, *Prêtres d'hier et d'aujourd'hui* (n.2), 153–81.

11. R.R.Post, *Kerkelijke verhoudingen in Nederland voor de Reformatie*, Utrecht and Antwerp 1954, 410. What is said here about the Netherlands also applies, with slight differences, to other European countries.

12. For the different categories of priests see e.g. M.Aubrun, *La paroisse en France des origines au XVe siècle*, Paris 1986. Prebends (whose income came from church property or a church ministry) and benefices (leases from which one had the produce) were often decisive factors in appointments in the

Middle Ages. In later centuries the system as such was to disappear, but often the financial aspect was a factor in the recognition of a function.

13. Post, *Kerkelijke verhoudingen* (n.11), 41; id., *Kerkgeschiedenis van Nederland in de Middeleeuwen*, Utrecht and Antwerp 1957, II, 278. See also G.LeBras, *Institutions ecclésiastiques de la chrétienté médiévale*, Paris 1959.

14. J.Loehr, *Methodisch-Kritische Beiträge zur Geschichte der Sittlichkeit des Klerus besonders der Erzdiözese Köln am Ausgang des Mittelalters*, Reformationsgeschichtliche Studien und Texte 17, Münster 1910, 67.

15. For the Netherlands see Post, *Kerkelijke verhoudingen* (n.11), 136.

16. One might think of the irony with which Erasmus depicted the shortcomings of the clergy in his *In Praise of Folly*. In passing, it might be mentioned that Thomas More in his *Utopia* outlined a portrait of the priest as he dreamed of him. He saw priests as men with a way of life which was beyond criticism and therefore (this 'therefore' is typical!) very few in number. He spoke of the wives of priests, thus taking it for granted that they could be married, and did not exclude the wives themselves from priestly office.

17. J.Huizinga, *The Waning of the Middle Ages*, London 1924. For the training of priests in Germany see F.W.Oediger, *Über die Bildung der Geistlichen im späten Mittelalter*, Leiden 1943.

18. For a good picture of the Christian community in the district around Florence see C.M.de la Roncière, 'Les communautés chrétiennes et leurs curés', in J.Delumeau, *Histoire vécue du peuple chrétien* I, Toulouse 1979, 281–314.

19. R.Gryson, *Les origines du célibat ecclésiastique du premier au septième siècle*, Recherches et Synthèses, Coll.Hist.2, Gembloux 1970.

20. '. . . *ne cum uxoribus suis possent carnale exercere commercium*', Migne, PL 56, 558.

21. Post, *Kerkelijke verhoudingen* (n.11), 100; cf. also P.Adam, *La vie paroissiale en France au XIVe siècle*, Paris 1964, 151–8.

22. *Ons geestelijk erf* 2, 1928, 218.

23. J.Lortz, *Die Reformation in Deutschland* II, 241.

24. According to Post, when the Counter-Reformation began, around 25% of the priests in the Netherlands may have been living with concubines; cf. *Kerkelijke verhoudingen* (n.11), 125.

25. H.Jedin, 'Das Leitbild des Priesters nach dem Tridentinum und dem Vatikan II', *Theologie und Glaube* 60, 1970, 102–24.

26. '*Ut habitu, gestu, sermone aliisque omnibus rebus, nil nisi grave, moderatum ac religione plenum prae se ferant*', Sessio XXII, cap.1.

27. Sfora Pallavicino, *Istoria del Concilio di Trente* II, Rome 1657, 254. The decree *Cum adolescentium aetas* was promulgated during the twenty-third session (cap.18U). On this see J.O'Donohoe, *Tridentine Seminary Legislation. Its Sources and Its Formation*, Louvain and Boston 1957; H.Jedin, 'L'importanza del

Decreto tridentino sui seminari nella vita della Chiesa', *Seminarium* 15, 1963, 396–412.

28. H.Pourrat, *Jean-Jacques Olier, fondateur de Saint-Sulpice*, Paris 1932.

29. In the introduction to the *Directoire* he wrote: 'The first and last end of this institution is to live in a sovereign way for God, in Christ Jesus Our Lord, in such a way that the inner dispositions of his Son penetrate the depths of our heart and each one can say of himself what St Paul affirms of himself with confidence: "Christ is my life." That will be the unique hope of each person, his unique mediation, his unique practice: to live inwardly the life of Christ.'

30. M.Olier popularized the pattern of the spirituality of the French school in a number of works, e.g. *La journée chrétienne* (1655), *Catéchisme chrétien pour la vie intérieure* (1656) and *Introduction à la vie et aux vertus chrétiennes* (1657).

31. Jean Eudes (1601–1680) belonged to the Bérulle school. He founded his own congregation and established numerous seminaries for priests in France.

32. Quoted by P.Pourrat, *La sacerdoce. Doctrine de l'École française*, Paris 1931, 101.

33. A.Molinier, 'Curés et parioissiens de la Contre-Réforme', in Delumeau (ed.), *Histoire vécue* (n.18), 69–91, has sketched a good portrait of the Counter-Reformation priest.

34. A typical example from the first half of the century is the long episcopate of Bishop A.Triest. See M.Cloet (ed.), *Itinerarium visitationum Antonii Triest episcopi Gandavensis (1623–1654)*, Louvain 1976.

35. B.Plongeron, *La vie quotidienne du clergé français au XVIIIe siècle*, Paris 1974.

36. A.de Roskovany, *De coelibatu et Breviario* (5 vols), Supplementa ad collectiones monumentorum et litterature 3, 4, Nitro 1888.

37. E.Keller, *Die Konstanzer Liturgiereform unter Ignaz Heinrich von Wessenberg*, Freiburg 1965.

38. Among them were various people (in England, Spain and Germany) who left behind memoirs with reflections on the life-style of the priests and the adaptations forced on them. Cf. P. de la Gorce, *Histoire religieuse de la révolution française* IV, Paris 1923, 260–1.

39. J.Leflon, *Monsiur Emery* (2 vols), Paris 1944.

40. J.LeClercq, 'Le "Memoriale vitae sacerdotalis" de Claude Arvisenet', *Collectanea Mechliniensia* 23, 1934, 321–6. Migne published the *Oeuvres complètes d'Arvisenet* in 1856.

41. *Vie de l'abbé Caron*, by a Benedictine of the Congrégation de France (2 vols.), Paris 1886.

42. P.Broutin, 'La piété sacerdotale au début du XIXe siècle', *Revue d'ascétique et de mystique* 20, 1939, 158–80.

43. *Theologische Quartalschrift* 150, 1970, 401. For a study of celibacy in a broader framework cf. W.Leinweber, *Der Streit um den Zölibat im 19. Jahrhundert*, Münster 1978.

44. We hear a different voice in P.Boll, Archbishop of Freiburg. Cf. *Theologische Quartalschrift* 1, 1832, 594–603.

45. It was published a year later in book form: W.Talmadge, *Letters from Florence on the Religious Reform Movement*, London 1866.

46. In Malines and other Belgian diocese forms were printed: '*conceditur Rev.mo Domino . . . licentia utendi rota dicta "bicyclette" (non motocyclette) in opem ministerii intra propriae paroeciae fines exercendi.*'

47. M.Nuyttens, *Camille Looten (1855–1941), Priester, Wetenschapsman en Frans-Vlaams regionalist*, Louvain doctoral thesis 1978; E.Defoort, 'Jean-Marie Gantois et le mouvement flamand en France (1909–1939)', in C.Gras and G.Livet (eds.), *Régions et régionalisme en France du XVIIIe siècle à nos jours*, Paris 1977, 327–36.

48. For France cf. G.Cholvy, 'Régionalisme et clergé catholique au XIXe siècle', in Gras and Livet (eds.), *Régions et régionalisme en France du XVIIIe siècle* (n.46), 187–202.

49. R.Murri, *Battaglie d'Oggi II, La cultura del clero*, Rome 1904, 30–1.

50. R.Aubert, 'Aspects divers du néo-thomisme sous le pontificat de Léon XIII', in *Aspetti della cultura nell'età di Leone XIII*, Bologna 1962, 132–227; G.Martina, 'Il neo-tomismo', in R.Aubert, *Il pontificato di Pio IX*, Turin 1964, 808–11.

51. *Praelectiones theologicae dogmaticae* (9 vols.), 1835–42.

52. P.Scavini, *Theologia moralis universa ad mentem S.Alphonsi de Ligorio*, Milan 1869.

53. *Theologia moralis*, Naples 1824.

54. Another work which enjoyed a certain popularity was that of L.Turchi, *Utriusque foederis bibliorum subsidia exegetica* (4 vols.), Bologna 1841.

55. P.del Signore, *Storia della Chiesa* (4 vols.), Rome [2]1837–46.

56. G.Giovanni Fornici, *Institutiones liturgicae*, Rome 1825.

57. Murri, *Battaglie d'oggi II* (n.49), Rome 1904, 30–1.

58. R.Boudens, 'Image and Training of the Priest in Italian Modernism', *Louvain Studies* 4, 1973, 351–61.

59. Murri, *Battaglie d'oggi II* (n.49), 71–2.

60. For information we are dependent on monographs.

61. There are examples of the low level of studying for the priesthood in France in E.Vacherot, 'La théologie catholique en France', *Revue des deux Mondes* 70, 1868, 294–318.

62. J.R.Geiselmann, *Lebendiger Glaube am geheiligter Überlieferung. Der Grundgedanke J.A.Möhlers und der katholischen Tübinger Schule*, Mainz 1942.

63. V.Conzemius, *Von Döllinger Briefwechsel 1820–1890* (3 vols.), Munich 1963; R.Boudens (ed.), *Alfred Plummer. Conversations with Dr Döllinger*, Louvain 1985.

64. For the development of pastoral work see e.g. P.Broutin, 'Histoire et tradition pastorales', *NRT* 77, 1955, 725–36.

65. J.Faupin, *La mission de France*, Paris 1960; A.Dansette, *Destin du*

catholicisme français 1926–1956, Paris 1957; P.Pierrard, *L'Eglise et les ouvriers en France* 1940–1990, Paris 1991.

66. G.Michonneau, *Paroisse communauté missionaire*, Paris 1946, is another influential work from the time.

67. Emile Poulat drew attention to this in an article in *Le Monde* which appeared on the ocasion of the fortieth anniversary of the final abolition in 1959, I follow his argument closely.

68. R.Rogellio Docastella, 'Rapport sur les effectifs sacerdotaux d'Espagne', in *Die europäische Priesterfrage. Bericht der Internationalen Enquête in Wien 10–12 Oct.1958*, Vienna 1959, 174–93. This also contains details of the geographical distribution of vocations to the priesthood.

69. See F.Boulard, *Essor ou déclin du clergé français*, Paris 1950.

70. P.Winninger, *Construire des Eglises*, Paris 1957.

IV. Ministry in the Church: Changing Identity

1. The development of the ministries took place in the framework of the embedding of the church in history, and precisely in this respect proved both necessary and a consequence of the church's mission. At the beginning of this century, A. Loisy already refered to this function of the ministry as ensuring fidelity to the church's origins. He rejected Harnack's theory put forward in *What is Christianity?* that 'mediocrity was the basis of authority': 'In important moments the church becomes what it must be, so as not to fall into decay and drag down the gospel with it. But it does not create any essential part of its constitution' (*L'Évangile et l'Église*, Paris [5]1930, 135).

2. For the apostle and his function of continuity cf. P.Neuener, 'Ekklesiologie', in *Glaubenszugänge. Lehrbuch der katholischen Dogmatik*, ed. W.Beinert, Paderborn etc. 1995, 436–8.

3. For pseudepigraphy and its significance for the doctrine of ministry cf. N.Brox, *Die Pastoralbriefe*, RNT 7,2, Regensburg [4]1969, 60–6.

4. The reflections on the concept of apostle are based on E.Schlink, 'Die apostolische Sukzession', in id., *Der kommende Christus und die kirchliche Traditionen*, Göttingen 1961, 160–95. Here it becomes clear that the concept of apostolicity, which has long been a bone of contention between the confessions, is open to an ecumenical perspective.

5. The description of the fellowship in the earliest community in Acts 4.32–37 is not simply a situation report, but certainly also has a paraenetic purpose, not seeking to undermine the function of the first Christians as models.

6. Cf. *Texte zur Theologie, Ekklesiologie*, ed. P.Neuner, Graz, Vienna and Cologne 1994f., I, nos.41,42.

7. Cf. ibid., I, no.31.

8. For this reason the testimony of the apostles as set down in scripture is understood to be inspired; cf. K.Rahner, *Über die Schriftinspiration*, QD 1, Freiburg 1948.

9. The notion of the apostolicity of the church as a whole has proved particularly fertile for ecumenical dialogue. The non-episcopal churches also understand themselves to be apostolic in the sense of the Creed. Cf. P.Neuner, *Kleines Handbuch der Ökumene*, Düsseldorf [2]1987, 148f.

10. W.Kasper, 'Ökumenischer Konsens über das kirchliche Amt?', *Stimmen der Zeit* 191, 1973, 219–30: 30.

11. J.Ratzinger and K.Rahner, *Episkopat und Primat*, Freiburg, Basel and Vienna [3]1963, 49.

12. *Texte zur Theologie* (n.6), I, no.31.

13. This notion is constantly emphasized in Vatican II, including what is said in the *nota explicativa praevia*. So it should be understood not only in the sense of the special authority of the Pope but in particular of his incororation into the College of Bishops.

14. Therefore the model of delegation, in which the minister could be understood simply as a representative of the community, is also rejected in ecumenical dialogue. Cf. Gemeinsame römisch-katholische/evangelisch-lutherische Kommission, *Das geistliche Amt in der Kirche*, Paderborn and Frankfurt 1981, nos.20,23.

15. Thus against F.Schleiermacher and his statement: 'It is not he who believes in a holy scripture that has religion, but he who needs none and could make one for himself' (*Speeches on Religion*, 1799).

16. For the interpretation of this process of translation in terms of inculturation cf. P.Neuner, 'Die Hellenisierung des Christentums als Modell von Inkulturation', *Stimmen der Zeit* 213, 1995.

17. If the universal church is realized in the local church, it is wrong to identify the world church with Rome. Ratzinger has summed up this notion in the statement: 'To be Catholic means ... to have cross-connections' (*Das Neue Volk Gottes*, Düsseldorf 1969, 215).

18. Augustine, *Sermo* 340.1, quoted in *Lumen Gentium* 32.

19. *Lumen Gentium* 10.

20. In this interpretation of sacramental character Catholic and Protestant theology agree; the text *Das geistliche Amt in der Kirche* can even speak of a consensus, if reifying misunderstandings are overcome and the ministry is not seen as a means of personal sanctification (ibid., nos.37–39).

21. The manifold theological interpretations and historical forms of realization of the church are documented in *Texte zur Theologie* (n.6), I and II.

22. 'From ancient times have been called bishops, priests and deacons' (*Lumen Gentium* 28). Here the council refers to the Tridentine statement 'the hierarchy appointed by divine ordinance which consists of bishops, priests and deacons' (Denzinger 1776). This is a telling instance of the Vatican II hermeneutics, in which the Tridentine statement *divina ordinatione institutam* becomes proof of its *ab antiquo*. Here it should be noted that in view of the historical problem, Trent itself already avoided the technical term *de iure divino*.

23. *Texte zur Theologie* (n.6), II, no.158, from J.A.Möhler, *Die Einheit in der Kirche, oder: Das Prinzip des Katholizismus* (1825), 52.

24. Thus Döllinger's dogmatic criticism of Vatican I. Cf. P.Neuner, *Döllinger als Theologe der Ökumene*, Paderborn, etc. 1979, 72–7.

25. *Lumen Gentium* 27. For the whole section cf. P.Neuner, 'Zwischen Primat und Kollegialität. Das Verhältnis von Papst und Bischofen auf dem Ersten und dem Zweiten Vatikanischen Konzil', in F.König (ed.), *Zentralismus statt Kollegialität?*, Düsseldorf 1990, 82–113.

26. *Lumen Gentium* 21.

27. *Lumen Gentium* 28.

28. *Presbyterorum Ordinis* 2.

29. *Lumen Gentium* 31. On this see P.Neuner, *Der Laie und das Gottesvolk*, Frankfurt 1988, esp.115–32.

30. *Apostolicam Actuositatem* 6.

31. *Apostolicam Actuositatem* 3.

32. *Lumen Gentium* 33.

33. Published by the Secretariat of the German Conference of Bishops, Bonn 1977.

34. For an account of the controversy over the lay theologians and their participation in ministry cf. Neuner, *Der Laie und das Gottesvolk* (n.29), 198–203.

35. K.Rahner, 'Pastorale Dienste und Gemeindeleitung', *Stimmen der Zeit* 195, 1977, 733–43: 738.

36. P.Hünermann, 'Ordo in neuer Ordnung? Dogmatische Überlegungen zur Frage der Ämter und Dienste in der Kirche heute', in F.Klostermann (ed.), *Der Priestermangel und seine Konsequenzen*, Düsseldorf 1977, 58–94: 91.

37. W.Kasper gives a survey of the present possibilities in canon law in his report for the German Conference of Bishops, *Der Leitungsdienst in der Gemeinde*, published by the Secretariat of the German Conference of Bishops (Arbeitshilfen 118), Bonn 1994, 13.

38. On this cf. H.B.Meyer, 'Liturgischer Leitungsdienst durch Laien', in *Heiliger Dienst*, published by the Institutum Liturgicum, Erzabtei St Peter, Salzburg, 47, 1993, no.3, 173–201: 197.

39. ' "Die Kirche entwickelt heute neue Ämter". Ein Gespräch mit dem Münchner Dogmatiker Peter Neuner', *Herder-Korrespondenz* 49, 1995, 128–33: 133.

V. Leadership in a Voluntary Movement

1. A.Faivre, *Ordonner la fraternité. Pouvoir d'innover et retour à l'ordre dans l'Église ancienne*, Paris 1992.

2. G.Alberigo et al, *La chrétienté en débat. Histoire, formes et problèmes actuels, Colloque de Bologne 11–15 Mai 1983*, Paris 1984.

3. According to the European Values Study, in Western Europe 77% said that they were members of a religious confession, and 81% of these claimed to

be Catholic. Of the Catholics, 44% believed in the resurrection, 39% did not and 17% did not know (1990).

4. J.J.Vollebergh, 'Religious Leadership', in L.Grollenberg et al., *Minister? Pastor? Prophet? Grass-roots Leadership in the Churches*, London 1980, 41–56.

5. In this context see also *Episcopal Leadership*, Pro Mundi Vita Bulletin 65, 1977.

6. See e.g. G.Schmidtchen, *Was den Deutschen heilig ist. Religiöse und Politische Strömungen in der Bundesrepublik Deutschland*, Munich 1979, 94.

7. According to the European Values Study, in the Netherlands 51% said that they no longer belonged to any religious confession, as opposed to 23% who were core members, i.e. practising regularly and active in a parish (as compared to e.g. Belgium, with 32% and 9% respectively, or Sweden, with 19% and 4%).

8. In the Netherlands in the 1901 census 1% said that they were not members of a church; in 1990 the number in the 18–24 age group had risen to 61% (EVS); only 23% of the population said that they were regularly involved in a church (the highest percentage in Western Europe).

9. See R.Bellah et al., *The Habits of the Heart*, New York 1985, 219–49: 232.

10. L.Moulin, *Le monde vivant des religieux*, Paris 1966.

11. L.Renoir (ed.), *Le Temps de la responsabilité*, Paris 1991 (with a remarkable 'Postface' by P.Ricoeur), is a secular plea for a greater sense of responsibility.

12. See many articles in *Ethical Perspectives*, Quarterly Review, Centre for Christian Ethics, Catholic University of Louvain.

13. R.Bellah (ed.), *The Good Society*, New York 1992.

14. The title of the conciliar constitution *Lumen Gentium* refers primarily to Jesus Christ and the first lines refer to the Holy Spirit. See also W.Kasper and G.Sauter, *Kirche – Ort des Geistes*, Freiburg 1976.

15. Much disappointment was expressed in 1985 in the evaluation of the German Synod (Würzburg 1972–1975). After the 1994 Roman Synod on the Religious Life, Cardinal Danneels pleaded for a thorough reflection on method; another cardinal even asked for a synod devoted to the synod. By contrast, at a diocesan level much more has been achieved within the possibilities (albeit limited) of such a synod (above all in France but also in Germany).

16. J.Kerhofs, 'Christenen zonder kerk', *Streven* 58, 1991, 675–84.

17. G.Alberigo and J.-P.Jossua (eds.), *La réception de Vatican II*, Paris 1985.

18. The document *Dialog statt Dialogverweigerung. Wie in der Kirche miteinander umgehen?*, produced by the Central Committee of German Catholics at the end of 1991, which made a sharp protest against the lack of dialogue, met with an enormous response (*Herder Korrespondenz* 46, 1992, 497–9). Bishop K.Lehman, President of the German Conference of Bishops, joined in this protest (1994).

19. Thus for example in the very numerous French diocesan synods (in 1993, including areas overseas, of 107 dioceses 43 held a synod and 6 were preparing for one); see a bibliography and discussion in *Esprit et Vie* 104 (11th series), 42, 1994, 561–7.

20. In the European Values Study, for ten countries of Western Europe in general little difference could be noted between Catholic, Protestants, regular churchgoers and those who were not members of a church when it came to membership of a voluntary social organization (around 5% in all) or voluntary involvement in one (around 2%). But there were striking differences when it came to church or religious organization. Here, as with sports organizations, we find the highest figures: 13% of Catholics and 23% of Protestants say that they are members (of the 25% who are regular churchgoers); 7% of Catholics and 8% of Protestants say that they are involved as volunteers (14% of those attending church weekly, above all in the Netherlands and Belgium). This means that voluntary church work scores very highly in Western Europe.

21. See *Pastoraat in gedeelde verantwoordelijkheid: Een workboek over het funktioneren van het vrijwilligerskader in der pastoral werk*, Zeist (Utrecht Diocesan Pastoral Centre) 1985.

22. 'De gemengde pastorale teams', *Pro Mundi Vita Bulletin* 78, 1979.

23. For self-help groups see e.g. *The Future of Voluntary Organizations. Report of the Wolfenden Committee*, London 1978; D.Pancoast, P.Parker, C.Froland, *Rediscovering Self-help*, Berkeley 1983; R.Wuthnow, *Acts of Compassion. Caring for Others and Helping Ourselves*, Princeton 1991; D.Ferrand-Bechmann, *Bénévolat et solidarité*, Paris 1992; U.Rausch, *Kreative Gemeinde*, Frankfurt am Main 1994.

24. *La pastorale des grandes villes: le diocèse de Madrid*, Pro Mundi Vita Dossiers, Europe-Amérique du Nord, 20, 1983, 21–2.

25. In the Middle Ages, people were regarded as adult by the age of thirteen to fifteen, according to existing law (R.Delort, *La vie au Moyen Age*, Paris 1982, 110).

26. The difference is increasing both in the recruitment and in the formation (and mentality) of candidates for the priesthood (see above all C.Flipo, 'Les jeunes prêtres de France', *Études* 381, 1994, 513–34); these candidates know that 'Christendom' is a thing of the past.

27. D.F.Gillespie (ed.), *Burnout Among Social Workers*, New York 1987; see above all the dossier 'Stress et équilibre de vie. A propos du prêtre catholique', *Le Supplément* 179, 1991, 7–100.

28. L.J.Cardinal Suenens, *Souvenirs et espérances*, Paris 1991, 121.

29. W.Seibel, 'Verwaltete Kirchen in einer verwalteten Welt', *Stimmen der Zeit* 212, 1994, 721–2.

30. In the USA 60% of Catholics give one dollar per week and per family to the church (it is estimated that in 1991 all Catholics together gave less than 1% of their income to the church, as compared with 6% in the case of Mormons, 2.9% in the case of Baptists and 1.3% in the case of Lutherans; see also the special issue of *Concilium* 117, 1979, *The Finances of the Church*).

31. D.B.Barrett (ed.), *World Christian Encyclopaedia. A Comparative Study of Churches and Religions in the Modern World AD 1900–2000*, Nairobi 1982; R.Michiels, *Het Wereldchristendom*, Averbode 1991.

32. C.Duquoc, *Provisional Churches. An Essay in Ecumenical Ecclesiology*, London 1986.

33. Y.Congar already pointed this out in his first great study *Chrétiens désunis. Principes d'un 'oecuménisme' catholique*, Paris 1937.

34. See e.g. the special numbers of *Concilium* (*Geistliche Erweckungs-bewegungen*, 9/1973 [not published in English]; *New Religious Movements*, 161, 1983; and some 'Bulletins' in 1972/8); D.Hervieu-Léger, *Vers un nouveau christianisme?*, Paris 1986 (Ch. IV, 'Les nouveaux mouvements religieux'); M.Hébrard, *Les nouveaux disciples dix ans après. Voyage à travers les communautés charismatiques*, Paris 1986; S.Abbruzzese, *Communione e liberazione*, Paris 1989. And of course the numerous publications of and about Opus Dei.

35. See the special number of *Concilium, Die Kirche als Institution*, 10/1974 (this never appeared in English); Avery Dulles, *The Resilient Church. The Necessity and Limits of Adaptation*, New York 1977 (especially Ch.2, 'Church Reform through Creative Interaction').

36. In the concluding statement of the synod mention was made first of the parishes, then of the new movements and finally of the base communities as important levers for the new evangelization, but nothing was said about the relationship betwen them and the questions raised by leadership in all three.

VI. Where Now? Possible Scenarios

1. J.Dellepoort, *Die europäische Priesterfrage*, Vienna 1959, 341.

2. A permanent commission was appointed for this (*La Documentation Catholique* 2035, 1991, 864).

3. In many countries of the southern hemisphere an important minority of the clergy come from Europe.

4. Belgium still has relatively more priests than Poland, but the structure of the age pyramid in the two countries is very different.

5. It is estimated that Poles make up one third of the priests in the archdiocese of Vienna. Many priests from Croatia and Slovenia are employed in Germany and Austria and many Irish priests in Great Britain. In 1994 Bishop P.Iby of Eisenstadt, Austria, started an exchange programme with two Indian dioceses, on a three to one basis.

6. *The Base Communities in the Church*, Pro Mundi Vita Bulletin 81, Brussels 1980.

7. According to c.517§2 of the Code of Canon Law. In this connection see A.Loretan, *Laien im pastoralen Dienst. Ein Amt in der kirchlichen Gesetzgebung: Pastoralassistent(in), Pastoralreferent(in)*, Fribourg 1994.

8. According to the European Values Study (1990), in Western Europe (Belgium, France, West Germany, the United Kingdom, Ireland, the Nether-lands, Spain, Italy and Portugal), 70% of the total population said that they would want a religious ceremony for births (in the Netherlands 46%, in Ireland 93%), 72% for marriages, and 77% for funerals. In Central Europe the

percentages differ more strongly (with e.g. Poland at one extreme with 94, 95 and 93% respectively and at the other extreme Czechia with 41, 40 and 50%). Belgium can serve as an illustration of the general development in north-west Europe: in 1967 94% were baptized, 86% married and 84% buried in the Catholic church; in 1990 75%, 59% and 81% respectively.

9. The great majority of those who have a church funeral in northern and western Europe were rarely churchgoers, if ever (with the exception of Ireland and parts of Italy).

10. In the Code of Canon Law see c.861§2 and 230§3 for baptism; c.112§§1 and 2 for marriage; c.230§3 for the liturgy of the word; c.766 for preaching. For the liturgy of the word with the distribution of communion see also the instruction *Inter oecumenica*, no.37 (AAS 56, 1960, 877–900) and the instruction *Liturgicae instaurationes* no.6 (AAS 62, 1970, 692–704). For the funeral service see *Ordo obsequiarum (Rituale Romanum,* 1969), Praenotanda no.19.

11. J.Ratzinger, *De christelijke broederlijkheid,* Hilversum and Antwerp 1963.

12. As the Pontifical Biblical Commission confirmed in 1993 (cf. *The Interpretation of the Bible in the Church,* London 1995, 35).

13. B.Sesboüé, 'Les animateurs pastoraux laïcs. Une prospective théologique', *Études* 377, 1992, 253–65.

14. The problems raised by a 'parallel clergy' are described in a study by A.van der Helm (*Un clergé parallèle,* Cerdic, Strasbourg 1994). He recognizes the unclear status of laity who work full time or part time on the basis of a comparison between France (where they are often called 'pastoral animators', are usually women, and are not paid very much: around Ffr 6,200 per month), and the Netherlands (where they are called pastoral workers, are usually men, and receive a respectable salary from the church of around Ffr 16,500 per month). The definition of their place in the church and their legal safeguards are much weaker in France than in Germany (G.Duperray, 'Ministères laïcs. Une nouvelle tradition', *Études* 378, 1993, 63–74). The uncertainty over the specific 'office' of the laity and leaders of communities is also recognized in Germany both by the conference of bishops (*Herder Korrespondenz,* 1994.5, 226–8) and by canon lawyers (H.Schmitz, in *Archiv für Katholisches Kirchenrecht* 161, 1992, 329); cf. P.-M.Gy, 'La célébration du baptême du mariage et des funérailles confiée à des laïcs?', *La Maison-Dieu* 194, 1993/2, 13–25.

15. For North American models see *Diocesan Guidelines, Policies and Job Descriptions for Alternative Forms of Pastoral Leadership,* Institute for Pastoral Life, Kansas City 1988 (this is a survey of 24 dioceses). In 1933 B.O'Sullivan, President of the National Conference of Priests of England and Wales, made a plea for more collaboration between priests and laity ('Collaborative Ministry: Not Just Words', *The Tablet,* 18 September 1993, 1211–12). In 1994 Bishop A.Conti of Aberdeen made a similar plea for his extended diocese containing few Catholics and a handful of priests ('Working Together in Christ', *Priests and People* 8, 1994, 57–60).

16. Graph produced by P.-M.Zulehner. See also id. (ed.), *Vom Untertan zum*

Freiheitskünstler. Eine Kulturdiagnose anhand der Untersuchungen 'Religion im Leben der Oesterreicher 1970–1990'. Europäische Wertestudie, Oesterreich-Teil 1990, Vienna 1992.

17. The German bishops, *Zur Ordnung der pastoralen Dienste,* Bonn 1977. For a commentary see W.Kasper, 'Die Schädliche Nebenwirkungen des Priestermangels', *Stimmen der Zeit* 195, 1977, 129–35; P.J.Cordes, 'Pastoralassistenten und Diakone', ibid., 389–401; K.Rahner, 'Pastorale Dienste und Gemeindeleitung', ibid., 733–43.

18. See e.g. G.Wollmann, *Die ständigen Diakone. Berufswirklichkeit und Selbstverständnis,* Mainz 1983. In Canada, too, there are few deacons among the pastoral workers paid by the church: in 1987–88 there were only 85, as opposed to at least 1,714 religious (sisters and brothers) and 1,934 lay people (*Les ressources humaines de l'Église catholique au Canada en 1987–88* [*Personnel rémunéré*], Conférence des évêques catholiques au Canada, Ottawa 1988).

19. M.Brulin, 'Les Assemblées Dominicales en l'Absence de Prêtre. Situation Française en 1987. Les résultats d'une enquête nationale', *La Maison-Dieu* 175, 1988, 111–67. Since 1977 the ADAP have increased by 79% in the south-west and by 297% in the north.

20. 6.3% of the ADAPs take place in communities with less than 100 inhabitants, 48% in communities of between 100 and 499 inhabitants, 24.7% in communities of between 500 and 999 inhabitants, and 20.9% in communities with more than 1,000 inhabitants. This makes 2,103 communities in total. The attendance in more than half the ADAPs is less than 50 (and in some areas more than half the ADAPs have attendances of between 10 and 30). According to the European Values Study 17% of the French practise once a month (J.Lambert, 'Un paysage religieux en profonde évolution', in H.Riffault, *Les valeurs des français,* Paris 1994, 138). It is important to note that in 1969–70 there were 37,962 communities in France, 30,000 of them with less than 1,000 inhabitants, 808 with less than 50 and even 8 which were uninhabited . . .

21. The Church of England also comes up against this problem. According to a report by Lord Templeman, commissioned by David Hope, Bishop of London, 36 churches in the City of London needed to be closed. The 22 current parishes had to be amalgamated into four. This 'mission strategy' was felt necessary to counter present-day frustrations and achieve an approach in solidarity in which each 'leaves his own jealously guarded ivory tower', under one central dean with four parish priests (*The Tablet,* 5 February 1994, 155).

22. In Germany a distinction is made between 'associated parishes', in which particular tasks of general concern are co-ordinated for different parishes but the parishes continue to have a legal existence, and 'integrated parishes', in which different parishes are fused. This is the difference between clustering and closing. See P.M.Zulehner, 'Auswege aus dem Pfarrenmangel', *Stimmen der Zeit,* 1992, 615–16.

23. J.P.Jaeger, 'Laïcs animateurs', *Pastorale,* 9 February 1994.

24. R.Bouchex, 'L'avenir des paroisses dans notre diocèse', *L'église d'Avignon*, 17 October 1993.

25. Similarly, the episcopal council of the diocese of St-Dié published an orientation text *Les nouvelles unités pastorales* (September 1993) in which the existing parish model was abandoned to keep a series of small faith communities viable. A 'pastoral unit' can even cover a whole present-day deanery. Everything depends on the number of inhabitants, the number of committed believers, the distance to be covered and the number of priests available. In each case each 'unit' will have a pastoral council and an economic council.

26. *L'Église communion missionnaire*, Paris 1991.

27. Ibid., 148: 'Are our parishes more French than Catholic? What is the place of linguistic parishes?'

28. In 1988 a directory of the ADAP was published by the Congregation for Divine Worship *(Osservatore Romano*, 30 June/1 July 1988); it appeared in a French translation: *Directoire pour les Assemblées Dominicales en l'Absence de Prêtre*, Commission Episcopale de Liturgie, Paris 1988.

29. For centuries Christians officially administered unction to the sick with chrism, blessed by the bishop. The Indonesian conference of bishops has urgently asked the Holy See for permission to be given to catechists to administer it in the many remote villages where almost everyone dies without receiving unction and the last sacraments. How far can one take the 'universal priesthood' in sacramental terms? Believers may marry and administer marriage to one another. See R.Béraudy, 'Le sacrement des malades', *Nouvelle Revue Théologique* 96, 1974, 600–34; P.Rouillard, 'Le ministre du sacrement de l'onction des malades', ibid. 111, 1979, 394–402; I.Riedel-Spangenberger, 'Das Gewohnheitsrecht in der katholischen Kirche. Zur Spendung der Krankensalbung durch Diakone und Laien', *Trierer Theologische Zeitschrift* 103, 1994, 188ff.; P.de Clerck, 'Des laïcs ministres des sacrements?', *La Maison-Dieu* 194, 1993/2, 27–45.

30. See T.Cloïn, 'Een nieuw type priester', in *Nieuwe ambtsvormen in christlijke gemeenschappen*, Pro Mundi Vita Bulletin 50, 1974, 78–81.

31. In *Herder Korrespondenz*, 1994, 5, 226–8. For the complete text see *Der Leitungsdienst in der Gemeinde*, Arbeitshelfen 118, Sekretariat der Deutschen Bishofskonferenz, Bonn 1994.

32. Concern about the preservation of priestly identity in the midst of this process of transferring tasks to the laity clearly emerges from recent episcopal publications: from the Dutch bishops (*In Christus' naam. Herdelijk schrijven over woord, sacrament, ambt en wijding*, Utrecht 1992), the German bishops (*Schreiben der deutschen Bischöfe über den priesterlichen Dienst*, Bonn 1992), and the French bishops (*Les ministres ordonnés dans une Église-communion*, Paris 1993, to be compared with *Ministères et charges ecclésiales des baptisés, évaluation et orientations. Rapport présenté au Conseil permanent de l'Episcopàt*, February 1982). All these texts in fact make use of the brief *Sacerdotium ministriale* of the Congregation for the Doctrine of Faith, 6 August 1983.

33. *Viri probati* are understood to be married men who through marriage, professional training and quality of faith have proved sufficiently that they could be considered for possible priestly ordination.

34. P.Hebblethwaite, *Paul VI, the First Modern Pope*, London 1993, 441–2.

35. Roman Synods of Bishops 1971, 1974, 1985, 1990; the national synods of Denmark (1989), the Federal Republic in Würzburg (1972–1975), the Swiss synod (1972–75), the Dutch Pastoral Council (1969), the Flemish Inter-diocesan Pastoral Council (1970–71); through diocesan synods (Rottenburg in Germany and many French diocesan synods).

36. E.g. the Scandinavian conference of bishops (1971 synod and after-wards), Cardinal Hume, then president of the Council of European Con-ferences of Bishops ('Perspectives sur l'Église locale', *La Maison-Dieu* 165, 1986, 101–16), H.Vogel, Bishop of Basel ('Den ganzen Auftrag der Kirche im Blick bekommen', in *Kirche, Schweizerische Kirchenzeitung* 24, 1994, 348–9). Questions have been raised about compulsory celibacy by Cardinals G.Ster-zinsky (Berlin), F.König (Vienna), and the Austrian bishops J.Schoiswohl, F.Zak, H.Krätzl and F.Kuntner. Archbishop R.Weakland (Milwaukee), who defended this open standpoint, was censured by the Secretariat of State. Of course others have vigorously defended compulsory celibacy. e.g. Cardinals A.Simonis, J.-M.Lustiger, A.Decourtray, etc. In Indonesia the conference of bishops has repeatedly pleaded for the ordination of married men, as also happened with a group of bishops in Brazil. This was also one of the desiderata of the 'Asian Colloquium on Ministries' organized by the Federation of Asian Bishops' Conferences in Hong Kong in 1977 (P.S.Achutegui SJ [ed.], *Asian Colloquium on Ministries in the Church*, Manila 1977).

37. E.g. K.Rahner, H.Küng, E.Schillebeeckx, C.Duquoc, etc. Y.Congar pointed this out with special urgency (*Entretiens d'automne*, Paris 1987, 65–6). See also R.Gryson, 'Quels prêtres pour demain?', *Lumen Vitae* 49, 1993, 407–15.

38. A survey among committed Catholics in Wallonia (Belgium) organized by the inter-diocesan pastoral council, in which 10,000 answers were received, indicated that not only would 61% accept other than celibate priests but even more (76%) would accept the co-existence of celibate and married priests, and 79% were in favour of the ordination of married men ('Enquête: 10,000 chrétiens repondent pour le changement', *L'Appel* 136, 1990, 8–9). In June 1990 a representative survey in *La Vie* gave the following answers for France: 76% for the ordination of *viri probati*, 78% for the possibility of reintegrating married priests into the ministry. According to an opinion poll in Ireland (*Sunday Press*, May 1992), 69% of the Irish are in favour of optional celibacy; a poll by the 'Katholieke Radio Omroep' in the Netherlands (1992) indicates that 84% of all Dutch Catholics are in favour, and all the surveys in the USA and Canada point in this direction.

39. J.Kerkhofs, 'Le People de Dieu est-il infaillible? L'importance du "sensus fidelium" dans l'Église postconciliaire', *Freiburger Zeitschrift für Philosophie und Theologie* 35, 1988, 3–19.

40. *Gemeinsame Synode der Bistümer in der Bundesrepublik Deutschland, Offizielle Gesamtausgabe,* Freiburg 1976, 628.

41. Ibid., 269.

42. *Katholischer Erwachsenenkatechismus,* German conference of bishops, 1985, 385.

43. Although it cannot be said *a priori* that they may not have this. Many small abbeys and communities of sisters for centuries had one priest (or more) at their disposal.

44. Of course the key problem is the presence of a living community. More and more people find themselves in a vicious circle: they have a weak community because there is no dynamic priest in the team, and there is no such priest because the commnity is to small and old.

45. Not only Bishop H.Vogel of Basel but also for example the authorities in the diocese of Speyer have recognized this: 'However, the diocesan authorities have noted the clear wish for a change in the conditions of admission expressed by the communities and will hand it on to the responsible superior bodies and decision-makers', in *Kirche leben in der Pfarrgemeinde. Für die Seelsorge, Verordnungsblatt für das Bistum Speyer* 1, 1993, 25.

46. How far progress has been made can be seen from the following quotation from the encyclical *Vehementer* (1906) of Pope Pius X: 'The church is by nature an unequal community; it comprises two categories of persons, the pastors and the flock; those who occupy a rank in the hierarchy and the mass of believers. These categories are so different from each other that only in the group of pastors is there the right and authority necessary to guide all members towards advancing the aim of the community. The mass has no other right than to accept leadership and submissively to follow the orders of their leaders.' For a commentary on this see R.Aubert, 'De kerk van de crisis van 1948 tot Vaticanum II', in *Geschiedenis van de kerk* X, Bussum 1974, 172.

47. For the Church of England see e.g. P.Baelz and W.Jacob (eds.), *Ministers of the Kingdom. Exploration in Non-Stipendiary Ministry,* London 1988.

48. In the French-speaking Protestant churches in Switzerland 10% of pastors are involved in divorces (1991), among the Lutherans in Germany one in three (*Evangelische Kommentare,* December 1990). According to the *Nachrichten der Evangelisch-Lutheranische Kirche in Bayern* (1991), between 1960 and 1990 there were 177 divorces involving pastors (117 of them between 1980 and 1990); however, this proportion is substantially lower than the average in the rest of the population. For the situation of the wives of priests in the Eastern and Reformation churches and their reaction to their husbands' ministry see *Women and the Priesthood,* Pro Mundi Vita, Brussels 1970.

49. There are no known official figures. For the period 1965–1975 estimates range between 40,000 and 100,000 out of a total of 400,000. In Spain the estimate is one in three priests. According to E.Colagiovanni, rector at the Rota in Rome, between 1963 and 1969 9,804 dispensations were given, 5,184 for diocesan priests and 4,620 for priests in religious orders (*Crisi vere a falsi nel*

ruolo del Prete oggi, Rome 1973, 156–7). According to the *Annuarium Statisticum*, between 1969 and 1980 at least 24,489 priests left the ministry (there are no facts about dispensations, and facts about religious have been given only since 1975, when almost as many priests in religious orders as secular priests left). The total for 1975 was 3,001 and it declined steadily to 1,200 in 1981. We know that under John Paul II dispensations have been drastically cut back. The impact on the state of the priesthood in earlier years is evident from the following figures: in 1969 1,382 dispensations were granted to diocesan priests (and at least 400 others left) and 1,277 to priests in religious orders; 5,156 were ordained and 5,014 died (F.Pycroft, *Catholic Facts and Figures*, London 1977, 9). For France, see J.Potel, *'Ils se sont mariés . . . et après'*, Paris 1986.

50. Despite a number of publications in the Netherlands, Germany, etc., no reliable figures are available.

51. It ties in with this that in the preparation of the Roman Synod of Bishops on the Religious Life (October 1994), many proposals by religious superiors argued for a rethinking of the place and significance of 'temporal vows'.

52. A married priesthood in the Latin church would at the same time have a symbolic function for the Catholic churches of the Eastern rite: these would see that more recognition was being made of them and not continue to feel that they were in effect second-class. In a wider context this is also true of dialogue both with the Orthodox churches and with the churches of the Reformation. As ecumenism becomes real and specific, the Catholic Church, too, will have to integrate the 'style' of the ministry in these churches.

53. According to a survey among 100 pastors (average age sixty-five) in the Haute-Saône (diocese of Besançon), in which 60% were in favour of the ordination of *viri probati* and 59% of the reintegration of married priests, 80% thought that this would not be a solution.

54. In his studies *Religion in Leben der Österreicher* (Vienna 1981) and *Vom Untertan zum Freiheitskünstler* (Freiburg 1991), P.M.Zulehner found that the faithful first and foremost looked for a 'pastor'. In 1990, a priest would be asked for advice: by 58% on religious problems, 54% over personal doubts, 45% over problems of conscience, 16% over marriage problems, 3% on political questions. In the survey in Wallonia (Belgium) mentioned above, seven characteristics were suggested that people might find important in a priest: 41% put spiritual training first, 23% human maturity, 10% the capacity to live in a community. Asceticism, missionary spirit, openness to the problems of the world and sensitivity to social and economic life were hardly mentioned. The following positive percentages appeared in the answers to the question asked in the European Values Study for Western Europe, 'Do you think that the church in your country is giving the right answer?' on certain issues like 'human spiritual need, the moral problems of the individual, family problems, the social problems of your country?': 54%, 36%, 32% and 27%.

55. Retirement should not be put at between 65 and 70. Many people – e.g. teachers – have a pension between the ages of 50 and 55 or work only part-time; they have around fifteen years of potential activity as priests in a team.

56. The total number is not known to us and is doubtless very limited. In 1990 in the United Kingdom 5 Anglican married priests were ordained Catholic priests (more cases are likely to follow the Church of England's decision to ordain women to the priesthood). This also happened elsewhere sporadically. There were 29 cases in the USA, and in Sweden 3 former Lutheran priests were ordained Catholic priests. There have also been a number of cases in Germany and Australia,. This transition of course raises severe 'assimilation' problems for Protestant priests who become Catholics (see J.H.Fichter, 'The Ordination of Episcopal Priests', *America* 159.9, 1988, 157–61). Of course there are also Catholic priests who go over to another church – how many? See J.Moorhead, 'Two-way Traffic', *The Tablet*, 12 February 1994.

57. However, it would be premature to say that celibate diocesan priests will disappear. In Hungary, Slovakia, the Ukraine, Lebanon, etc., in the Catholic Church, alongside married priests of the Eastern rite one also finds celibate priests of the Eastern and Latin rites.

58. On the one hand it has to be recognized that between 1965 and 1975 many priests in religious orders also left the church, and on the other hand that a number of candidates for the priesthood entered a religious institution in order to find more support in their choice of the priesthood with its implication of obligatory celibacy.

59. At a congress of Greek Orthodox priests and laity of the very far-flung Greek Orthodox archdiocese of North and South America, the bishops of the Patriarchate were asked also to allow married priests to become bishops, but it is expected that such a change would have to be decided at a pan-Orthodox level *(Christ in der Gegenwart* 51, 1990, 418). As early as 1969, in dialogue with Olivier Clément, Athenagoras I of Constantinople raised the possibility of the marriage of celibate priests and the consecration of married priests as bishops in the distant future *(Dialogues avec le patriarche Athénagoras,* Paris 1969).

60. For example, Gregory of Nyssa first had a church career, followed by a secular profession and a marriage; for thirteen years he was a bishop and a married man, and then as a widower entered a monastery. The father of Gregory of Nazianzus was also consecrated bishop (G.Denzler, *Die Geschichte des Zölibats*, Freiburg 1993).

61. The discussion of the theological significance of 'ordination' has certainly not come to an end. See K.Rahner, 'Ordination in the Life and Reflection of the Church', *Theological Investigations* 20, London and New York 1982; A.Faivre, *Ordonner la fraternité. Pouvoir d'innover et retour à l'ordre dans l'Église ancienne*, Paris 1992.

62. See Chapter 1 above.

63. 'Die Frau in Kirche und Gesellschaft. Ein Wort der deutschen Bischöfe', *Herder Korrespondenz* 36, 1982, 26–34.

64. For the diaconate see e.g. *Diakonia*, special issue, Internationales Diakonatszentrum, Freiburg 1985 (with a preface by Bishop G.Moser of Rottenburg); D.Ansorge, 'Die wesentlichen Argumente liegen auf dem Tisch. Zur neueren Diskussion um der Diakonat der Frau', *Herder Korrespondenz* 47, 1993, 581–6. On ordination to the priesthood see *The Situation of Women in the Catholic Church*, Pro Mundi Vita Bulletin 83, 1980; M.Hébrard, *Les Femmes dans l'Église*, Paris 1984; *Femmes prêtres fait-il dire jamais?* Special number of *Actualité religieuse dans le monde* 108, 15 February 1993.

65. See e.g. K.Rahner, 'Priestertum der Frau', *Stimmen der Zeit* 195, 1977, 291–301; J.Field-Bibb, *Women towards Priesthood*, Cambridge 1991; W.Beinert, 'Dogmatische Überlegungen zum Thema Priestertum der Frau', *Theologische Quartalschrift* 173, 1993, 3, 186–204 (and the whole issue); W.Beinert, 'Priestertum der Frau', *Stimmen der Zeit* 212, 1994, 723–8; J.Moingt, 'Sur un débat close' (editorial), *Recherches de science religieuse* 82, 1994, 321–33.

66. *Synod 87*, prepared by the General Secretariat of the Bishops' Conference of England and Wales, London 1987, 17f.

67. J.Homeyer, 'Der Priestermangel, und die Hoffnung, auf eine neue Art Kirche zu sein'. *Diakonia* 23, 1992, 177; see also H.J.Spital, Bishop of Trier, and K.Nientiedt, 'Das fundamentale Problem ist nicht der Priestermangel', *Herder Korrespondenz* 46, 1992, 70–75.

68. U.Rausch, *Kreative Gemeinde, Der Pfarrermangel – und das Ende? Analysen-Modelle-Visionen*, Frankfurt am Main 1994; H.Wieh, *Konzil und Gemeinde, Eine systematisch-theologische Untersuchung zum Gemeindeverständnis des Zweiten Vatikanischen Konzils in pastoraler Absicht*, Frankfurter Theologische Studien 25, Frankfurt 1978; *Réflexions sur l'Église locale*, special number of *La Maison-Dieu* 165, 1986. K.Rahner, *Strukturwandel der Kirche als Aufgabe und Chance*, Freiburg 1972, continues to be inspiring.

69. They will be able to base themselves here on the resolution of the 1975 Joint Synod in Germany: 'A community which receives pastoral care must become a community which shapes its life in the common service of all and with the non-transferable personal responsibility of each individual' (*Gemeinsame Synode, Würzburg 1975*, Beschluss: Dienste und Ämter, 602).